a Minute

Contents

A Laugh a Minute

A Laugh

Introduction

Doctor: "I have some bad news and some worse news. The bad news is that you have only 24 hours left to live."

Patient: "That is bad news. What could be worse?"

Doctor: "I've been trying to reach you since yesterday."

This familiar joke made millions of people laugh when we published it in Reader's Digest magazine. And every time you laugh, it's like taking a miracle cure for your health. According to doctors and scientific researchers, laughter can reduce stress, lower blood pressure, boost the immune system, improve brain functioning and even protect your heart. Maybe that's why the average person laughs around 17 times a day. When you think about humour and health, it's no wonder that we have a "funny bone", that humour is "contagious" and that laughter is "infectious".

Humour is also an "antidote" to everyday problems, like trying to make sense of a computer error. You can get angry about it, or you can respond with a joke, like making up your own on-screen error messages:

ERROR: Keyboard Not Found!
Press any key to continue ...

Press any key ... no, no, no
NOT THAT ONE

Press any key to continue or any key to quit ...

Enter 11-digit prime number to continue ...

Smash forehead on keyboard to continue ...

And when we're afraid of something, the best thing to do is laugh our way through it. Let's say you need an operation. You're scared. You're worried. You don't know if you'll come through it. So your friend takes you aside, gives you a pep talk and says don't worry unless you hear the following during the operation:

"Better save that. We'll need it for the autopsy."

"Bo! Bo! Come back with that! Bad dog!"

"Oh, no! I just lost my Rolex."

"Wait a minute ... if this is his spleen, then what's that?"

Reader's Digest has always believed in the power of laughter. Our well-known magazine column, "Laughter, the Best Medicine," has appeared in every issue of the magazine for more than half a century. Over the years, we have published more than 100,000 jokes, quotes and funny stories from the more than 20 million people who have submitted them. We receive around 35,000 submissions each month, so we know that there is many a funny anecdote to be told and many a laugh to be had. It's true to say that when we started the column, we knew that we could brighten people's day but we didn't realise that we were actually in the business of healing. Now that science has put us there, we couldn't be happier.

As you read through this book, remember to share the humour with your family and friends. And make sure that you keep it handy. You never know when you or those around you might need another uplifting dose of the best medicine. Or, as Groucho Marx once said, "A laugh is like an aspirin, only it works twice as fast."

Life in these times

It's fast, complicated and confusing, but it's rarely dull – here are the absurdities and ironies of modern-day living in all their glory!

My boyfriend and I met online and we'd been dating for over a year. I introduced Hans to my uncle, who was fascinated by the fact that we met over the internet. He asked Hans what kind of line he had used to pick me up.

Ever the geek, Hans naïvely replied, "I just used a normal 56K modem."

ANNE MCCONNE

Kids have a greater need for speed than classroom computers can deliver. Impatient to turn in his essay, one restless student kept clicking the "Print" command. The printer started to churn out copy after copy of the ten-page report.

The topic? "Save Our Trees."

KEN CUMMINGS

I am five feet, three inches tall and pleasingly plump. After I had a minor accident, my mother accompanied me to the accident and emergency department.

The triage nurse asked for my height and weight, and I blurted out, "Five-foot-eight and ten stone."

While the nurse pondered this information, my mother leaned over to me. "Sweetheart," she gently chided, "this is not the internet."

M. M.

During a visit to the ladies' room, my friend Addy heard the woman in the next cubicle suddenly ask, "So how are you?"

Startled, Addy said that she was fine.

"So what's new?" the woman continued.

Still confused, Addy said, "Not much. What's new with you?"

It was then that the woman snapped, "Do you mind? I'm on the phone."

MARION SPARER

I was visiting a friend who could not find her cordless phone. After several minutes of searching, her young daughter said, "You know what they should invent? A phone that stays connected to its base so it never gets lost."

MIRIAM SCOW

Trying to explain to our five-year-old daughter how much computers had changed, my husband pointed to our brand-new computer and told her that when he was in university, a computer with the same amount of power would have been the size of a house.

Wide-eyed, our daughter asked, "How big was the mouse?"

C. HINDS

Learning to use a voice-recognition computer program, I was excited about the prospect of finally being able to write more accurately than I type. First I read out loud to the computer for about an hour to train it to my voice, then I opened a clean page and dictated a nursery rhyme to see the magic.

The computer recorded: "Murry fed a little clam, its fleas was bright and slow."

CARRIE PITTS

TIMELESS HUMOUR

50s The big electronic computer in the accounting department performed admirably until summer weather arrived. Then it practically quit. A diagnosis of the trouble revealed that the machine was extremely sensitive to changes in temperature, so the only thing to do was to move it into an air-conditioned room.

Now, as we office drones perspire and droop, we are treated to the vision of the computer operating coolly and efficiently beyond the glass wall of its private office. What was that again about men being smarter than machines?

"It's guaranteed for the life of the product, which obviously ended when it broke."

When my printer's type began to grow faint, I called a local repair shop, where a friendly man informed me that the printer probably needed only to be cleaned. Because the store charged £50 for such cleanings, he told me, I might be better off reading the printer's manual and trying the job myself.

Pleasantly surprised by his candor, I asked, "Does your boss know that you discourage business?"

"Actually it's my boss's idea," the employee replied sheepishly. "We usually make more money on repairs if we let people try to fix things themselves first."

MICHELLE ST. JAMES

A pastor I know of uses a standard liturgy for funerals. To personalise each service, he enters a "find and replace" command into his word processor. The computer then finds the name of the deceased from the previous funeral and replaces it with the name of the deceased for the upcoming one.

Not long ago, the pastor told the computer to find the name "Mary" and replace it with "Edna." The next morning, the funeral was going smoothly until the congregation intoned the Apostles' Creed. "Jesus Christ," they read from the preprinted program, "born of the Virgin Edna."

ROBIN GREENSPAN

I returned from Russia after living there nearly two years. My sister decided to surprise me by creating "welcome home" signs in Russian. She went to a website that offered translations and typed in "Welcome Home, Cole." She then printed the translated phrase onto about 20 coloured cardboard signs.

When I got off the plane, the first thing I saw was my family, excitedly waving posters printed with a strange message. My sister gave me a big hug, and pointed proudly to her creations. "Isn't that great?" she said. "Bet you didn't think I knew any Russian."

I admitted that I was indeed surprised – and so was she when I told her what the signs actually said: "Translation not found."

C. CRITTENDEN

I purchased a new desktop-publishing program that surprised me by containing a make-a-paper-aeroplane option. I decided to give it a try. After I selected the plane I wanted, the software gave me a choice of accessories available for my plane, including a stick-up tail, adjustable flaps and an AM/FM radio. Out of curiosity I chose the AM/FM radio.

The program responded with a message box stating: "Come on, be serious. These are paper aeroplanes."

GREG SCOTT

Picking what felt like a good moment, I asked the man I was dating if he was serious about our relationship. Looking hurt, he said, "Do you know how special you are?" He held up his mobile phone. "I use my daytime minutes on you."

AMANDA POINTELIN

Our newer, high-speed computer was in the shop for repair, and my son was forced to work on our old model with the black-and-white printer.

"Mum," he complained to me one day, "this is like we're living back in the twentieth century."

DENISE DONAVIN

A DIY expert on one of those home-improvement TV programmes suggested putting coffee granules into pale beige paint to give it a "kick". Indeed, on the wall he painted it looked lovely, so I decided to give it a try.

My wall looked great, but there was a catch. The room I'd painted was the bathroom – and I had possibly used too many granules. For weeks afterwards, whenever we took a shower, the steam condensed on the wall, sweated out the additive, and thick black coffee ran down on to the floor.

GLORIA LEWIS

As a responsible parent, I was horrified when I found two white tablets in my son's jeans. Before confronting him, I decided to show them to our local pharmacist. On one side was printed "24–7". Could they be an illegal substance? I wondered.

Taking her eye-glass, the pharmacist admitted she hadn't come across them before, but returned them with comforting words. Printed on the other side in minute lettering was the word "TREBOR".

FIONA BIDDISCOMBE

One cold night my boiler died, so I went to my parents' house. In the morning, a neighbour called to tell me that my water pipes had burst and flooded my house and hers. I raced home – and on the way got a speeding ticket.

Then the boiler repairman arrived and told me he didn't think he had the proper fuse but would check in his van. Meanwhile, the plumber cut holes in my bathroom wall to locate the leak.

When the boiler repairman returned, he held aloft a fuse. "I had the right one," he said triumphantly. "This must be your lucky day."

C. PRESTWICH

I was preparing lunch for my granddaughter when the phone rang. "If you can answer one question," a young man said, "you'll win ten free dancing lessons."

Before I could tell him I was not interested, he continued. "You'll be a lucky winner if you can tell me what Alexander Graham Bell invented."

"I don't know," I replied dryly, trying to discourage him.

"What are you holding in your hand right now?" he asked excitedly.

"A sandwich."

"Congratulations!" he shrieked. "And for having such a good sense of humour … "

L. CANTRELL

Having lived in our house for four years we were moving on. My husband had backed the car up to our garage door so we could start loading all of the boxes. At that moment, one of our neighbours came walking across the lawn carrying a plate of cakes.

"Isn't that thoughtful," my husband said to me. "They must have realised we've packed away our kitchen stuff."

The neighbour stuck out his hand and boomed, "Welcome to the neighbourhood!"

GWEN MOSER

Splashing out on a luxury holiday in Spain, my wife and I arrived at our five-star hotel. When we walked into the marble foyer, we began to feel out of place, as the other guests all looked so wealthy.

"McDonald," I said to the receptionist when we checked in. Looking us up and down in disdain, the receptionist answered, "Down the road, first street on the right."

ALEX MCDONALD

It is so rare to be offered a meal on airlines these days that I was surprised to hear the flight attendant ask the man sitting in front of me,

"Would you like dinner?"

"What are my choices?" he responded.

"Yes or no," she said.

KERVYN DIMNEY

The lift in our building broke down one day, leaving several of us stranded. Seeing a sign that listed two emergency phone numbers, I dialed the first and explained our situation.

After what seemed to be a very long silence, the voice on the other end said, "I don't know what you expect me to do for you; I'm a psychologist."

"A psychologist?" I replied. "Your phone is listed here as an emergency number. Can't you help us?"

"Well," he finally responded in a measured tone. "How do you feel about being stuck in a lift?"

CHRISTINE QUINN

Soon after arriving at our holiday cottage, my wife discovered a problem with the oven. I consulted the manual but had no joy. So, we contacted the owner, who in turn consulted her husband.

After he had been reading the instructions for a few minutes I joked that you'd need a degree in nuclear physics to understand them.

"No," he lamented. "I'm afraid it doesn't help."

PETER GROSSMAN

I provide technical support for the computer software published by my company. One day, over the phone, I was helping a customer install a product on a Macintosh. The procedure required him to delete an old file. On the Mac there is an icon of a trash can that is used to collect items to be permanently deleted.

I told the customer to click on the old file and drag it to the trash. Then I had him perform a few other steps. As a reminder, I said, "Don't forget to empty the trash."

Obediently he replied, "Yes, dear."

CYNTHIA KAINU

One Saturday night my boss and her family came to our house. As they were driving away at the end of the evening, I discovered that she had left her handbag in a corner next to the dining-room hatch. I was about to call her house, intending to leave a message on the answering machine, when my son reminded me that they had a mobile phone.

As I dialed the number, I marveled at the technology that would alert them before they had driven all the way home. A few seconds later the handbag began to ring.

P. DUNHAM

My mother began getting calls from men who misdialed the similar number of an escort service. Mum, who had had her number for years, asked the telephone company to change the organisation's number. They refused. The calls kept coming day and night.

Finally, Mum began telling the gentlemen who called that the company had gone out of business. Within a week, the escort service voluntarily changed its number.

MARIAN BURGESS

I was browsing in a military surplus shop when a young couple walked in with a little boy in a pushchair. I couldn't help noticing the father was in full punk regalia: spiked hair, black leather gloves, snake tattoos visible on his arms. Later I spotted him running through the shop, frantically calling for his son. Relieved when he found the boy in another aisle, he embraced him and admonished, "Don't go where Mummy and Daddy aren't able to see you. A scary man might grab you."

D. AGENA

13

YOU DON'T USE CHEMICALS, DO YOU?

FARMER'S MARKET

VEGETABLES

The memo about the company's revised travel policy dictated that we were no longer allowed to buy cheap tickets via the internet. Instead, we were instructed to use the more expensive company travel department. Furthermore, to show how much money we were saving, we were asked to compare fares – by looking on the internet.

I thought the typing error in the last line of the memo summed it up accurately: "The new process is ineffective today."

K. HARTMAN

A friend of mine always carries sweets with her and offers them to anyone she feels has been particularly helpful. Going through a supermarket checkout, she put a sweet down on the counter in front of the friendly man at the till. He refused politely, but she insisted and pushed the sweet back towards him and he accepted it. When my friend arrived home, she checked her receipt and found she'd been charged for confectionery from the pick-and-mix selection.

JOHN DICKINSON

After I bought my mother a compact-disc player and some CDs, she was excited to discover she no longer needed to rewind or fast-forward tapes or move the needle on her record player.

Knowing she was not that technically astute, I called her a few days later to see how she was managing. "Fine. I listened to Shania Twain this morning," she said.

"The whole CD?" I asked.

"No," she replied, "just one side."

C. DYER

A phone company representative called to ask if I was interested in caller ID. Since I'm blind, I asked, "Does it come in Braille?"

The rep put me on hold. When she returned, she replied, "I'm sorry, sir, but the caller ID box doesn't come in that colour."

ED LUCAS

"What sound does a dog make?" my friend, who is a teacher, asked her class.

"Woof woof," came the reply.

"And a cat?"

"Meow," said the children.

"And what sound does a mouse make?" she asked.

"Click," chorused the class.

GRAEME BRETHERTON

QUOTABLE
QUOTES

Part of what makes a human being a human being is the imperfections. Like, you wouldn't give a robot my ears. You just wouldn't do that.

WILL SMITH in InTouch

A computer lets you make more mistakes faster than any invention in human history – with the possible exceptions of handguns and tequila.

MITCH RATCLIFFE

The trouble with the rat race is that even if you win, you're still a rat.

LILY TOMLIN

Just think how far we've come in the 20th century. The man who used to be a cog in the wheel is now a digit in the computer.

ROBERT FUOSS
in The Wall Street Journal

A bank is a place that will lend you money if you can prove that you don't need it.

BOB HOPE

Why do they call it rush hour when nothing moves?

ROBIN WILLIAMS

Instant gratification takes too long.

CARRIE FISHER

You can't write poetry on the computer.

QUENTIN TARANTINO

A modern computer is an electronic wonder that performs complex mathematical calculations and intricate accounting tabulations in one ten-thousandth of a second – and then mails out statements ten days later.

PAUL SWEENEY

In the fight between you and the world, back the world.

FRANZ KAFKA

Modern manners

Peace and quiet

As I grow older I long for extensive periods of absolute silence. There is no such thing where I live. One can only experience calm wearing ear-plugs and heavily sedated.

Last Saturday I was woken at 3 a.m. from a divine sleep by my mother honking her emergency hooter. Was it a robber or a heart attack? I staggered to her bedroom and there she was at the open window, hooting wildly into the night air. She had been driven to the borders of madness by a party raging behind our house and thought, in her crazed, exhausted state, that they might hear her hooter, realise how annoying they were and shut up.

We phoned the Town Hall to alert the noise officers, but lucky them, they go home to bed at 3a.m.

At least my mother sleeps at the back of the house. Stuck at the front I am woken every hour or so by people wandering up and down the street at all hours,

carousing, arguing and laughing loudly as if it were lunchtime. I would like to rush out there, hold them up at gunpoint and place them in the stocks, gagged, until morning.

Nor can one rest during the day, what with the odd car alarm going off at dawn, thunderous pop music blaring from windows, the house shaken and blasted by passing cars throbbing with noise, Rosemary's Perfect Son practising his drumming and the Daughter and her chums galloping up and down the stairs relentlessly.

And because of the heat we must all have our windows open while the noise of enervated families shrieking within pours out and annoys all the other boiling and exhausted families who are trying to control themselves.

But it isn't just the hot weather. I suspect that the world is growing generally noisier and many of the public are partially deaf. Last night Daughter and I went out to dinner in a restaurant of her choice.

Michele Hanson, *Living with Mother*

Over the thunderous pop music, waitresses shouted cheerfully and Daughter and I lipread or roared at each other in order to converse. Being one of the new hearing-impaired generation, her ears terminally damaged and senses banged flat by clubbing and very loud music, the Daughter thought this a relaxing venue. Why was I scowling?

We had an uninhibited row about it. Luckily no on could hear us.

Out and about

I open the front door and see a desperate figure. Is that the first Mrs Rochester standing screaming and wailing at the top of the stairs in her nightie with her hair awry? No. It is my poor mother in a panic. Where have I been, why am I so late, she thought I was dead! But how, on a dog walk? Easy, thinks my mother: crashed on the way home, drowned in a pond, gobbled up by Rottweilers. She is the Anxiety Queen on overdrive.

She knows that if there is a psychopath on the loose, he is bound to home in on her only child.

She cannot help this. It runs in the family. I do it myself when Daughter goes off the radar, but luckily Daughter has a mobile. That has to be the answer. I must get one, programme my number into my mother's phone and she will be able to send out a mayday call at the touch of one button. Even the news of this plan soothes her. She is happy, but I feel rather glum. I must break my vow never to have a ghastly mobile.

I hate the pesky things. Remember that horrid advert in which the poor unfashionable mobile falls from the table? It is unattractive, isolated, unloved and probably seriously injured, but what happens? Everybody laughs themselves sick. Who would want to approve such callous behaviour and buy such a product?

Returning from York on the train Rosemary saw just how the mobile phone aids wickedness. A drunken soldier on leave borrowed his chum's mobile to phone three women and line them up for three consecutive bonking opportunities that very night, the last one being his wife, who he advised not to wait up. "The train's delayed," he lied, when really it was just pulling up into Euston.

So goodbye moral standards and resolutions, I am off to buy a mobile. Within hours I own one of the little horrors. I take it on our walk. Soon I am bellowing into it, just like all those people I have mocked for years. "Hello! I'm still on the Heath, we're having a coffee, back in half an hour." My mother is relaxing in heaven but Rosemary is scarlet with shame.

"Marvellous," I say, overexcited. "That's calmed her down."

"D'you know what you just said?" snaps Rosemary. "You said marvellous!"

"Did I?"

**"Beautiful day out there, folks. Don't miss it.
Complete coverage, coming up next."**

While walking through a car park, I tripped and fell flat on my face. As I was lying there, a woman motorist stopped and called out from her vehicle, "Are you hurt?"

"No, I'm fine," I said, touched by her concern.

"Oh, good," she said. "Does that mean you'll be leaving your parking space?"

HARRIETT WELLING

The car auction I attended was selling cars to benefit charity. Vehicles were classified as either "Running" or "No Start." On the block was a No Starter.

It had a shattered windshield, two missing tyres, a sagging front bumper, a bonnet that was sprung up at an angle, and bumps and dents all over the body.

Before he started the bidding, the auctioneer announced the car's year, make and model, and then read the owner's comments: "Please note – the radio does not work."

C. MANSUR

Friends and I were chatting over dinner in a restaurant. A man at the next table told his mobile phone caller to hold on. Then he stepped outside to talk.

When he returned, I said, "That was very thoughtful."

"I had no choice," he replied. "You were making too much noise."

N. BLUMENTHAL

Our flight was about to take off when the passenger behind me immediately launched into a loud and annoying conference call on his mobile phone. "Sally, get the customer lists. Charlie, pull all the data together we have on … Bob, can you bring us up to date … " and on and on.

As the flight attendant began the preflight safety instructions, the executive's voice was drowned out by the PA system. While the safety speech continued, I heard him mutter into the phone, "Hold on a second. Some people just like to hear themselves talk."

G. BORMAN

After we got broadband internet, my husband decided to start paying bills online. This worked well; in fact all our bill companies accepted online payments except one – our internet service provider.

SARAH LIBERA

I dialed a wrong number and got the following recording: "I am not available right now, but I thank you for caring enough to call. I am making some changes in my life. Please leave a message after the beep. If I do not return your call, you are one of the changes."

ANTONIO CURTIS

Security and peace of mind were part of the reason we moved to a gated community. Both flew out the window the night I called a local pizza shop for a delivery. "I'd like to order a large pepperoni, please," I said, then gave him the address of our house.

"We'll be there in about half an hour," the voice at the other end replied. "Your gate code is still 1238, right?"

MARY MCCUSKER

I heard the following over the PA system in a supermarket:

"A wallet has been found containing a large sum of cash but no ID. Will those laying claim to it please form a double line at the customer service desk?"

L. IANNARELLI

My sister isn't good with technology. So when she mastered her first mobile phone, she proudly sent the following text message to her daughter:

"Betyouareamazedthatimanagedtosendyouthistextallihavetodonowisworkouthowtogetspaces".

JOYCE WEBB

I realised the impact of computers on my young son one evening when there was a dramatic sunset. Pointing to the western sky, David said, "I wish we could click and save that."

THERESA KLEIN

My mother, a master of guilt trips, showed me a photo of herself waiting by a phone that never rings.

"Mum, I call all the time," I said. "If you had an answering machine, you'd know." Soon after, my brother installed one for her.

When I called the next time, I got her machine: "If you are a salesperson, press one. If you're a friend, press two. If you're my daughter who never calls, press 999 because the shock will probably give me a heart attack."

SUSAN STARACE BALDUCCI

"I've got to take this call."

"It's me. Just checking to see if the phone number
you gave me was real."

As an engineer in an upmarket hotel, I was asked to repair or replace the television in a guest room. When I arrived, the couple was watching a picture one-third the size of the screen. I knew all our spare sets were in use, so I figured what the hell: I struck the side of the TV with the heel of my hand. The picture returned to full size.

"Look, darling," said the wife to her husband. "He went to the same repair school as you."

WILLIAM OLLER

I was with a friend in a café when a noisy car alarm interrupted our conversation. "What good are car alarms when no one pays any attention to them?" I wondered aloud.

"Some are quite effective," my friend corrected me. "Last summer, my son spent a lot of time at the neighbours'. Whenever I wanted him home, I'd go out to our driveway and jostle his car."

SHEILA MOORE

My husband, a computer-systems trouble-shooter, rode with me in my new car one afternoon. He had been working on a customer's computer all morning and was still tense from the session. When I stopped for a traffic light,

I made sure to leave a safe distance from the stop line to keep oncoming drivers from hitting the car.

I couldn't help but laugh when my husband impatiently waved at me to move the car forward while saying, "Scroll up, sweetie."

GEORGIA HARVEY

While my wife was in the gynecologist's busy waiting room a mobile phone rang. A woman answered it, and for the next few minutes, she explained her symptoms to the caller in intimate detail, and what she suspected might be wrong.

Suddenly the conversation shifted, and the woman said, "Him? That's over." Then she added, "Can we talk about this later? It's rather personal, and I'm in a room full of people."

ALAN ROBERTS

In these days of teenage internet entrepreneurs, it's easy to forget, when shopping online, that you may not be dealing with a large, highly organised corporation. I recently e-mailed one website to enquire why my goods had not arrived a week after I had paid for them. A little later, I received a charming telephone call. "Sorry for the delay," said a young male voice. "I'll check

and get back to you. I can't access the Net at the moment because my mum's doing the hoovering and this room only has one socket."

TERESA HEWITT

People don't like to look fat in their own snapshots, which is why my husband, a professional photographer, gets a lot of requests asking him to retouch photos. So I wasn't surprised when one woman, pointing to a family portrait, asked him, "Can you take two stone off me?" until she added, "And put it on my sister?"

JEAN CUNDICK

21

Opening the box containing my new portable television, I removed the remote and turned it over to install the batteries.

Molded into the device was this message:

"Made in Indonesia – Not Dishwasher Safe."

M. WIER

Jolly holidays

Ancient proverb
It's not the travelling that's important –
It's the not getting there on time.

Pockets of surprise
Always be sure to carry four pairs of keys,
fifteen different coins,
a corkscrew, a lighter,
two discarded ring-pulls,
a metal dog-whistle and three small spoons
distributed about your person
before passing through
the airport security gate.

Is this one taken?
When boarding the train for
the long journey,
Wait until everyone else is sitting comfortably
before going up to the man who looks most content, his
possessions spread over
the neighbouring seat.
Then smile broadly and say,
"Excuse me: is this one taken?"

Mood music
If you are the Captain of an aeroplane
Ensure your passengers remain alert
as you joy-ride around the runway
before take-off
by playing Phil Collins's
"Something In The Air Tonight"
over the intercom.

Think of others
Has your neighbouring passenger
fallen into a deep sleep?
Re-angle his air vent
so he is refreshed by a blast
of cool air
on his left eyelid
before he awakes.

The perfect picnic
In search of the perfect place
for your picnic?
Be sure to speed past the first
seventeen sites
saying, "We can do better than that!"
At 2.50pm, you will realise that
the children are crying, the dog
is dehydrated,
the cassettes have all melted
and the
car is about to boil over.
"The perfect place!" you must
exclaim triumphantly,
as you drive into a field full of bulls.

A good squeeze
Early morning.
Sun ablaze.
Relax.
Reach out for the bottle of
sunscreen.
Give it a good squeeze.
Whoosh!
Your palm now contains enough
ointment
for your face
and thirty others.

Keep your eyes open
In the most beautiful part of the city,
or at the top of the highest
mountain;
in a leafy glade
or beside the most magnificent
cathedral,
don't worry.

Craig Brown, *This is Craig Brown*

You're only two minutes from a
McDonald's.

Four-legged friend
Cheer up a mangy dog in a muzzle
by giving him a
hearty pat.

A necessary calculation
You wish to buy a pair of espadrilles.
The price tag says 575 escudos.
There are 289.51 escudos to
the pound.
You try to do the sum in your head,
switch to a pencil and paper,
then nip back to your hotel
for a pocket calculator.
Ah! Good news!
Less than £2 for a pair of espadrilles!
You rush back to the shop.
They're out of your size.

Roots
Don't forget your roots.
On holiday, always remember
what the time is
in the UK.
So that when your family is
relaxing over lunch
You can glance at your watch
and say,

"At home, *Birds of a Feather* would
be just starting."

A grasp of language
Never let a foreign menu show
you up.
Point with a self-confident smile
at the seventh dish down.
And sit back, ready to enjoy your
Fritters of Raw Squid and Whole
Chillies in a Jellyfish Purée.

Away from it all
A little village in the Dordogne.
The office seems a million
miles away.
But who's that waving hard at you
across the street?
Why, if it isn't
Frank from the Fifth Floor
And
Maureen from Accounts.

Le Mot Juste
Never mind that the ticket-seller,
the hotel receptionist, the courier,
the shopkeeper
and the air stewardness
all speak fluent English.
They will be delighted to linger while

you flick through your selection
of phrasebooks
in search of
Le Mot Juste.

Life is a carousel
When picking up luggage
from the airport carousel
remember to
grab the handle of your heaviest bag
as it whirls round, sending
others flying
as you struggle
to keep up with it.

23

Jesus and Satan were arguing over who was better with computers. Finally God suggested they settle it: Each would spend two hours using spreadsheets, designing web pages, making charts and tables – everything they knew how to do.

The two sat down at their keyboards and began typing furiously. Just before the two hours were up, a thunderstorm knocked the power out. Once it came back on, they booted up their computers.

"It's gone! It's all gone!" Satan began to scream. "My work was destroyed!"

Meanwhile, Jesus began quietly printing out his work. "Hey, he must have cheated!" Satan yelled. "How come his stuff wasn't lost?"

God shrugged and said simply, "Jesus saves."

LAURA MASON

Shortly after I had my car repaired, the mechanic who fixed it asked me to bring it back. I watched as he opened the bonnet and removed a tool he had left behind. In a conspiratorial voice I said, "If you were a surgeon, I'd sue for malpractice."

"Yeah, but if I was a surgeon," he replied, "I'd charge you for having to go back in."

JEANIE LOVELADY

I feel inadequate when talking with a mechanic, so when my vehicle started making a strange noise, I sought help from a friend. He drove the car around for a few minutes, listened carefully, then told me how to explain the difficulty when I took it in for repair.

At the garage I proudly recited, "The timing is off, and there are premature detonations, which may damage the valves."

As I smugly glanced over the mechanic's shoulder, I saw him write on his clipboard "Lady says it makes a funny noise."

KATE KELLOGG

An undertaker friend organised the funeral of a man who was to be buried on his birthday. To mark the sad irony, the man's young grandson asked if he could put a card in the coffin. My friend happily agreed – not realising it was a musical card. As the coffin was carried through the church, the movement knocked the card off the departed's chest and triggered its mechanism.

The service remained dignified, but its solemnity was somewhat undermined by a tinny voice singing "Happy birthday to you, happy birthday to you" from somewhere inside the coffin.

ALAN HASKEY

Listening to my husband praise the virtues of internet shopping, I remarked that in five years' time there would be an entry in the dictionary for those who panic at the thought of visiting the shops and will only make their purchases over the internet.

"There already is," replied my husband. "They're called 'men'."

JAN MORPHET

After shopping at a busy supermarket, another woman and I happened to leave at the same time, only to be faced with the daunting task of finding our cars in the crowded car park. Just then my car horn beeped, and I was able to locate my vehicle easily.

"Wow," the woman said. "I sure could use a gadget like that to help me find my car."

"Actually," I replied, "that's my husband."

KATHY BEHRENBRINKER

My 50-something friend Nancy and I decided to introduce her mother to the magic of the internet. Our first move was to access the popular "Ask Jeeves" site, and we told her it could answer any question she had.

Nancy's mother was very skeptical until Nancy said, "It's true, Mum. Think of something to ask it."

As I sat with fingers poised over the keyboard, Nancy's mother thought a minute, then responded, "How is Aunt Helen feeling?"

CATHERINE BURNS

"I've figured out how to send e-mails and faxes, take photos, play games, and film videos, but what I'd really like to do is make a phone call."

TIMELESS HUMOUR

60s We were browsing through our local record shop when the proprietor, also a stereo fan, walked up to make suggestions about some recordings he thought we might enjoy. As we were engrossed in this conversation, a teenager came along and asked "Where can I find the rock-'n'-roll records?" With a disarming smile the proprietor replied, "Right over there, son. We try to keep them separate from the music."

B.M.

My husband works for a high-tech company that uses a sophisticated robotic mail-delivery system. The robot makes mail stops by following a clear painted line on the hallway floor. Recently the line had to be recharged by applying special paint. While it was drying, signs were posted warning, "Please don't step on the invisible line."

J. BADIK

On holiday on one of the Hebridean islands, my husband went to a nearby farm to buy milk. He asked the owner what he thought the weather would be like that day.

The farmer gazed up at the sky and looked off at the far horizon. **"It'll be fine,"** he replied.

"How can you tell?" asked my husband, intrigued by the man's understanding of nature.

"It said so on the radio."

ALISON THIRKELL

My sister Darlene has the confidence – but not always the skills – to tackle any home-repair project. For example, in her garage are pieces of a lawn mower she once tried to fix. So I wasn't surprised the day my other sister Jesse and I found Darlene attacking her vacuum cleaner with a screwdriver.

"I can't get this thing to cooperate," she explained.

"Why don't you drag it out to the garage and show it the lawn mower?" Jesse suggested.

J. NORTON

The computer in my classroom recently started acting up. After watching me struggle with it, one of my students took over. "Your hard drive crashed," he said. I called the computer services office and explained, "My computer is down. The hard drive crashed."

"We can't just send people down on your say-so. How do you know that's the problem?"

"A student told me," I answered.

"We'll send someone over right away."

ROLF EKLUND

"That sounds expensive. Is there any way you could ship it without handling it?"

My wife and I get along just great – except she's a back-seat driver second to none. On my way home from work one day, my mobile phone rang as I merged onto the motorway. It was my wife. By chance, she had entered the motorway right behind me.

"Sweetheart," she said, "your indicator is still on. And put your lights on – it's starting to rain."

W. HAIRSTON

Heard on my cable company's answering machine: **"We realise you are still holding. Please do not hang up, as this will further delay your call."**

EDGAR NENTWIG

To keep their active two-year-old from roaming onto the busy street in front of their home, my sister and brother-in-law decided to put a gate across the driveway. After working over two weekends on the project, Robert was ready to attach the lock to complete the job. He was working on the garden side of the gate, with his daughter nearby, when he dropped the screwdriver he was using and it rolled under the gate, out of his reach.

"I'll get it, Daddy," Lauren called, nimbly crawling under the newly erected barrier.

JANICE DECOSTE

Our office building's only lift was acting up. When I rode it to the ground floor on my way to lunch, the door refused to open. Trying not to panic, I hit the emergency button, which triggers an automatic call to the repair service.

Through the speaker in the elevator, I heard the call going through and then a recorded announcement: "The area code of the number you dialed has been changed. The new area code is 810. Please hang up and dial again."

DIANE MASTRANTONIO

My wife's mother, who is in her nineties, lives in sheltered housing not far from us. She manages very well, but sometimes modern technology confuses her.

One day she phoned to say that despite pressing the button on the remote control several times, the TV would not turn off. And for reasons she couldn't understand, she kept falling out of her chair. Puzzled, my wife and I decided to go round to her house to see what was going on.

Sitting in her electric recliner, she gave us a demonstration. But rather than picking up the TV remote, she pointed her chair's controller at the screen and pressed one of the buttons. The recliner rose slightly towards the upright position.

"See?" she said. "The television's not working," and she continued to press the button, rising a little each time, until the chair reached its full height and gently tipped her out.

DAVID WRIGHT

27

Over the years I have heard my share of strange questions and silly comments from people who call the computer software company where I work as a technical support telephone operator. But one day I realised how absurd things can sound on the other end of the line when I heard myself say to one caller, "Yes, sir, you must first upgrade your download software in order to download our upgrade software."

CARLOS MEJIA

I was delighted to discover that I could play compact discs in the new computer I had received at work. One morning I was enjoying the sound of Beethoven when an administrative assistant stopped by to deliver a stack of papers.

Hearing classical music filling the air, she stopped and exclaimed, "Poor you. They put you on hold?"

KEITH BRINTON

I thought I had finally found a way to convince Susan, my continually harried friend, that she needed to find ways to relax. I invited her to dinner and, while I was busy cooking, she agreed to watch my videotape on stress management and relaxation techniques. Fifteen minutes later,

My wife's car horn began to beep in cold weather and would only stop when she disconnected it.

So she disabled the horn and drove to the dealership, whose garage had its door shut to keep out the cold. Outside was a sign: **"Honk horn for service."**

JEFF ROMANCZUK

"and this one's for people who've hurt their wrists wearing too many wristbands."

she came into the kitchen and handed me the tape.

"But it's a 70-minute video," I replied. "You couldn't have watched the whole thing."

"Yes, I did," Susan assured me. "I put it on fast-forward."

JEAN KELLY

A colleague asked if I knew what to do about a computer problem that was preventing her from getting e-mail. After calling the help desk, I told my colleague that e-mail was being delayed to check for a computer virus.

"It's a variant of the I Love You virus, only worse," I said.

"What could be worse?" my single colleague asked wryly. "The Let's Just Be Friends virus?"

A. ORCHEL

When I heard sirens outside our block of flats, I looked out of the window and saw two fire engines coming down the road. A few minutes later, I heard more sirens as a couple of ambulances arrived, followed by several police cars. A few moments passed and another vehicle pulled up with its bells ringing – the local ice-cream man hoping to cash in on the crowd gathered at the scene.

BRIAN WOODROW

During the mortgage closing on our house, my wife and I were asked to sign documents containing small print. When I asked if I should read it, my lawyer replied, "Legally, you should. But here's the bottom line: If you pay your installments on time, there is nothing in there that could harm you. Should you stop paying, however, there is definitely nothing in the small print that can save you."

MILLORAD DEVIAK

TIMELESS HUMOUR

70s A solar-powered computer wrist watch, which is programmed to tell the time and date for 125 years, has a guarantee – for two years.

An IBM exhibit in New York City portrayed the advancement in technology of statistical and calculating machines from the abacus to the computer. After completing the tour, I stopped at the reception desk to ask a question. There, a distinguished elderly gentleman was keeping track of the number of visitors in the old tried-and-true method of drawing ̶H̶H̶ ̶H̶H̶ on a sheet of paper.

EMIL BIRNBAUM

My five children and I were playing hide-and-seek one evening. With the lights turned off in the house, the kids scattered to hide, and I was "it." After a few minutes I located all of them. When it was my turn to hide, they searched high and low but could not find me.

Finally one of my sons got a bright idea. He went to the phone and dialed; they found me immediately because my pager started beeping.

LELAND JENSEN

All my husband wanted was to pay for some batteries, but none of the assistants in the electronics shop seemed interested in helping him.

"I've got an idea," I said, and pulled a tape measure out of my bag. I stepped over to one of the giant plasma-screen TVs and started to measure it. Faster than you can say high definition, a young man came running over.

"May I help you?" he asked breathlessly.

"Yes," I replied. "I'd like to buy these batteries."

TASIA DALE

All in a day's work

Put a group of people together and see how they get the job done.
When you're all aiming for the same goal, what could possibly go wrong?

"We're considering outsourcing your job. Could you explain to this guy in Guatemala whatever it is you do around here?"

I hate the idea of going under the knife. So I was very upset when the doctor told me I needed a tonsillectomy. Later, the nurse and I were filling out an admission form. I tried to respond to the questions, but I was so nervous I couldn't speak. The nurse put down the form, took my hands in hers and said, "Don't worry. This medical problem can easily be fixed, and it's not a dangerous procedure."

"You're right. I'm being silly," I said, feeling relieved. "Please continue."

"Good. Now," the nurse went on, "do you have a living will?"

EDWARD GRIFFIN

While on holiday, my husband and I decided to see a film at the little local cinema nearby. The old woman working in the box office was resplendent in a scarlet tunic with gold epaulettes. "Have you worked here long?" my husband asked her.

"Twenty-seven years," she replied proudly.

"You must like it," I smiled.

"Oh, I love it," she said, picking up her torch to show us to our seats. "Once you've been in show business, you can't settle for any other kind of life."

B. ANDERSON

Most people would be angry if their company was bought and the new owners replaced them with their own people. Not our neighbour Andy. "You know how it goes," he said, waxing philosophical. "Every circus brings its own clowns."

CHRIS GULLEN

I had a job cleaning the home of an older couple. Among other duties, I had to dust their many imported carvings and petrified collectables as well as clean up after their pets.

One day I was astonished to find two ivory fossils lying on the floor beside the bookcase. I picked them up and put them back on the shelf. The next week, the same thing happened. That afternoon, my employer came into the room, her faithful canine behind her. Looking round, she eyed the bookcase.

"Tippy," she asked, "how do your bones keep getting up there?"

JENNIFER GORDON

Working in the training section of a government department, I organised a team-building exercise about resolving conflict between management and staff.

Employees were asked to think about the subject and jot down keywords on a flip chart. One participant complained about the management's tendency to interfere and wrote "nitpicking". Jumping to his feet, one of the managers queried, "Shouldn't there be a hyphen between 'nit' and 'picking'?"

E. HOWSON

I worked hard planting shrubs and flowers to create the tumbling effect of a cottage garden and was very pleased with the results. A friend remarked one day on how pretty it looked. "I hope you don't mind my copying your idea," she said, "next year, I think I'll just chuck plants in and see what happens."

CHRISTINE BYFORD

33

SIGN LANGUAGE

Noted at the bottom of a receipt for funeral arrangements:
"Thank you.
Please come again."

CARMELA HENRIQUEZ

Everyone at the company I worked for dressed up for Halloween. One fellow's costume stumped us. He simply wore trousers and a white T-shirt with a large 98.6 printed across the front in glitter. When someone finally asked what he was supposed to be, he replied, "I'm a temp."

BRIAN DAVIS

I'm dyslexic, and attended a conference about the disorder with a friend. The speakers asked us to share a personal experience with the group. I told them stress aggravates my condition, in which I reverse words and letters when I'm tense. When I finished speaking, my friend leaned over and whispered to me, "Now I know why you named your daughter Hannah."

CHARLES JEHLEN

Teaching is not for sensitive souls. While reviewing future, past and present tenses with my English class, I posed the question "'I am beautiful' is what tense?" One student raised her hand. "Past tense."

REEMA RAHAT

While I was on duty as an assistant in the casualty ward a father brought in his son, who had managed to poke a tyre from one of his toy trucks up his nose. The man was embarrassed, but I assured him children were always putting all sorts of things up their noses. I quickly removed the tyre and then sent them on their way.

A few minutes later, the father was back in Casualty asking to talk to me in private. Mystified, I led him to an examining room.

"While we were on our way home," he began, "I was looking at that little tyre and wondering, how on earth did my son get this thing stuck up his nose and then ... "

It took just a few seconds to get the toy tyre out of Dad's nose.

LEAH BEACK

Working as a secretary at an international airport, my sister had an office adjacent to the room where security temporarily holds suspects. One day security officers were questioning a man when they were suddenly called away on another emergency. To the horror of my sister and her colleagues, the man was left alone in the unlocked room. After a few minutes, the door opened and he began to walk out.

Summoning up her courage, one of the secretaries barked, "Get back in there, and don't you come out until you're told!" The man scuttled back inside and slammed the door. When the security people returned, the women reported what had happened. Without a word, an officer walked into the room and released one very frightened telephone repairman.

RUSS PERMAN

My builder friend was doing some repairs on a house when he and his workmate spotted a revolving summerhouse in the garden and decided to see how fast they could turn it. So they spun it round faster and faster.

It was only when they looked up that they realised there was an old lady sitting inside holding on for dear life.

AUDREY ROBERTS

Touring Ireland's countryside with a group of travel writers, we passed an immaculate cemetery with hundreds of beautiful headstones set in a field of emerald green grass. Everyone reached for their cameras when the tour guide said the inventor of the crossword puzzle was buried there. He pointed out the location, "Three down and four across."

STEVE BAUER

One of my friends, a musician, is always upbeat. Nothing gets her down. But when she developed ringing in one ear, I was concerned it might overwhelm even her. When I asked if her condition was especially annoying to a musician, she shook her head. "Not really," she said cheerfully. "The ringing sound is in the key of B flat, so I use it to tune my cello a half-tone lower."

KATHLEEN CAHILL

The 104-year-old building that had served as the priory and student lodgings of the small Catholic college where I work was about to be demolished. As the wrecker's ball began to strike, I sensed the sadness and anxiety of one of the older monks whose order had founded the college.

"This must be difficult to watch, Father," I said. "The tradition associated with that building, the memories of all the students and monks who lived and worked there. I can't imagine how hard this must be for you."

"It's worse than that," the monk replied. "I think I left my PalmPilot in there."

P.J. BROZYNSKI

My colleagues and I decided to remove the small, wooden suggestion box from our office because it had received so few entries. We stuck the box on top of a seven-foot-high metal storage cabinet and promptly forgot about it. Months later, when the box was moved during remodelling, we found a single slip of paper inside. The suggestion read, "Lower the box!"

FRANK MONACO

A man rushed to the jewellery counter in the shop where I work soon after the doors opened one morning and said he needed a pair of diamond earrings. I showed him a wide selection, and quickly he picked out a pair. When I asked him if he wanted them gift-wrapped, he said, "That'd be great. But can you make it quick? I forgot today was my anniversary, and my wife thinks I'm taking out the rubbish."

A. PAYSON

TIMELESS HUMOUR

50s When a fellow piano tuner was ill, I took over his assignment of tuning a piano in a girls' boarding-house. While I was at work, several of the girls strolled casually through the room in various states of undress. The climax came when a young lady in startling déshabillé appeared to pay the bill.

As I was writing the receipt, she suddenly gave me a bewildered look, then fled, screaming, "That's not our regular man!"

Their regular man is blind.

ALEX BYRNES

It took five years at university to become an archaeologist and I am proud of my job. It's just a pity not everyone appreciates it. My colleague and I were on a dig in a local town when a woman walked by with her son. Seeing us in our hole, covered in mud with pickaxes in hand, the mother told her child, "See what happens if you don't work hard at school? You'll end up like them."

NICHOLAS MARQUEZ-GRANT

35

Each year our company holds a training session in the conference room of the same hotel. When we were told we would not be able to reserve our usual location, my secretary, Gail, spent many hours on the phone trying to work out alternative arrangements. Finally, when the details were ironed out, she burst into my office.

"Great news, Scott!" she announced. "We're getting our regular room at the hotel!"

All eyes were on Gail and me as she suddenly realised she had interrupted a meeting

SCOTT DUINK

A friend and I used to run a small temporary-staffing service. Our agency did mandatory background checks on all job candidates, even though our application form asked them if they'd ever been convicted of a crime. One day after a round of interviews, my colleague was entering information from a young man's application into the computer.

She called me over to show me that he had noted a previous conviction for manslaughter. Below that, on the line listing his skills, he had written, "Good with people."

JANA RAHRIG

The company where I work provides four-foot-high cubicles so each employee can have some privacy.

One day a colleague had an exasperating phone conversation with one of her teenage sons. After hanging up, she heaved a sigh and said, **"No one ever listens to me."**

Immediately, several voices from surrounding cubicles called out, **"Yes, we do."**

JO JAIMESON

My husband, a teacher, had a meeting with the mother of a pupil who was easily distracted in class. He asked if she had noticed that in her daughter. The mother looked thoughtfully at him and then, pointing to the far wall, asked "Are those aluminium windows?"

M. JONES

I worked different shifts as a chef at two restaurants in the same area. One Saturday night, I was about to finish the evening shift at one restaurant and hurrying to report to work at the second place. I was delayed because one table kept sending back an order of hash browns, insisting they were too cold. I replaced them several times, but the customers were still not satisfied.

When I was able to leave, I raced out the door and arrived at my second job. A waitress immediately handed me my first order. "Make sure these hash browns are hot," she said, "because these people just left a restaurant down the street that kept serving them cold ones."

BILL BERGQUIST

Finally, after years of testing business software, I landed my dream job – trying out computer games. On my first day I was listing various ideas in a spreadsheet programme when my manager walked past.

He looked at my screen for a moment, then issued a stern warning: "I'd better not catch you using spreadsheets in company time when you know you should be playing games."

JON BACH

"Thanks to wireless technology, I can hate my job almost anywhere."

Mango delight

The computer decided that the three most popular ice cream flavours were book-ends, West Germany and pumice stone. This was found to be due to an electrical fault, the cards were rapidly checked by hand, and this time the three most popular flavours were found to be mango delight, cumquat surprise, and strawberry and lychee ripple.

Reggie held a meeting of the exotic ices team in his office at ten-thirty. Tony Webster wore a double-breasted grey suit with a discreetly floral shirt and matching tie. His clothes were modern without being too modern. Esther Pigeon wore an orange sleeveless blouse and a green maxi-skirt with long side vents. Morris Coates from the advertising agency wore flared green corduroy trousers, a purple shirt, a huge white tie, a brown suede jacket and black boots.

"What is this?" said Reggie. "A fashion show?"

David Harris-Jones telephoned at ten thirty-five to say that he was ill in bed with stomach trouble, the result of eating forty-three ice creams.

Joan provided coffee. Reggie explained that there would be trial sales campaigns of the three flavours in two areas – Hertfordshire and East Lancashire. David Harris-Jones would be in control of Hertforshire and Tony Webster of East Lancashire, with Reggie controlling the whole operation.

"Great," said Tony Webster.

Esther Pigeon gave them the results of her survey. 73% of housewives in East Lancashire and 81% in Hertfordshire had expressed interest in the concept of exotic ice creams. Only 8% in Hertfordshire and 14% in East Lancashire had expressed positive hostility, while 5% had expressed latent hostility. In Hertfordshire 96.3% of the 20% who formed 50% of consumer spending potential were in favour. Among the unemployed only 0.1% were in favour. 0.6% had told her where they could put the exotic ice creams.

"What does this all mean in laymen's terms?" said Reggie.

"This would be regarded as a reasonably satisfactory basis for introducing the product in the canvassed areas," said Esther Pigeon.

The sun was streaming in on to the dark green filling cabinets, and Reggie watched the bits of dust that were floating around in its rays. He could feel his shivering again, like a subdued shuddering from his engine room. Suddenly he realized that Esther Pigeon was talking.

"Sorry," he said. "I missed that. I was looking at the rays of dust in the sun. They're rather pretty."

There was a pause. Morris Coates flicked cigarette ash on to the floor.

"I was saying that there were interesting variations from town to town," said Esther Pigeon, who had huggable knees but an indeterminate face, and was usually ignored by 92.7% of the men on the Bakerloo Line. "There was a lot of interest in Hitchin and Hertford,

David Nobbs, *The Fall and Rise of Reginald Perrin*

but Welwyn Garden City was positively lukewarm."

"Hitchin has a very nice church," said Reggie. It slipped out before he could stop it. Everyone stared at him. He was sweating profusely.

"It's very hot in here," he said. "Take your jackets off if you want to."

The men took their jackets off and rolled up their sleeves. Reggie had the hairiest forearms, followed by Esther Pigeon.

He was very conscious of his grubby white shirt. The sartorial revolution had passed him by. He resented these well-dressed men. He resented Esther Pigeon, whose vital statistics were 36-32-38. He resented Tony Webster who sat quietly, confident yet not too confident, content to wait for his inevitable promotion. He resented the film of skin which was spreading across their forgotten coffees.

They turned to the question of advertising.

"I was just thinking, off the top of the head, beautiful girl," said Morris Coates. "Yoga position, which let's face it can be a pretty sexy position, something like, I'm not a writer, I find it much easier to meditate – with a cumquat surprise ice cream – one of the new range of exotic ice creams from Sunshine."

"Ludicrous," said Reggie. Morris Coates flushed.

"I'm just exploring angles," he said. "We'll have a whole team on this. I'm just sounding things out."

It wasn't any use being angry with Morris Coates. It wasn't his fault. Somebody had to man the third-rate advertising agencies. If it wasn't for him, it would be somebody else.

"What about sex?" said Morris Coates.

"What about something like, off the top of the head, I like to stroke my nipple with a strawberry and lychee ripple," said Reggie.

Morris Coates turned red. Esther Pigeon examined her finger nails. Tony Webster smiled faintly.

"All right, fair enough, sex is a bum steer," said Morris Coates. "Perhaps we just go for something plain and factual, with a good up-beat picture. But then you're up against the fact that an ice cream carton *per se* doesn't look up-beat. Just thinking aloud. Sorry."

"Well I'll be interested to see what you come up with," said Reggie.

"Incidentally," said Morris Coates, "is the concept of a ripple, in the ice cream sense of the word, fully understood by the public?"

"In the Forest of Dean, in 1967, 97.3% of housewives understood the concept of a ripple in the ice cream sense of the word," said Esther Pigeon.

"Does that answer your question?" said Reggie

"Yes. Fine," said Morris Coates.

39

"We're going to have to let you go, but I'm confident that you'll land on your feet."

On duty as a customer-service representative for a car rental company, I answered a call from a driver who needed a tow. He was stranded on a busy motorway, but he didn't know the make of the car he was driving. I asked again for a more detailed description beyond "a nice blue four-door".

After a long pause, the driver replied, "My car is the one on fire."

 and a DAEMIEN O'KEEFFE

Our daughter Helen worked in a local government office. As part of her job she had to check through the various accident-report forms that had been received.

One from the municipal swimming baths described how a little boy had bumped his head on the side of the pool. Under the heading of "Action taken" the attendant had written "Kissed better".

ANTHONY THOMAS

I was halfway through a meeting with a photocopy salesman, when he suddenly mentioned his wife and children, and how contented he was. I was puzzled, but let him continue. It was only when I glanced down that I understood his reason for imparting this personal information: the table leg against which I had been rubbing my itchy foot wasn't a table leg at all!

EILEEN GASKIN

Have you ever wondered what medical personnel scribble on those clipboards attached to the foot of the bed? Here are some comments taken from hospital charts:

"The patient refused autopsy."

"The patient has no previous history of suicides."

"She has had no shaking chills, but her husband states she was very hot in bed last night."

"She's numb from her toes down."

"Patient has two teenage children but no other abnormalities."

"Discharge status: alive but without my permission."

WILLIAM MURPHY

A Catholic priest I once knew went to the hospital to visit patients. Stopping at the nurses' station, he carefully looked over the patient roster and jotted down the room number of everyone who had "Cath" written boldly next to his name. That, he told me, was a big mistake.

When I asked why, he replied, "It was only after I had made the rounds that I learned they were all patients with catheters."

DENNIS SMYTH

SIGN LANGUAGE

Seen in a dentist's office:

"Be kind to your dentist. He has fillings too."

CHRISTY CRITCHFIELD

Any time companies merge, employees worry about layoffs. When my company was bought out, I was no exception. My fears seemed justified when a photo of the newly merged staff appeared on the company's website with the following words underneath: **"Updated daily"**.

DIANNE STEVENS

Our plane had a number of children on board who required a lot of attention from very patient flight attendants. As if that weren't enough, the plane had mechanical problems and was forced to return to the airport.

An hour later we were finally taking off. In the dimmed cabin, the voice of a male attendant came soothingly over the intercom. "You are getting sleepy ... very sleepy. You don't want any snacks. You don't want any drinks. You want to be left alone."

PAMELA OLSCHEWSKI

During a business trip to a Boeing factory in America, I noticed several 747 and 777 airliners being assembled. Before the engines were installed, huge weights were hung from the wings to keep the planes balanced. The solid-steel weights were bright yellow and marked "14,000 lbs". But what I found particularly interesting was some stencilling I discovered on the side of each weight. Imprinted there was the warning: "Remove before flight".

KEVIN HAW

Regulations at the hospital where I work state that a wheelchair must be provided for patients being discharged. However, while working as a student nurse, I found one elderly gentleman – dressed and sitting on the bed with a suitcase at his feet – who insisted he didn't need my help. After a chat about rules being rules, he reluctantly let me wheel him to the lift.

On the way down I asked if his wife was meeting him. "I don't know," he said. "She's still upstairs changing out of her hospital gown."

P. DANSEY

"Which brings us to my next point."

"I want to try something, Caruthers – come at me like you're asking for a raise."

My husband, Daniel, had been promoted to a newly created position. He was eager to find out what his official title was so when his business cards finally arrived I was surprised that he seemed reluctant to show me. After some persuasion, Daniel gave me one, naming him director of product efficiency. "Wow," I responded, "that sounds impressive."

"Not really," Daniel replied as he removed my thumb from the acronym underneath. It read DOPE.

SANDY GERVAIS

The chef of the restaurant I manage collided with a waiter one day and spilled coffee all over our computer. The liquid poured into the processing unit, resulting in a symphony of crackling and popping sounds. After mopping up the mess, we gathered round the terminal as the computer was turned back on.

"Please work," begged the waiter.

A waitress replied, "It should be faster than ever before – that was a double espresso."

BRIAN KOHLER

One of the irksome things for a musician in a symphony orchestra is trying to follow the erratic beat of guest conductors. I didn't realise how strongly the rest of the musicians felt until we were talking to someone from a university physics department at a reception.

When I asked him what his field was, he answered, "I work with semiconductors."

"So do we," I heard a colleague mutter.

BERNARD GOLDSTEIN

During the latter stages of my pregnancy, I brought a cushion in to work to make my chair a little more comfortable. One afternoon I returned from lunch and found that my chair had been pushed to the other side of my work area.

"Looks like someone's been sitting in my chair," I commented to one of my colleagues.

Glancing down at my stomach, she said, "It looks like someone's also been sleeping in your bed."

RUTH MALLARD

Excerpts from actual employee evaluations. Hope none of these rings a bell:

- "Works well when under constant supervision and cornered like a rat in a trap."
- "His men would follow him anywhere, but only out of morbid curiosity."
- "When she opens her mouth, it is only to change feet."
- "He doesn't have ulcers, but he's a carrier."
- "If you see two people talking and one looks bored, he's the other one."

It was an unusually hectic evening at the emergency department where I work. The doctor on duty was simultaneously bombarded with questions, given forms to sign, and even asked for his dinner order. I was in the next room, cleaning up a newly sutured wound, when I realised he hadn't given instructions for a bandage. I poked my head out the door and asked, "What kind of dressing do you want on that?"

"French," he replied.

BRENDA TODD

As a 999 operator, I speak to people in various states of panic. One day, a woman called saying that a family member had fallen and needed help.

"Do you know what caused the fall?" I asked.

"No," the woman nervously replied. "What?"

REBECCA PARKS

Our copier was broken so I put a note on it: "Service has been called." When the technician told me he had to order parts, I added a second note: "Parts have been ordered." During the next five days, when we had to use an older copier on the other side of the building, someone taped a third note to the machine: "Prayers have been said."

JENNIFER HARRISON

The aquarium shop where I work has been in business for more than 20 years. One Sunday a customer called wanting to buy a larger aquarium. "And by the way, I've spent a lot of money at your shop over the years," he said. "I think I should get a discount."

"Only our owner can give a discount," I explained, "and he won't be in until tomorrow."

When the customer said that he'd come in the next day, I asked him if there was anything else I could help him with.

"Yes," he said. "Where is your shop located?"

DAVID BILLINGTON

The company I work for supplies materials to picture-framing shops. One of our customers told me about a woman she had served who wanted to purchase a green frame. She had shown her a large selection of sample corner pieces, holding them up to the picture. However, the woman didn't feel any of them was quite what she wanted. "Could you be more precise about what you had in mind?" my customer asked.

"You don't seem to understand," the shopper replied. "I want a frame that goes right round the picture."

A. MORGAN

One of the most difficult tasks I had to perform as a paediatric nurse was immunising children.

One day I entered the examining room to give a four-year-old called Lizzie her jab. "No, no, no!" she screamed. Her mother scolded her, complaining that she ought to be more polite. With that, the girl shouted even louder, "No thank you! No thank you!"

CAROL VARTANIAN

Sometimes I wonder whether the world is being run by smart people who are putting us on, or by imbeciles who really mean it.

MARK TWAIN

You're not famous until my mother has heard of you.

JAY LENO

The grass may be greener on the other side, but it's just as hard to cut.

LITTLE RICHARD

It is impossible to enjoy idling thoroughly unless one has plenty of work to do.

JEROME K. JEROME

A peacock that rests on his feathers is just another turkey.

DOLLY PARTON

Money won't buy friends, but you get a better class of enemy.

SPIKE MILLIGAN

When people ask if I do my own stunts, I always answer, "Not on purpose."

BILLY BOB THORNTON

You've got to be original, because if you're like someone else, what do they need you for?

BERNADETTE PETERS on "Inside the Actors Studio" (Bravo)

If you can see a bandwagon, it's too late to get on it.

JAMES GOLDSMITH

My nephew, a flight attendant, split the back of his trousers one day during a flight. To save embarrassment, he decided to work in front of the beverage cart, facing forward.

The arrangement worked perfectly until he got to the last row and a passenger leaned over to him and said in a low voice, "Your fly is open."

RICHARD MARKS

My husband Jeff and I had several problems while assembling our new computer system, so we called the help desk. The man on the phone started to talk to Jeff in computer jargon, which confused us even more. "Sir," my husband said politely, "please explain what I should do as if I were a four-year-old."

"OK," the computer technician replied. "Son, could you please put your mummy on the phone?"

LENA WORTH

While on holiday, my wife and I stopped for lunch at a diner. We sat at the counter, right next to the grill. The cook was a young man who was very busy flipping pancakes. Every so often, he would

"Damn it, Peterson, you've got to try and fit in!"

stop and hit the grill with the handle of the spatula. Finally I asked him facetiously, "Does that improve the taste of the pancakes?"

"No," he replied. "That keeps the handle from falling off."

NORMAN SMEE

The insurance company I work for gets business from a retirement community. Once, when applying for car insurance for a client, I asked him how many miles he drives in a year. He said he didn't know.

"Well, do you drive 10,000 miles a year?" I asked, "or 5,000?"

He said the numbers sounded

high. "What month is this?" he asked. I told him it was July.

"Maybe this will help," he said. "I filled the car with petrol in February."

LYNN BEBEE

Our nephew was getting married to a doctor's daughter. At the wedding reception, the father of the bride stood up to make his speech, which he had scribbled on a piece of scrap paper. Several times during his address, he halted, overcome with what I assumed was a moment of deep emotion. But after a particularly long pause, he explained, "I'm sorry. I can't seem to make out what I've written down." Looking out into the audience, he asked, "Is there a pharmacist in the house?"

TONY BELMONTE

Each new patient at the clinic where I work must fill out a questionnaire asking basic health and personal-history questions. One query that inevitably gets a "No" answer is, "Do you now use or have you ever used recreational drugs?"

We were unprepared for the response of a young newlywed who wrote: "Yes – birth-control pills."

FRANCES BOWEN

45

"We need to focus on diversity. Your goal is to hire people who all look different but think just like me."

How many chiropractors does it take to change a lightbulb?
Only one, but it takes six visits.

It was our new receptionist's very first job, and it showed in the way she dressed – her revealing clothes screamed "university" more than "office". As diplomatically as he could, our boss sat her down and told her that she would have to dress more appropriately.

"Why?" she asked. "Are we going out to lunch?"

CLAUDIA SMELKO & MARION ABEL

The salesman at the megastore had only one sale that day, but it was for a staggering £158,762. Flabbergasted by such a massive sale, the manager asked him to explain. "First, I sold the man a fishhook," the salesman said. "Then I sold him a rod and reel. When I found out he was planning on fishing down the coast, I suggested he'd need a boat. Then I took him to the car department and sold him our biggest car to pull the boat."

"You sold all that to a guy who came in for a fishhook?" asked the boss.

"Actually," said the salesman, "he came in for a bottle of aspirin for his wife's migraine. I told him, 'Your weekend's shot. Might as well go fishing.'"

After regular Thursday night phone calls to a colleague to arrange a meeting the following evening, I surprised him by turning up at his home in person. His wife answered the door. "It's Howard!" she shouted up the stairs to her husband. Seconds later, as I stood in the hall, my colleague charged downstairs stark naked and picked up the phone.

HOWARD ASMAN

While I was waiting in a queue at a checkout, I noticed the woman in front of me rifling through her purse for some change to pay her bill. After producing a couple of notes, she nodded towards her partner, indicating that he would have to find the rest. "I'm afraid we don't accept husbands," interrupted the cashier. "They don't fit in the till."

TRACY MORRISON

Having finished our stint at a trade show in San Diego, my colleague Maureen and I decided to do a little shopping and bought a few pieces of clay kitchenware. Later, when we were going through customs, an official asked if we had anything of value to declare. "Not really," Maureen replied, digging in her bag for her recent purchase. People around us froze as she continued, "I only bought a little pot."

R. TOMPKINS

Doctors are used to getting calls at any hour. One night a man phoned, waking me up. "I'm sorry to bother you so late," he said, "but I think my wife has appendicitis."

Still half asleep, I reminded him that I had taken his wife's inflamed appendix out two years earlier.

"Whoever heard of a second appendix?" I asked.

"You may not have heard of a second appendix," he replied, "but surely you've heard of a second wife."

JAMES KARURI MUCHIRI

I thought I wanted a tattoo, so I had a friend come with me to the tattoo parlour. As I nervously paused outside the door, I noticed the T had slipped off their sign. Now it read:

"Creative ouch."

KAREN BLOUNT

My wife and I run a small restaurant where we often name our specials after our employees – dishes like "Chicken Mickey", after our dishwasher who gave us the recipe, and "Rod's Ribs", after a waiter who had his personal style of barbecue. One evening after re-reading the menu, I broke with this tradition and changed the description of the special we had named after our chef.

Despite her skills and excellent reputation, somehow I didn't think an entrée named "Salmon Ella" would go over well with our customers.

BRETT LEHIGH

47

"Do you want a salary or benefits?"

After a lengthy session with a customer who had been having difficulties with a computer program, a support technician at my mother's company turned in his report:

"The problem resides between the keyboard and the chair."

NICOLE MILLIGAN

In the surgery where I work, the doctors press a buzzer when they are ready to see the next patient. One day an elderly woman came in. The receptionist told her to take a seat and wait for the buzz. After a while, the poor patient popped her head around the door.

"But where is the bus taking me?" she asked.

JEAN LEWIS

Because I was processing my first accident report at the transport company where I worked, I was being particularly attentive. A driver had hit a deer on the motorway, resulting in a severely damaged bonnet and bumper. My concentration wavered when I reached the section of the report that asked, "Speed of other vehicle?"

The driver had written "Full gallop".

DOUGLAS WAKEHAM

As part of a scuba-diving course, a friend of mine had to locate the instructor on the murky ocean floor and "rescue" him. The instructor assured her that, like a panicking person, he would struggle.

After allowing her quarry a minute's start, my friend found him, removed his air regulator, clasped him firmly and ascended slowly to the surface while giving him air from her regulator every second breath. True to his word, he kicked and fought strenuously – and revealed on pulling off his mask that he was a complete stranger.

TRACEY GREENWOOD

Strolling through the corridors at the school where I work, I saw a new teacher standing outside his classroom with his forehead pressed against a locker. I heard him mutter, "How did you get yourself into this?"

Knowing he was assigned to a difficult class, I tried to offer moral support. "Are you okay?" I asked.

He lifted his head and replied, "I'll be fine as soon as I get this kid out of his locker."

HELEN BUTTON

After a lecture, our tutor found some paper aeroplanes on the floor of the room. At the start of our next talk, he asked the person responsible to come forward, but we all sat there in silence. Picking up the planes, our tutor threw them into the air, but they crashed after flying just a few feet.

"For goodness sake," he exclaimed. "You're engineers. You can do better than that!"

CAROLINE PLUMB

SIGN LANGUAGE

Sign above the scales in a doctor's office:

"Pretend it's your I.Q."

LYNN MICLEA

"I'll need the saw again, sir."

I'm a life-and-career coach and one morning, when a prospective client called for an appointment, I asked him what he wanted to get out of our sessions. "Clarity," he said very firmly.

"And on what issues are you looking for clarity?" I probed.

"Well," he said in a less confident tone, "I really don't know."

SHANA SPOONER

Four students walked in halfway through the history test my father was holding at the local community college. "Sorry," they said, "we had a flat tyre."

An understanding man, Dad said that if they could all answer just one question correctly, he would give them each an "A" for the exam. The students agreed. So my father handed each one a piece of paper, placed them in four different corners and said, "Write down which tyre was flat."

KURT SMITH

My husband and I arrived at the car dealership to pick up our new car, only to be told that the keys had been locked inside. We went to the service department, where a mechanic was working to unlock the driver's side door. Instinctively, I reached for the passenger door and – voilà! – it was unlocked. "Hey," I shouted to him. "It's open!"

"I know," yelled the mechanic. "I already got that side. Now I'm working on this door."

B. PHILLIPS

My friend applied for a job as an insurance salesperson. Where the form requested "prior experience," he wrote "lifeguard". That was it. Nothing else.

"We're looking for someone who can not only sell insurance, but who can also sell himself," said the interviewer. "How does working as a lifeguard pertain to selling yourself?"

"I couldn't swim," my pal replied. He got the job.

TEDD HUSTON

My dad works as a photocopier engineer and meets a lot of people. In one small office, a kindly but rather deaf old lady introduced him to the rest of her team. "Andrew, this is Neville. Neville, Andrew," she said, then left the two men to get aquainted. When she was out of sight, my father said, "Erm, actually my name is Neal."

"Don't worry," the other man replied. "I'm Alan. Nice to meet you."

SUSANNAH DAVIS

SIGN LANGUAGE

On the door of the post office:

PULL. If that doesn't work, PUSH. If that doesn't work, we're closed. Come again.

VERA KASSON

A young boy came to the optician's where I work to have his vision checked. He sat down and I turned off the lights. Then I switched on a projector that flashed the letters F, Z and B on a screen. I asked the boy what he saw.

Without hesitation he replied, **"Consonants."**

STEPHEN DOWNING

Hard to believe, but many of our customers at the bank still don't know how to put their card into the cashpoint. Because of this, my fellow cashiers and I often find ourselves having to explain how it's done. One cashier complained that she kept getting odd looks every time she explained it. I found out why when I overheard her tell one man, "Strip down facing me."

VICKI STONE

While editing announcements for a newspaper, I came across an item promoting a camp for children with asthma. Aside from all the wonderful activities the kids could enjoy, such as canoeing, swimming, crafts and more, it promised that its lakefront property offered something the kids probably did not expect: "breathtaking views".

CHRISTY NICHOLS

A neighbour had invited some friends, including our minister, over for dinner. On the menu were mashed potatoes, stuffing, buttery peas and roast chicken. As we prepared to eat, we were serenaded by a crowing cockerel. "Listen to that cockerel," said one of the guests.

Glancing at our pastor digging into his chicken, the host said, "You'd crow too if your child was going into the clergy."

E. MILLER

My friend and his rock band were playing a concert at the psychiatric hospital where he worked as a musical therapist. The audience was a little quiet, so the guitarist decided to do something about it. He grabbed the microphone, pointed to the group and shouted, "Are you ready to get a little crazy?"

STEPHAN DERVAN

A guy shows up late for work. His boss yells, "You should've been here at 8:30!"

The guy replies, "Why? What happened at 8:30?"

51

"Good news, Mr. Hawkins. Companies have laid off too much deadwood, and now there's a shortage."

Insider tips

Dress to impress

Dress-Down Friday used to mean the carpeting you got from your boss at the end of the week for not having done any work in the rest of the week. Nowadays, Dress-Down Fridays are an incredibly generous gesture by companies that let you wear casual clothing on Fridays as long as you don't have a meeting or any meaningful work. Which means if you dress casually you're obviously not working hard enough.

Since the collapse of communism, Dress-Down Fridays have done more than anything else to impair the smooth running of capitalism. Business suits are for doing business in. If you're wearing a welder's helmet people expect rivets, if you're wearing a suit people expect business but if you're wearing shorts and sandals people expect you to be on your way to San Francisco with flowers in your hair.

Of course, when the managing director says you can dress down that doesn't mean you can come to work in a luminous thong. You have to wear smart-casual clothing. Smart-casual is a particular kind of attire not found anywhere outside the working environment. It's been specifically designed not to be smart or casual. It is in fact more of a uniform than a suit because if you're a man smart-casual can only mean polo shirt and chinos. If you're a woman it means anything under the sun except four-inch black stilettos.

In trendy companies that are permanently dressed down, the introduction of Dress-Down Friday would lead to the rapid establishment of a nudist colony. Instead they should have Dress-Up Fridays, where everyone has to come to work in a twelve-piece suit, spats and a monocle. This would also give them a valuable insight into what it's like working in a rural solicitor's office.

Day dreaming

When we look at the future of the office, one thing is absolutely crystal clear. But no one knows what that one thing is, so we'll just have to blunder on as usual.

However, there are some predictions we can make with complete confidence. The first is that there will be more and better ways of communicating, all of which we will continue to ignore, and instead we'll keep people in the dark until something goes disastrously wrong.

The other thing that will happen is that offices will become more like home and home will become more like the office. Offices will get incredibly cosy with trendy cafés, soft furnishings, casual clothing, crèches and sympathetic lighting, while an increasing part of the home is taken up with computers, printers, filing and desks. Eventually people will be desperate to get to

Guy Browning, *Office Politics*

work, where they can drop off their kids, sink into some soft furnishings, get some decent food and generally kick back and relax.

Bosses will disappear. When everyone's working from home, no one's going to want a boss in the spare room. Everyone will be their own boss. Bosses will become good communicators so we'll all have bosses that listen to us rather than the other way round. The downside of this is that we'll have to think of something worth saying.

The big question is, will people still have desks? If you have a palm device that computes, communicates and does absolutely everything electronically, desks will need to be completely redesigned. They will have coffee cup holders and Chocolate HobNob dispensers; a buttock rest for passing gossipers; a pop-up video display of your loved ones (updatable); a range of drawers designed to hold a banana, yoghurt and copy of *Heat* magazine; and a single sheet of A4 paper and a pen in a glass case that you can break in an emergency.

The even bigger question is, will we, in thirty years' time, still be struggling to work on unreliable, over-crowded trains, working in teeming, peeling offices for rude and unpleasant bosses, doing repetitive and largely useless work? Given the state of our pensions, the answer is yes, we probably will.

A young man asked for a job with the circus, any job at all. The manager decided to give him a chance to become an assistant lion tamer and took him to the practice cage.

The head lion tamer, a beautiful young woman, was just starting her rehearsal. Entering the cage, she removed her cape with a flourish and, standing in a gorgeous costume, motioned to a lion. Obediently the lion crept towards her and then rolled over twice.

"Well," said the manager to the young man, "do you think you can learn to do that?"

"I'm sure I could," he replied, "but first you'll have to get that lion out of there."

SCOTT RIVA

Late one night I stopped at one of those 24-hour petrol station shops to get myself a freshly brewed cup of coffee. When I picked up the pot, I noticed that the brew was as black as Tarmac and just about as thick. "How old is this coffee?" I asked the woman who was standing behind the counter.

She shrugged. "I don't know. I've only been working here two weeks."

PETER CULVER

Since I was first to arrive at our high-tech company one morning, I answered the phone. When the caller asked for field engineering, I explained that it was before normal business hours but that I would help if I could. "What's your job there?" the caller asked. "I'm the manager," I replied.

There was a pause. Then he said, "I'll call back later. I need to talk to someone who knows something."

KEITH SWANSON

I am an obstetrician and sometimes see unusual tattoos when working in maternity wards. One patient had some type of fish tattoo on her abdomen.

"That's a pretty whale," I commented.

With a smile she replied, "It used to be a dolphin."

RON NORRIS

When employees of the restaurant where I work attended a fire-safety seminar, we watched a fire official demonstrate the proper way to operate an extinguisher. "Pull the pin like a hand grenade," he explained, "then depress the trigger to release the foam."

Later, an employee was selected to extinguish a controlled fire in the car park. In her nervousness, she forgot to pull the pin.

Our instructor hinted, "Like a hand grenade, remember?"

In a burst of confidence, she pulled the pin – and hurled the extinguisher at the blaze.

BECKI HARRIS

TIMELESS HUMOUR

70s My friend John and I, determined to see the world, signed on a Norwegian freighter as deckhands. We were being trained as helmsmen, and John's first lesson was given by the mate, a seasoned but gentle white-haired seafarer. John was holding the heading he had been given, when the mate ordered, "Come starboard."

Pleased at knowing which way starboard was, John left the helm and walked over to his instructor.

The mate had an incredulous look on his face as the helm swung freely, but he merely asked politely, "Could you bring the ship with you?"

BRUCE INGRAHAM

**QUOTABLE
QUOTES**

Responsible, who wants to be responsible?
Whenever something bad happens, it's always,
Who's responsible for this?

JERRY SEINFELD

**If an idea's worth having once,
it's worth having twice.**

TOM STOPPARD, Indian Ink

When I hear about people
making vast fortunes
without doing any
productive work or
contributing anything to
society, my reaction is,
How do I get in on that?

DAVE BARRY in The Miami Herald

The key to success? Work hard,
stay focused and marry a Kennedy.

ARNOLD SCHWARZENEGGER

Many an optimist has become rich
by buying out a pessimist.

ROBERT G. ALLEN, Multiple Streams of Income (John Wiley & Sons)

**Money doesn't
talk, it swears.**
BOB DYLAN,
"It's Alright Ma (I'm Only Bleeding)"

**If men can run the world, why can't they stop wearing
neckties? How intelligent is it to start the day by tying
a little noose around your neck?**

LINDA ELLERBEE in The Seattle Post-Intelligencer

I like work; it fascinates me; I can sit
and look at it for hours.

JEROME K. JEROME

55

then a boy confidently raised his hand. "One means fast-forward," he said, "and the other means rewind!"

TERESA DONN

My musical director wasn't happy with the performance of one of our percussionists. Repeated attempts to get the drummer to improve failed. Finally, in front of the orchestra, the director said in frustration, "When a musician just can't handle his instrument, they take it away, give him two sticks and make him a drummer!"

A stage whisper was heard from the percussion section: "And if he can't handle that, they take away one of his sticks and make him a conductor."

QUINCY WONG

Desperate for registered nurses, my colleagues and I in hospital administration often share ideas to recruit employees. Out of exasperation, I made a joking plea to two of my colleagues, asking them to send me six nurses from each of their hospitals. That request prompted one of them to suggest a unique solution: "Send six nurses to the top three names on the list of hospital administrators, and then send your request to five other colleagues. In 14 days you will have received 1,567 nurses."

DAVID PARKS

While reviewing maths symbols with my pupils, I drew a greater-than (>) and a less-than (<) sign on the blackboard and asked, "Does anyone remember what these mean?" A few moments passed, and

Fed up with running a business from home, my wife decided to look for a staff job. One day when she was out, our telephone rang. A woman asked for my wife and explained she was with an investor's magazine. Because of my wife's business, we often got sales calls for such periodicals, so I quickly said, "She's not really interested in your magazine." "That's odd," replied the woman, "because she's just sent us her CV."

STEPHEN DUFRESNE

SIGN LANGUAGE

Seen on the door of a repair shop:

WE CAN FIX ANYTHING. (Please knock on the door – the bell doesn't work.)

VICTORIA GOLDEN

On the job as a dental receptionist, I answered the phone and noticed on the caller-ID screen that the incoming call was from a car-repair shop. The man on the line begged to see the dentist because of a painful tooth.

"Which side of your mouth hurts?" I asked the patient.

He sighed and answered, "The passenger side."

CHERYL SATTERWHITE

Part of my job as a policeman involves explaining court procedures to visitors. One day I was showing a group of secondary school children round. The court wasn't in session, so only a clerk and a young man in custody were in the courtroom.

"This is where the judge sits," I began, pointing to the bench. "Lawyers sit at these tables. A court clerk sits over there. The recorder, or stenographer, sits over here. Near the judge is the witness stand and over there is where the jury sits.

"As you can see," I finished, "there are a lot of people involved in making this system work." At that point, the prisoner raised his cuffed hands and said, "Yeah, but I'm the one who makes it all happen."

MICHAEL MCPHERSON

A livestock truck overturned in my town, and the accident made the local news. The young reporter who covered the story declared on camera, "Two cows, Black and Gus, escaped into nearby woods."

At the studio there was muffled laughter as they cut to a commercial. After the break, the reporter sheepishly added, "About that overturned truck – make those Black Angus cattle."

JULIANA KEMP

The boss placed a sign directly over the sink in the men's room at work. It had a single word on it: "Think!"

The next day when the boss went to the men's room, he saw another sign had been placed immediately above the soap dispenser.

It read: "Thoap!"

MURIEL NAYLOR

TIMELESS HUMOUR

60s Another man and I share a locker at work. Noticing that it needed a new combination lock, my partner said he would pick one up on his way to work the next day. It occurred to me later that I might not see him in the morning. How would I find out the combination? I needn't have worried.

When I arrived at work I found that he had used the locker before me and had left a note reading: "To find the first number subtract 142 from your high score the last time we went bowling. The second number is 16 less than that. To find the third number subtract 1.87 from the amount you owe me."

MICHAEL KLABER

"Technically, we're not firing you. We're just moving you into an exit-level position."

A woman recently brought her two cats to my husband's veterinary clinic for their annual checkup. One was a small-framed, round tiger-striped tabby, while the other was a long, sleek black cat. She watched closely as I put each on the scale. "They weigh about the same," I told her.

"That proves it!" she exclaimed. "Black does make you look slimmer. And stripes make you look fat."

SUSAN DANIEL

I was inspecting communications facilities in Alaska. Since I had little experience flying in small planes, I was nervous when we approached a landing strip in a snow-covered area. The pilot descended to just a couple of hundred feet, then gunned both engines, climbed and circled back. While my heart pounded, the passenger next to me seemed calm. "I wonder why the pilot didn't land," I said.

"He was checking to see if the landing strip was ploughed," the man replied.

As we made a second approach, I glanced out the window. "It looks ploughed to me," I commented.

"No," my neighbour replied. "It hasn't been cleared for some time."

"How can you tell?" I asked.

"Because," the man informed me, "I'm the guy who drives the plough."

LAWRENCE WEISS

"How much do you charge?" a man asked a lawyer.

"I get £50 for three questions," the lawyer answers.

"That's awfully steep, isn't it?" says the man.

"Yes, it is," replies the lawyer.

"Now, what's your final question?"

The customer ordering a floral arrangement from my shop gave very specific guidelines. "I don't want anything fragrant," she instructed. "Nothing too tall or wild and no bright colours. My house is beige and cream. Here's a sample of my wallpaper." She handed me a square of tan-coloured paper.

"Can I have your name, please?" I asked.

"Mrs. Bland," came the reply.

STEPHEN STANLEY

At the busy dental surgery where I work, one patient was always late. Once when I called to confirm an appointment, he said, "I'll be about 15 minutes late. That won't be a problem, will it?"

"No," I told him. "We just won't have time to give you an anaesthetic."

He arrived early.

T. SPACCAROTELLI

Corporate managers are always a good source of memorable quotes. Here are some examples of mediocrity rising to the top.

- "As of tomorrow, employees will only be able to access the building using individual security cards. Pictures will be taken next Wednesday, and employees will receive their cards in two weeks."
- "What I need is a list of specific unknown problems we will encounter."
- "E-mail is not to be used to pass on information or data. It should be used only for company business."
- "This project is so important, we can't let things that are more important interfere with it."
- "We know that communication is a problem, but the company is not going to discuss it with the employees."

E. T. THOMPSON

My brother Jim was hired by a government agency and assigned to a small office cubicle in a large area. At the end of his first day, he realised he couldn't see over the panels to find his way out, so he waited until he saw someone else leaving and followed him. He did the same the next day. On the third day he had to work late, long after his colleagues had left. He wandered around lost in the maze of cubicles and corridors, but then, just as panic began to set in, he came upon another employee in a cubicle.

"How do you get out of here?" Jim asked.

The fellow looked up from his desk, smiled and said, "No cheese for you."

CHRISTINE PROBASCO

Giving a sermon one Sunday, I heard two teenage girls in the back giggling and disturbing people. I interrupted my sermon and announced sternly, "There are two of you here who have not heard a word I've said." That quietened them down.

When the service was over, I went to greet people at the front door. Three adults apologised for going to sleep in church, promising it would never happen again.

WILLIAM RUSS

"There's an important job I'd like you to tackle, Haffner – yours."

59

When my daughter was preparing for her school's "career week", a time when career options are discussed and often led by representatives of different professions, we talked about my job as an airline customer-services representative. I mentioned that one of my responsibilities was to load passengers' luggage at the check-in counter. I later found out to my dismay that my daughter had listed my occupation as "Bag Lady".

VICKI FREEMAN

As the office supervisor, I had to have a word with a new employee who never arrived at work on time. I asked if there was a reason for her lack of punctuality and explained that other employees had noticed that she was walking in late every day. After listening to my complaints, she agreed that this was a problem and even offered a solution.

"Is there another door I could use?"

BARBARA DAVIES

During a shopping trip to a department store, I was looking around for a salesperson so I could pay for my purchase. Finally I ran into a woman wearing the store's ID tag and told her I was trying to locate a cashier.

"I can't help you," she briskly replied, barely slowing down. "I work in customer service."

S. HEARTZ

I'm an attendant in a launderette. A woman came in, sat near my counter and chain-smoked cigarette after cigarette. The smoke was bothering me, so I turned on a fan. "Could you please point that thing in another direction?" she asked. "I'm just getting over pneumonia and the last thing I need is a breeze blowing on me."

HOLLY SNAPP

In my job as an electronics salesman, I've seen the rise in popularity of sport-utility vehicles and minivans, which has created a market for rear-seat entertainment. Monitors that keep passengers occupied with movies and television have been selling like crazy. One day as I was showing a young couple how a monitor could play videos, DVDs, and even pick up local TV stations, the husband asked matter-of-factly, "Does it get cable?"

JOSEPH WADE

After harvesting a bumper crop of vegetables last year, I took some into the office and piled them on the table in the coffee area. Then I posted a sign advertising that they were free. The next day I noticed an addition to my note. Below "Free Courgettes", someone had written, "Save the Whales".

DAN ARCHEY

"Sanders, I just sold your soul. You weren't using it, were you?"

A kid's world

They're innocent, inquisitive, and often hilarious. You'll love the priceless things that kids say and the hilarious things they do.

"Can you hear me now?"

We had been trying to have a third child for some time. The day I was due to take a home pregnancy test, my husband was called away on business. My two young daughters and I decided if it was positive, we would buy a baby outfit to surprise their father when he got home. The three of us stood in the bathroom eagerly waiting for the result.

When it was negative, my seven-year-old hugged me. "Don't worry, Mummy," she said. "The next time Daddy goes away, you can try to get pregnant again."

J. MACDONALD

One evening after dinner, my five-year-old son Brian noticed that his mother had gone out. In answer to his questions, I told him, "Mum is at a Tupperware party."

This explanation satisfied him for only a moment. Puzzled, he asked, "What's a Tupperware party, Dad?"

I've always given my son honest answers, so I figured a simple explanation would be the best approach. "Well Brian," I said, "at a Tupperware party, a group of ladies sit around and sell plastic bowls to each other."

Brian nodded, indicating that he understood. Then he burst into laughter. "Come on, Dad," he said. "What is it really?"

KENNETH HOLMES

I was telling my three boys the story of the Nativity and how the Wise Men brought gifts of gold, frankincense and myrrh for the infant Jesus.

Clearly giving it a lot of thought, my six-year-old observed, "Mum, a Wise Woman would have brought nappies."

ANGIE FLAUTE

One Saturday, my house-proud mother told my brother and I that we couldn't go out until we had tidied the spare room. We were desperate to get it done quickly. Finally, exhausted after what we thought was an excellent job,

---

I took my two small nieces to church and the children's address that morning was about sharing. After the service, I bought some sweets for the girls.

"First I'll eat mine," I heard one saying to the other, "then we'll eat yours."

JOAN GRAHAM

---

we said we were finished.

Mum came in, ran her fingers along the shelves, and peered under the furniture. Clearly dissatisfied, she turned to my brother and ordered "Go and get me the broom."

As he handed it to her he asked, "Is this for sweeping the floor or are you going somewhere?"

MARK BERMAN

Our son, a doctor, and his wife were expecting their second child. They already had a three-year-old son, Adam. They decided to prepare him for the new arrival. Little hands were put on mother's tummy, little ears listened to heartbeats.

The day arrived and a second son, Robert, was born. Before going to the hospital, Adam's father said: "Your mother has a brother for you called Robert. He's out of mummy's tummy now and is waiting for you in the hospital. Do you understand, Adam?"

"Oh yes, yes!" said Adam.

When they arrived at the hospital, there was an elderly man in a wheelchair awaiting discharge. Adam marched up to him, threw his arms around him and said, "Hello! You must be Robert."

MRS W. FLOOK

63

My 12-year-old daughter asked me, "Mum, do you have a picture of yourself as a baby? I need it for a school project".

I handed one over without thinking to ask what the project was. A few days later I was in her classroom for a parent-teacher meeting when I noticed my face pinned to a mural which had been created by the students. The title of their project was "The oldest thing in my house".

A. KENT

While queueing in a theme park for a hair-raising ride, I heard my two nephews arguing.

"Aunt Staci's going with me!" insisted Yoni.

"No," said his brother. "She's coming with me!"

Flattered at being so popular, I promised Yoni, "You and I can go on the merry-go-round."

"But I really want you to come on this ride," he protested.

"Why?" I asked.

"Because the more weight there is, the faster it goes."

STACI MARGULIS

My niece, delivering her first child, requested that her mother and I come into the delivery room with her. During one violent contraction she looked up at my sister and said, "Mum, please help me. The pains are really bad."

"Darling," my sister replied, "there isn't anything I can do."

My niece then turned to me. "Marisela, please help me," she implored. "Mum doesn't understand what I'm going through."

MARISELA BOBO

Luke, our venturesome 14-month-old son, was at my mother-in-law's house. He was playing with her car keys when the phone rang. After hanging up, my mother-in-law realised that Luke had put the keys down somewhere, but she couldn't find them anywhere. Thinking quickly, she gave him another set of keys.

As she pretended not to look, Luke toddled around the corner and into her bedroom. Then she watched as he carefully placed the second set of keys under her bed – right next to the original car keys.

TONY BECKER

"As your mother, I took the liberty of making your wishes and blowing out your candles."

Having trouble getting my one-year-old son to take a nap, I tried singing him a lullaby. I have a terrible singing voice though, so halfway through the song, my son took his dummy out of his mouth and shoved it into mine. Then promptly fell asleep.

Z. AHMET

My friend took her five-year-old daughter shopping with her.

The girl watched her mother try on outfit after outfit, loudly exclaiming each time, "Mummy, you look beautiful!"

A woman in the next dressing room called out, "Can I borrow your daughter for a moment?"

JEAN STAMMET

At the tanning salon I was under the lights for so long that the protective shades left a big white circle around each eye. Gazing in the mirror the next day, I thought, "I look like a clown."

I had almost convinced myself that I was overreacting – until I got in the queue at the supermarket. I felt a tug at my shirt and looked down to see a toddler staring up at me. "Are you giving out balloons?" he asked.

NINA SECVIAR

Travelling to a funeral with my two young boys, I tried to prepare them by initiating a discussion about burial and what we believe happens after death.

The boys behaved themselves during the service, but at the grave site I discovered my explanations weren't as thorough as I'd thought. In a loud voice, my four-year-old asked, "Mum, what's in the box?"

GINNY RICHARDS

My teenage niece, Elizabeth, was nervous as she took the wheel for her first driving lesson. As she was pulling out of the driving centre car park, the instructor said, "Turn left here. And don't forget to let the people behind you know what you're doing."

Elizabeth turned to the students sitting in the back seat and announced, "I'm going left."

RACHEL NICHOLS

I began thinking about mortality after I was widowed. One day my daughter rang from university and I announced that I thought it was time for us to talk about where I'd like to be buried. "It's too soon to think of anything like that," she snapped.

Then there was a pause. "Wait a second, did you say 'married' or 'buried'?"

I repeated "buried" and she said, "Oh OK, fine."

W. WEINERT

65

Suddenly, without warning, Warren ate up all his dinner.

Despite several reprimands, my four-year-old, Sophie, continued her new habit of lying and spinning tall tales. So I decided to tell her the story of the boy who cried wolf.

"He kept telling the villagers a wolf was about to attack, but there was no wolf at all," I explained. "Wasn't that naughty?"

"Oh, yes!" replied my daughter sincerely.

"And then there really was a wolf and he cried out, but everyone thought he was lying, and the wolf ate him up. Silly, huh?"

I looked down hopefully at Sophie to see if she had got the point. She seemed deep in thought for a moment then looked up at me and said, "I was eaten by a wolf once, you know."

VAL KEOGH

When my son was learning to read, he absorbed everything he saw: books, signs – anything.

One day at the beach, he asked why anyone would want to put him in the rubbish. Surprised, I asked why he thought someone might. "There's a sign that says I shouldn't let anyone put me in the bin."

Sure enough, listed in the beach rules was one stipulating, "Refuse to be put in waste disposal units."

B. SHANNON

When we moved to a new city, my wife and I decided to drive both our cars. Nathan, our eight-year-old, worriedly asked, "How will we keep ourselves from getting separated?"

"We'll drive slowly so one car can follow the other," I reassured him.

"Yeah, but what if we get separated?" he persisted.

"Then I guess we'll never see each other again," I quipped.

"Okay," he said, "I'm going with Mum."

JAMES BUSH

"I've discovered that I'm homework intolerant."

My retired husband, Jim, has been attending a beginners watercolour class. During one session the instructor asked the class what they planned to do with their paintings when they were finished. Virtually all of the students were undecided, but Jim knew exactly what he would do with his.

"I'm going to send them to my children," he said with a smile, "so they can put them on their refrigerators."

BEVERLY LEE

A friend and his wife let their little boy open all his gifts at once on Christmas morning and were frustrated that the day's excitement was over in ten minutes. So the next year they decided to hold the big present back until after lunch.

They bought him a bike, but couldn't work out how to wrap it, so just tied a balloon to the handlebars.

Christmas Day arrived, lunch was eaten, then the mother said, "Look what else Santa has brought you," and my friend wheeled the bike in.

"Yippee," shouted the boy. "A balloon!"

JIM WATT

QUOTABLE QUOTES

My perspective on my mother has changed immensely. She was a lot taller when I was younger.

HOWIE MANDEL, in I Love You, Mom! by Kelly Ripa and Others (Hyperion)

All mothers have intuition. The great ones have radar.

CATHY GUISEWITE, quoted in The Joys of Motherhood by Jane Hughes Paulson (Andrews McMeel)

A perfect parent is a person with excellent child-rearing theories and no actual children.

DAVE BARRY

Parents are the last people on earth who ought to have children.

SAMUEL BUTLER

Familiarity breeds contempt and children.

MARK TWAIN

Raising kids is part joy and part guerilla warfare.

ED ASNER

There's no such thing as fun for the whole family.

JERRY SEINFELD

When you're eight years old, nothing is your business.

LENNY BRUCE

Just be good and kind to your children. Not only are they the future of the world, they're the ones who can sign you into the home.

DENNIS MILLER

67

"I appreciate your memo calling for more tolerant and forgiving parents. Now, what did you do this time?"

While I sat in the reception area of my doctor's office, a woman rolled an elderly man in a wheelchair into the room. As she went to the receptionist's desk, the man sat there, alone and silent. Just as I was thinking I should make small talk with him, a little boy slipped off his mother's lap and walked over to the wheelchair.

Placing his hand on the man's, he said, "I know how you feel. My mum makes me ride in the pushchair too."

STEVE ANDERSON

Since I am a busy mum of four, I rely on my children to help me out with everyday chores around the house. One morning I was running around trying to get the children and myself ready, when I suddenly realised it was rubbish day. So I handed a bag of rubbish to my sleepy seven-year-old son and told him to throw it in the bin on his way out of the door.

Glancing out my window moments later, I saw him wearily getting on the bus. He was carrying his rucksack, his lunchbox and a big black bag of rubbish.

LYNN PAREJKO

When my neighbour's grand-daughter introduced me to her young son, Brian, I said to him, "My grandchildren call me Mimi. Why don't you call me that too?"

"I don't think so," he retorted, and ran off after his mother.

Later I was asked to baby-sit for Brian, and we hit it off wonderfully. As he snuggled up to me, he said, "I don't care what your grandchildren say. I love you, Meanie."

MARILYN HAYDEN

My young son and I were looking at a poster advertising a mathematics conference. The theme was: "A Way With Maths".

"Mum," reflected my son hopefully, "do you think they'll really do away with maths?"

MARY ROUTLEY

Rushing to get to the cinema, my husband and I told the kids we had to leave "right now" – at which point our teenage daughter headed for the bathroom to apply make-up. Her dad shouted for her to get in the car immediately, and headed to the garage grumbling.

On the way to the multiplex my husband glanced in the rearview mirror and caught our teenager applying lipstick and blusher, which produced the predictable lecture. "Look at your mum," he said. "She didn't put on any make-up just to go sit in a dark cinema theatre."

From the back I heard, "Yeah, but Mum doesn't need make-up."

My heart swelling with the compliment, I turned back to thank this sweet, wonderful daughter of mine just as she continued, "Nobody looks at her."

D. BREWINGTON

At the Post Office queueing for some stamps while my four-year-old daughter chose some sweets, I suddenly heard her voice ring out,

"Mummy! The lady with the moustache says I need another penny."

D. ROOKWOOD

My husband was mending the roof when our five-year-old son rushed into the kitchen and said that his father had something really important to tell me.

I was busy cooking dinner, so I asked him to relay the message. Jacob thought for a few moments then said, "I can't remember all of it, but it started with 'Help!'"

CLAIRE PULLEY

One night about 10pm, I answered the phone and heard, "Dad, we want to stay out late. Is that okay?"

"Sure," I answered, "as long as you called."

When I hung up, my wife asked who was on the phone.

"One of the boys," I replied. "I gave them permission to stay out late."

"Not our boys," she said. "They're both downstairs."

L. WEISBERG

As I was nursing my baby, my cousin's six-year-old daughter, Krissy, came into the room. Never having seen anyone breastfeed before, she was intrigued and full of questions about what I was doing. After mulling over my answers, she remarked, "My mum has some of those, but I don't think she knows how to use them."

LOIS SINGER

My older son loves school, but his younger brother absolutely hates it. One weekend he cried and fretted and tried every excuse not to go back on Monday. Sunday morning on the way home from church, the crying and whining built to a crescendo. At the end of my rope, I finally stopped the car and explained, "Sweetheart, it's a law. If you don't go to school, they'll put Mummy in jail."

He looked at me, thought a moment, then asked, "How long would you have to stay?"

T. REES

"It's a painting. There is no sound."

69

You must all promise never to divulge what you are about to see.

During our computer class, the teacher chastised one boy for talking to the girl sitting next to him.

"I was just asking her a question," the boy said.

"If you have a question, ask me," the teacher tersely replied.

"Okay," he answered. "Do you want to go out with me on Friday night?"

TRACY MAXWELL

It began as an innocent game with my toddler Robert. I'd assume the fighter's stance and start shadowboxing. Jabbing with both fists, I'd say, "One-two, one-two," and he would imitate me over and over.

I never thought about the consequences until my wife took him to a birthday party. When the birthday boy's mother was handing out musical instruments, she leaned over to Robert and asked him, "Would you like one too?"

It took my wife a while to explain her way out of what happened next.

ALFRED ISNARDI

On a demographics survey given at our school, pupils were asked, "What disadvantages do you see in having children?" Usual answers included "It's expensive to raise children" and "They take up a lot of your time."

But one boy was not worried about money or responsibility. He wrote, "If I have children, I might have to drive a caravan."

C. DIEMERT

On holiday my nine-year-old son, Ryan, and I were at the pool, where two attractive young women wearing thong bikinis were sunning themselves. I noticed that Ryan kept staring at them, but he would occasionally glance back at me.

When they got up to leave, Ryan watched them particularly closely. I was bracing myself for questions he might have when he turned to me and whispered, "Dad, can I take that chocolate bar those girls left behind?"

PAUL DELUCA

My two-year-old cousin scared us one summer by disappearing during our lakeside holiday. More than a dozen relatives searched the forest and shoreline, and everyone was relieved when we found Matthew playing calmly in the woods.

"Listen to me, Matthew," his mother said sharply. "From now on when you want to go somewhere, you tell Mummy first, okay?"

Matthew thought about that for a moment and said, "Okay. Disney World."

LEAH HALLENBECK

When he joined our parish, the new priest took some time to meet the local children. He asked one little girl her name and she told him it was Jenny. The minister then explained that her proper name was actually Jennifer.

Next, he approached another child who, after a momentary hesitation, introduced herself as "Lucyfer".

J. HANLY

TIMELESS HUMOUR

60s On the first day of my career as a teacher, I made a firm statement about the kind of work I expected from the pupils. I closed my little speech by saying it would take far more than a mere "apple for the teacher" to receive a passing mark.

Apparently I had made my point. On the following morning one of my pupils presented me with a melon.

CECIL TISDELL

I overheard my nine-year-old son on the phone with a friend discussing a computer simulation game. The game involved creating a family, a house for them to live in, and so on.

My son, an old hand at the game, gave this warning: **"Whatever you do, don't get kids. They don't bring in any money, and all they do is eat."**

NICOLE KAULING

Near a hospital I noticed two firemen standing at the door of their vehicle.

A window was partly down and they were talking to a small child inside, instructing her how to unlock the door. Nearby, a young mother looked on patiently.

Assuming they had invited the curious girl into the vehicle to have a look round and she had locked the doors by mistake, I asked, "Has she locked herself in?"

"No, we locked ourselves out," said one of the men. "We borrowed her from her mother because she could fit through the back window."

GILBERT ROGIN

When I bought my new Lexus Sport Coupé, my two sons asked me who would inherit it if I met my demise. I pondered the question, then told them if I passed away on an even day, the son born on an even day would get it. If it happened on an odd day, the one born on the odd day would get it.

A few weekends later, while white water rafting with one of my sons, I was tossed out of the boat. As I floated in the rapids, I heard my son yelling, "It's the wrong day!"

GREG ZARET

Nothing seems to dim my 13-year-old son's sense of humour. And he's certainly not above being the butt of his own joke. Shortly after he was diagnosed with attention deficit disorder (ADD), he threw this at me: "Hey Dad – how many ADD children does it take to change a light bulb?"

"I give up," I said.

"Let's go and ride our bikes."

RICHARD HURD

Don't ever pay a surprise visit to a child in university. You might be the one getting the surprise. I learned this the hard way when I swung by my son's campus. Locating what I thought was his house, I rang the doorbell. "Yeah?" a voice called from inside.

"Does Dylan Houseman live here?"

"Yup," the voice answered. "Leave him by the front door. We'll drag him in later."

J. HOUSEMAN

Taking a group of nursery-school kids on a tour of our hospital, I overheard a conversation between one little girl and an X-ray technician.

"Have you ever broken a bone?" he asked. "Yes," the girl replied.

"Did it hurt?" "No."

"Really? Which bone did you break?"

"My sister's arm."

A. GRABER

SIGN LANGUAGE

Seen printed on the T-shirt of an obviously pregnant woman:

"Under construction"

W. BARNES

The day before I finally left school, the headmaster called an assembly. He wanted to say farewell informally, he explained, as he reviewed our years together. There was hardly a dry eye among us as he concluded, "We will remember you, and hope you will remember us; more importantly, we want you to remember each other. I want all of you to meet in this very hall 25 years from today."

There was a moment of silence; then a thin voice piped up, "What time?"

M. FRIEDE

A friend of mine has an adopted son who, at six-foot-one, loves to play basketball. The boy was applying to a basketball camp, and a section of the application called for him to write a brief essay about himself. My friend got a lump in his throat as he read his son's words: "Most of all I am thankful that I am adopted ... "

Then my friend got a cold dose of reality as he continued: "because my dad is so short."

R. LOCKERBIE

We live less than half a mile from the school, but my son proudly drove there in a car he bought with his own money. A typical first car, it had lots of little problems and was sometimes slow to start.

One morning I was surprised to see it still in front of the house, so after school I asked him about it. "I had to get to school early," he said, "so I just ran."

DENNIS DIGGES

My sister was busy getting ready to host our entire family for Easter. On her to-do list was a hair appointment for her daughter. "So, Katie," said the stylist as the little girl got up in the chair, "who's coming to your house this weekend with big ears and floppy feet?"

Katie replied, "I think it's my uncle Brian."

MARSHA ECKERMAN

Getting ready for school one morning I overheard my daughter Carole asking her father to put some toothpaste on her brush.

"How old are you?" he asked. She replied that she was seven.

"Well, you ought to be able to put on your own toothpaste by now," said her father.

"And you ought to know how old I am," Carole retorted.

ANN MOULT

"I'd like to work overtime till the kids are back in school."

Taking the school assembly one morning, I noticed that five-year-old Jenny was saying her own version of the Lord's Prayer: "Forgive us our trespasses and deliver us from Evelyn."

Later on I took her to one side and explained the word "evil". Jenny promised to get the prayer right next time. Out of curiosity, I asked who Evelyn was.

"My mum," she said proudly.

PATRICIA SIBLEY

My son Kris asked how he'd been born and I explained a Caesarean section as best I could to a child. Kris seemed happy with the explanation, so I saw no need to go into the details of natural childbirth.

A few weeks later, we were watching a documentary showing an elephant giving birth and I decided to expand Kris's knowledge. "Not all babies are born like you were," I told him. "Some are born like that."

"Wow!" exclaimed Kris. "Out of elephants?"

ELIZABETH ASHEN

My neighbour decided that it was time for her small son Joe to learn about privacy, so the next time she went into the bathroom, she shut the door. Joe was soon calling to his mother and pounding on the door.

"There's a lady in the bathroom," she yelled out to him. "You can't come in."

"Mum!" Joe replied. "Who's in there with you?"

QUENTIN MARSH

While working as a teaching assistant in a local primary school, my aunt fell pregnant.

After a few months, the bump started to show and one of the young pupils piped up, "Miss, you're getting fat!" Auntie explained that this was because a baby was growing in her tummy.

"I know," the inquisitive little girl replied, "but what's growing in your bottom?"

L. RICHFORD

My son Donald had been nicknamed "Donald Duck" at his old school. He learned to live with the name, but when we moved to a new area he was pleased to be rid of it.

One day, training for rugby at his new school, he heard somebody call "Donald Duck!" With his heart in his boots, he turned to see who had used the hated nickname, and the ball struck him on the head.

A.M. TRULUCK

I am a junior school teacher and a new empty nester. One night I was trying out an art project: making a person with simple materials. I took a coat hanger, attached a paper-plate face, put a shirt on the hanger and stuffed it. Then I sat it on the sofa to see how it looked.

Later that evening my son walked in the door, home for a surprise visit. Taking one look at my coat-hanger friend sitting on the sofa, he said, "Mum, it's not that bad, is it?"

LINDA ADAMS

TIMELESS HUMOUR

70s We sat glued to the television set during a space mission, listening eagerly to the exchange between ground control and the spacecraft each message ending with the customary "bleep-bleep".

My seven-year-old sister suddenly shattered the intense atmosphere. "They're awfully brave," she commented. "But I don't see why they have to swear so much."

P. THIRLING

QUOTABLE QUOTES

Setting a good example for your children does nothing but increase their embarrassment.

DOUG LARSON, United Feature Syndicate

If pregnancy were a book, they would cut the last two chapters.

NORA EPHRON, Heartburn (Knopf)

No matter how old a mother is, she watches her middle-aged children for signs of improvement.

FLORIDA SCOTT-MAXWELL,
The Measure of My Days (Knopf)

When I was born, I was so surprised I couldn't talk for a year and a half

GRACIE ALLEN

Like all parents, my husband and I just do the best we can, and hold our breath and hope we've set aside enough money for our kids' therapy.

MICHELLE PFEIFFER

You know your kids are growing up when they stop asking you where they came from and refuse to tell you where they're going.

P.J. O'ROURKE
in First for Women

When it comes to raising children, I believe in give and take. I give orders and they take 'em.

BERNIE MAC in People

There's an upside to grandparenthood. You play, you give, you love, then you hand them back and go to an early movie.

BILLY CRYSTAL in Good Housekeeping

75

"It's hard to believe that in just a few weeks, I'll be refusing to eat it."

Being a teenager and getting a tattoo seem to go hand and hand these days. I wasn't surprised when one of my daughter's friends showed me a delicate little Japanese symbol on her hip. "Please don't tell my parents," she begged.

"I won't," I promised. "By the way, what does that stand for?"

"Honesty," she said.

LINDA SINGER

Visiting his parents' retirement village, my middle-aged friend, Tim, went for a swim in the community pool while his elderly father took a walk. Tim struck up a conversation with the only other person in the pool, a five-year-old boy. After a while, Tim's father returned from his walk and called out, "I'm ready to leave."

Tim then turned to his new friend and announced that he had to leave because his father was calling. Astonished, the wide-eyed little boy cried, "You're a kid?"

JANICE PALKO

I asked our seven- and five- year-old grandchildren, who were staying for the weekend, what they would like for supper. "Hamburgers and chips!" they exclaimed. My husband lit the grill and the children watched me while I peeled and cut potatoes.

"Grandma," they asked, "what are you doing?"

"Making the chips," I replied.

"Out of potatoes?" they cried in horror

D. TEW

When my sister was unwell, I rang to check on her condition. My ten-year-old niece answered the phone in a whisper.

"How's your mother?" I enquired.

"She's sleeping," she answered, again in a whisper.

I asked if my sister had been able to visit the doctor.

"Yes, he gave her some medicine," my niece said softly.

"Well, just say I phoned. What are you doing, by the way?"

Again in a soft whisper, she answered, "Practising my trumpet."

S. DISBRO

As part of a life-skills class I was teaching, I got my class to discuss the various terms one might encounter in a restaurant.

I asked, "What does the phrase 'à la carte' mean?"

"It means," a student said, "you're in the wrong restaurant."

ALBERT GRANDE

Preparing my son for his first day of kindergarten, we were reviewing numbers and counting. Suddenly he asked, "What is the biggest number in the world?"

As briefly as possible, I tried to explain the concept of infinity. I thought I had done pretty well, but then he said, "Dad, what number comes just before infinity?"

SHAWN FOSTER

For years I had been telling my friend Pete that he ate too much fast food, but he always denied it. One day he admitted I was right.

"What changed your mind?"

"My grandson. When my daughter told him I was coming to visit, he asked, 'Grandpa from Florida, or Grandpa from Pizza Hut?' "

STEVE FRANK

A family named Morgan moved in to our street and when their four-year-old stopped his little bicycle outside our front garden, I said ,"How are you today, Mr Morgan?"

He replied, "I'm well, thank you." Then, looking a little puzzled, he asked, "Did you think I was my father?"

N. THORPE

One night there was a programme on television featuring an allegation that two Sesame Street characters, Bert and Ernie, were gay. The show's producer refuted this, pointing out that they were puppets, not humans. They argued with each other and then made up to show children how to resolve conflicts and remain friends.

While watching this report, my wife, Donna, noticed that our seven-year-old daughter was also listening. As Donna struggled to come up with an explanation for the term "gay," our crestfallen daughter said in dismay, "They're puppets?"

BILL DOERING

We rushed our four-year-old son Ben to Accident and Emergency with a terrible cough, high temperature and vomiting. The doctor carried out an examination, then asked Ben what bothered him the most.

After thinking it over, Ben said hoarsely, "I would have to say my little sister."

ANGELA SCHMID

As my five-year-old son and I were heading to McDonald's one day, we passed a car accident. Usually when we see something terrible like that, we say a prayer for whoever might be hurt, so I pointed and said to my son, "We should pray."

From the back seat I heard his earnest voice: "Dear God, please don't let those cars block the entrance to McDonald's."

S. LEARD

77

"Go ask your mother."

Only kidding

'm going to tell you about my children. Before they tell you about me. My children are eccentric. Surreal, sometimes. I expect they get this from their father. I'm very normal. After all, there's nothing eccentric about getting in the bath fully-clothed with a bottle of champagne, as I do every time one of them has a birthday.

Perfectly normal. Doesn't everyone?

It all began with Amy. She talked from a ludicrously early age. I was so proud of this one-year-old prodigy who would look out of the window and say, "What a gloomy day ... " At her fifteen-month check-up, I tried to show her off to the paediatrician. "Words?" I bragged to the enquiry, "Words? Whole sentences!"

The doctor then pointed her spatula at pictures of cats and houses and windows, asking Amy to identify each one, to verify the claims of her over-achieving

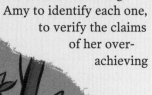

Maureen Lipman, *How Was It For You?*

parent. Amy steadfastly refused to utter a word. Finally, the doctor pointed to a picture of a dog (Snuffy by Dick Bruna, I recall) and said "Now, do we know what this is?"

"Yes," said the infant, with some weariness, "it's a spatula."

The doctor was rattled. "No, the picture. What's the picture of, Amy?"

"'S a dog, of course."

Once the expected reply came, the doctor prepared to wax lyrical. "Good girl!" she beamed.

"I've got a dog," said Amy.

"*Have* you? How lovely."

"But it can't walk."

"Oh, dearie me. Has he hurt his legs?"

"No. His batteries are flat."

Amy lived in an imaginary world called Flagleland. She had an imaginary friend called Doubt, and an invisible help-mate called Fairy Do-Good – a household treasure who apparently emigrated suddenly to America one day. I still miss her. My son, Adam, had an imaginary world called Boggyland, inhabited by a strange

and persistently-naughty playmate called Giggi. Giggi did all the wrong-doing in the house, which Adam got blamed for. We got used to taking him on journeys and leaving a place for him at dinner. One day, he too disappeared. "Who did this!" I yelled, scraping Boggyland mud off the new twistpile. "Bloody Giggi, I expect!"

"Don't say bloody-with-a-y and no, he didn't. Giggi's dead."

I stopped in mid-scrape. "Dead??" He nodded his three-year-old head. "Aha!" I thought, "his defence mechanism ... childhood fears of death, etc."

"Aaaah, poor Giggi," I murmured. "How did he die?"

Not an eyelid did he bat. "I pulled his skin off." Alas, poor Giggi. I knew him. Well!

My daughter, who could fell a stampeding herd of bison at twenty-five metres with one glance of her all-seeing, all-knowing almost greenish-brown eyes, suffers no such nonsense from her pipsqueak young brother. An overheard conversation in the car ...

Five-year-old He: "I can do

anything. I've got special extra-human powers. Me and Tom Dudderidge."

Seven-year-old She: "No, you have not, Adam."

He: "Anything on earth, I can do. And Tom Dudderidge. 'Cos of our amazing powers."

She: 'You haven't *any* amazing powers!"

He: "You don't know about them, that's all. Secret powers, so that I know everything in the world. Go on, ask me. Anything in the whole world."

Barrister-like, she rapped: "All right, then. Spell 'disillusionment'."

A silence followed, worthy of Charlie Brown at his most flattened. Amy rested her case. A minute later, he thumped her in the leg.

79

When my daughter was little, we took a flight to our holiday destination. Seated on the aeroplane near the wing, I pointed out to her that we were above the ocean. "Can you see the water?" I asked her.

"No," she said, peering out of the window at the wing, "but I can see the diving board."

REBECCA RICCI

While driving on the motorway, my daughter noticed a child in the window of a car in the next lane, holding up a handwritten sign that read "Help."

A few minutes later, the car passed again. The little boy held up the same sign and this time followed it with another, which read "My mother is singing!"

LIL GIBSON

80

My friend Susan was helping her young son do his maths homework while her teenager was in the kitchen making a snack.

"You have £4 and seven friends," Susan said. "You give £1 each to two of them but none to the others. What do you have left?"

From the next room the teenager called out, "Two friends."

DIANE KOH

Thinking his son would enjoy seeing the re-enactment of a battle, my niece's husband took the boy, Will, to the event. But the poor child was terrified by the booming cannons.

During a lull, Will's dad finally got him calmed down. That's when one of the generals bellowed, "Fire at Will!"

B. AMMAR

My daughter had our young grandchildren spellbound with stories about our Labrador, Sultan. His great delight was accompanying Grandpa in his boat on fishing trips to a nearby lake.

The children listened entranced as she told how one day, when Sultan had been left at home, Grandpa was all by himself, quietly fishing far out in the water. Suddenly he heard "splish-splash, splish-splash" and the sound of heavy breathing.

"And who do you think was trying to climb into the boat?" asked Mum.

In awed unison the children replied, "Granny!"

M. GILLANDERS

My grandson is obsessed with sport. I took him to church one day and he was particularly interested in the two ushers who were moving down each side of the aisle taking the collection. Watching them return to the altar, my grandson informed me excitedly, "Our man is winning, Grandma."

CYNTHIA STEWART

Our riding-instructor daughter began a lesson with a young girl who was seated astride a pony. "How much riding have you done?" she asked the eight-year-old.

No answer.

Again, "How much riding have you done?"

Still no answer.

In a very loud voice, in case the child was deaf, my daughter bellowed, "HOW MUCH RIDING HAVE YOU DONE?"

"Oh, sorry," said the girl. "I thought you were talking to the horse."

LYNN HUGHES

"Do you win every time?"

O n our way to my parents' house for dinner one evening, I glanced over at my 15-year-old daughter. "Isn't that skirt a bit short?" I asked. She rolled her eyes at my comment and gave me one of those "Oh, Mum" looks.

When we arrived, my mother greeted us at the door, hugged my daughter, then turned to me and said, "Elizabeth! Don't you think that blouse is awfully low-cut?"

ELIZABETH SCOTT

M y cooking has always been the target of family jokes. One evening, as I prepared dinner, the kitchen filled with smoke and the smoke detector went off. Although both of my children had received fire-safety training at school, they did not respond to the alarm. Annoyed, I stormed through the house in search of them. I found them in the bathroom, washing their hands.

Over the loud buzzing of the smoke alarm, I asked them to identify the sound.

"It's the smoke detector," they replied in unison.

"Do you know what that sound means?" I demanded.

"Yes," my oldest replied. "Dinner's ready."

D. CHRISTENSEN

M y sisters and I spent a fun afternoon working out the Chinese astrological signs for family members while our children played close by. A few weeks later we gathered for a wedding. At the reception the master of ceremonies asked for a volunteer to sing a song. To our surprise, my niece, a shy little girl, jumped up and went over to the mike. "Here's a charming songbird who's going to sing for us," said the MC.

"I'm not a songbird," said my niece indignantly into the microphone. "I'm a pig, just like my aunt and uncle."

MADELEINE COTE

I 'm aware that there are chores at home that I overlook. Recently, my 11-year-old son told me he had gained top marks for an essay entitled "My Home."

Embarrassed, I read: "I wake up in the morning just as the sun's rays are reaching the windowsill. I lie there until they shine on the big spider's web in the corner of my bedroom and then I know it's time to get up."

MRS V. STEYN

81

I had finished my Christmas shopping early and had wrapped all the presents. Having two curious children, I had to find a suitable hiding place. I chose an ideal spot – the airing cupboard. I stacked the presents and covered them with a blanket, positive they'd remain undiscovered.

When I went to get the gifts to put them under the tree, I lifted the blanket and there, stacked neatly on top of my gifts, were presents addressed to "Mum and Dad, From the Kids."

L. LONG

One of my young pupils asked my teacher's assistant, "How old are you, Mrs. Glass?"

"You should never ask an adult's age," I broke in. "That's okay," Harriett said smiling. "I'm fifty."

"Wow, you don't look that old," the boy said. I was breathing a sigh of relief when another child chimed in, "Parts of her do."

KATHERINE NORGARD

My mother was away all weekend at a business conference. During a break, she decided to call home. My six-year-old brother answered the phone and heard a stranger's voice saying, "We have a Marcia on the line. Will you accept the charges?"

Frantic, he dropped the receiver and came charging outside screaming, "Dad! They've got Mum! And they want money!"

RODNEY HOWELL

When a friend was planning her wedding she asked the four-year-old son of the matron of honour if he would like to be a page boy.

He agreed immediately and the bride-to-be told him that they would have to find a suitable outfit.

"That's OK," said the boy, "I've got two already. Which would you like – Spiderman or Superman?"

BRIAN INGLIS

Returning from work one evening, my husband noticed our neighbour's son sitting on the kerb outside his house. With some concern he asked the boy what he was doing there at that time of night. "I've run away from home," came the reply.

"You haven't got very far have you?" said my husband. The little boy looked at him and said, "I'm not allowed to cross the road."

SHEILA SCOTT

"I remind you that my client is nice until proven naughty."

Dumb and dumber

People do stupid things – it's a fact – and they can be very funny indeed!
These are the verbal fluffs and physical mishaps we love to laugh at.

My wife received a credit-card application in the mail that she had not requested. She didn't want it, but I did. So I crossed off my wife's name on the form, entered my own and returned the application. I soon got a phone call from a woman saying my application had been rejected.

I asked her why, and she told me the card could only be issued to the person originally solicited by the offer. However, she invited me to reapply, which I did during the same telephone call.

A few days later I got another call to tell me my second application had been rejected.

Why? The woman told me their files showed that I had previously applied for a card and had been denied.

S.P. BLANK

During a period of upheaval at the company where I worked, a number of office relocations were occurring. Having assisted with various moves, I considered myself quite the expert. So when I saw two colleagues struggling to carry a heavy desk up a flight of stairs, I went over and advised them that the desk would be much lighter if they removed the drawers. They duly took out the drawers. Then they balanced them on top of the desk and continued up the stairs.

DEBORAH HITCHIN

During our church service one Sunday, a parishioner was speaking about an emotionally charged topic and had trouble controlling her tears. Finishing her remarks, she told the congregation, "I apologise for crying so much. I'm usually not such a big boob."

The bishop rose to close the session and remarked, "That's okay. We like big boobs."

L.S.

On holiday, my step-mum, Sandy, called a café to make reservations for 7pm. Checking her book, the cheery young hostess said, "I'm sorry, all we have is 6:45. Would you like that?"

"That's fine," Sandy said.

"Okay," the woman confirmed. Then she added, "Just be advised you may have to wait 15 minutes for your table."

KELLY FINNEGAN

At the age of 14 I began a part-time job as a waiter. On my first night I took an order for steak. As I headed to the kitchen, the customer shouted after me, "Well done!"

I turned around and thanked him, proud of having done such a good job.

DAVID LANDER

I was out shopping in my local supermarket when a stranger came up and started chatting as if she knew me. When I could get a word in, I told her she must have mistaken me for someone else. She looked embarrassed, apologised and walked away. Five minutes later, she approached me for a second time and exclaimed, "You'll never guess what just happened to me!"

E. EAGLESTONE

TIMELESS HUMOUR

60s As a salesman, I was searching for a certain company in unfamiliar territory. I came to a likely-looking road marked with a small red sign reading: Industrial Centre. I was not certain that this was the right road, so I drove back to a petrol station to inquire.

The attendant took my arm and pointed to the sign that I had just read, now barely discernible in the distance. "See that little sign about three blocks away?" he asked.

"You mean the red one that says industrial centre?" I asked.

"Man!" he exclaimed. "You've got eyes like an eagle!"

EDWARD M. LONGAN

85

My husband decided life would be easier if he wired a new light switch in the master bedroom to save us from fumbling in the dark for the lamp. He cut through the partition wall and found a stash of bottles and small boxes inside the wall. "Sweetie!" he called excitedly. "Come and see what I've found!" I ran in and quickly realised that his next task would be to fix the hole that now led into the back of our medicine cabinet.

NOLA PIRART

It was the standard series of check-in questions that every traveller gets at the airline counter, including, "Has anyone put anything in your baggage without your knowledge?"

"If it was put there without my knowledge," I asked, "how would I know?"

The agent behind the counter smiled smugly. "That's why we ask."

KATE VETTER

An aching back sent me stumbling to the chemist for some relief. After a search, I found what I was looking for: a selection of heating pads designed for people with back pain – all on the bottom shelf.

KATHERINE JOHNSON

"It says, 'Separate two eggs.' Is that far enough?"

My mother, a meticulous housekeeper, often lectured my father about tramping dirt into the house. One day he came in to find her furiously scrubbing away at a spot on the floor and launching into a lecture. "I don't know what you've brought in," she said, "but I can't get it out."

He studied the situation for a moment and, without a word, moved a figurine on the windowsill where the sun was streaming in. The spot immediately disappeared.

MICHELE DONNELLY

One day while at the doctor's office, the receptionist called me to the desk to update my personal file.

Before I had a chance to tell her that all the information she had was still correct, she asked, **"Has your date of birth changed?"**

MARGARET FREESE

86

On a flight, the passenger next to me was clearly enjoying his first journey overseas. When given a disembarkation card, he pulled out his new passport and began to complete the form with great care.

When he came to the box which said "Passport No" he paused for a moment, then crossed out "No" and wrote "Yes".

SARAH PLANT

Dining out one evening, I noticed some teenagers celebrating at a nearby table. When one girl pulled out a camera, I offered to take a picture of the group. After one photo, I suggested taking another just in case the first one didn't come out.

"Oh, no, that's okay," she said, as she took back her camera. "I always get double prints."

D. GUY

Travelling on a minibus to a cricket match, I was passed a soft, flat, orange substance in a plastic wrapping. I recognised the object as a chemical hand warmer that gets hot as you manipulate it, but after several minutes of rubbing, the package failed to heat up. Just as I was losing patience, the bemused man next to me informed me that I was massaging a slice of Double Gloucester.

BOBBY DIX

I am a cook in an old people's home and was roasting a joint of beef one Sunday. But there was no plain flour for the Yorkshire puddings. A care worker assured me that self-raising would do just as well, so I went ahead and made them. But when I took them out of the oven, they were like biscuits. I mentioned this to the worker later that day. "Oh, I know," she agreed. "Mine turn out like that too."

TIM KILGETTY

During weekly visits to my doctor, I've noticed a lot of inattentive parents with badly behaved children in the waiting room. So I was impressed one day to see a mother with her little boy, helping him sound out the words on a sign.

Finally he mastered it and his mother cheered, "That's great! Now sit there. I'll be back in 15 minutes."

What did the sign say? "Children must not be left unattended."

D. HOVEL

87

"Reservations? No, we definitely want to eat here."

After I asked for a half-pound trout fillet at my local supermarket's seafood counter, the shop assistant picked one out of a pile and put it on the scale. It weighed precisely eight ounces.

Impressed, I asked, "How did you know?"

He proudly declared, "I'm psychotic."

G. HOCUTT

I was preparing to teach a course on the history of film censorship and went to the library to take out films that had been censored. "Do you have any banned movies in your collection?" I asked the librarian.

"Oh yes," she answered. "We have some really good ones. What would you like? Glenn Miller?"

PAUL STACY

Sometime around two in the morning our phone rang, waking us out of a sound sleep. "Wrong number," my husband growled and put down the receiver.

A few minutes later it rang again. I heard him say, "One with pepperoni and extra cheese and one with sausage. Pick up in 20 minutes."

"What was that?" I asked.

"I took his order. Now we can sleep."

JACKIE HUTH

I was getting into my car when I noticed a dent. On the windscreen was a note and a phone number from the driver.

"I feel terrible," the woman apologised when I called.

"I hit your car as I was pulling into the next parking spot."

"Please, don't worry," I said to her.

"I'm sure our insurance companies will take care of everything."

"Thank you for your understanding," she said.

"You're so much nicer than the man I hit on the way out."

L. PAYNE

I overheard two older women talking about their size on a bus recently.

"I never seemed to have a weight problem when I was younger," said one with a mixture of puzzlement and annoyance.

The other woman thought for a while before replying in all seriousness, "Well, they hadn't invented calories then."

"Of course," her friend said, looking relieved. "That explains everything."

LYNN HURTON

Our teenage daughter decided to learn the saxophone. She purchased a brand new tenor sax and retired to her room to start practicing.

However, despite her best efforts over the next few months, the only sounds she could produce were tuneless squeaks and wails. She reluctantly concluded that the saxophone wasn't the instrument for her and decided to sell it through the local paper.

The first prospective buyer was a pleasant woman in her twenties. She examined the instrument thoroughly. "It looks like it's new and hasn't been used," she cooed enthusiastically. "It's even still got the polystyrene protective packaging under the keys."

MICHAEL DELLER

The first day at my new health club I asked the girl at the front desk,
"I like to exercise after work. What are your hours?"
"Our club is open 24/7," she told me excitedly, **"Monday to Saturday."**

A. CAVENDER

No one is more cautious than a first-time parent. When our daughter was big enough to ride on the back of my bike, I bought her a little helmet and a special carrier with a seat belt.

The day of the first ride I put her in the seat, double-checked all the equipment, wheeled the bike to the end of our drive, carefully looked both ways and, swinging my leg up over the crossbar, kicked her in the chin.

ZACHARY GIBBS

My mother was discussing with my sister a relative's recent run of bad luck. "Why did she change her job?" Mother asked my sister. "Perhaps she has a subconscious desire not to succeed."

"Or maybe it just happened," sighed my exasperated sister. "Do you know you have a habit of over-analyzing everything?"

Mother was silent for a moment. "That's true," she said. "Why do you think I do that?"

B. CYPHERS

On the train to London, I realised that the businessman who had been sitting next to me had left the train and forgotten his briefcase. Hanging out of the window, I shouted over to a station employee as the train was pulling away and managed to hand him the case. About five minutes later the businessman reappeared carrying a coffee. He'd just been to the buffet car.

ROBIN THORNTON

While sitting in the emergency department of our local hospital, I watched as a panicked father-to-be rushed in and told a nurse that his wife had called him at work about 15 minutes earlier. She was going into labour prematurely, he said, and would be arriving at the hospital any minute now.

"How far along is your wife?" the nurse asked calmly.

Glancing down nervously at his watch, the man replied,

"Right now, she should be on London Road."

KAREN MORRIS

Clever cogs

This week scientists claimed that after years of research and billions of dollars they had finally developed a computer that could communicate with the linguistic skills of the average toddler. Which means that the computer just shouts "No!" at every reasonable suggestion you make and then throws itself to the floor of the supermarket while other shoppers look at you and tut.

"I know, PC, let's go to the swings after this!"

"I want Mummy!"

"Yes, well, Mummy's just having a little sleep because you woke her up four times last night … "

"I want Mummy!"

And eventually you just stick another floppy disk in the "A" drive to keep it quiet even though you haven't actually paid for them yet.

Computers have come a very long way in a very short space of time. Apparently there is more digital technology in the average mobile phone than there was on the spacecraft that put the first man on the moon. Which is why Neil Armstrong didn't spend his whole time annoying his fellow astronauts by braying, "Ya, hi, I'm on a lunar module – ya, we're just arriving at the moon now … " So while Apollo 11 may have looked impressive, there's no way it could ever have played an irritating electronic version of *The Entertainer*. It's amazing the things computers can do today. You can change the number of tropical fish on your screen saver, you can have the flying toasters go quick or slow, you can play solitaire on screen instead of with a pack of cards. How previous generations managed without such basic essentials is unimaginable. And following the week's breakthrough we are now promised microchips that will think and talk like real human beings. Cue a thousand crappy sci-fi films about computers taking over the world.

My PC already has its own personality – it is an unhelpful French bureaucrat; you try to reason with it but it just repeats the same thing back at you over and over again. I might try to get it re-programmed so that when it refuses to co-operate, it does so in a French accent. "Zere eez no disk een drive A."

"THERE IS A BLOODY DISK, LOOK, THERE IT IS! I'VE TAKEN IT OUT, NOW I'M PUTTING IT IN AGAIN, SO DON'T TELL ME THERE'S NO BLOODY DISK, OK?"

"Zere eez no disk een drive A."

"Look, is there anyone else I can talk to?"

Generally speaking, man is still the master of the machines, except when it comes to setting the timer on the video recorder. There was a scare a while back when the computer Deep Blue defeated Gary Kasparov at chess. The Grand Master had failed to make the most obvious move available to him, which was to lean across and pull the plug out. But there are various projects around the world that claim to have created genuine artificial intelligence. One team

John O'Farrell, *Global Village Idiot*

recently thought they'd cracked it when they asked their computer, "Can you recognize speech?" The machine said it could and proceeded to wreck a nice beach. And of course you can now buy electronic dictating programs that put the words up on the screen as you say them. I actually use this software to write with and it works perflkadnl.

If computers are going to have the intelligence of humans, the worrying question is which particular humans are we talking about? What's the point of going to all that effort if all you produce is the electronic equivalent of Tara Palmer-Tomkinson? Two e-mails and it thinks, "That's enough work for a month – I'm off skiing." Or a palm-top with the mind of a politician? "What's Tim's address?" Well, frankly I don't think that is the question you should be asking here ... " If the robots that make our cars are given brains we'll be straight back to the 1970s: mass walkouts and computerized shop stewards with huge collars talking about collective wage bargaining. With human sensibilities,

computers will get all depressed about the meaninglessness of it all. "I'm not just some machine, you know." "Um, well, you are actually."

Why is it presumed that the most desirable form of artificial intelligence is one modelled on the human mind? If you want the computers to do as they're told it would be far better to recreate the thought processes of a border collie. As long as you could put up with the PCs smelling one another's modem ports, the machines would be far more dependable. Millions of viewers could tune into *One Man and His Laptop* as the computer programmer shouted, "Cum-bye, lad, cum, bye. Now – print!"

But scientists are determined to press on with trying to recreate what they consider to be the ultimate in artificial intelligence – a computer that thinks like a person. We will know that we've got there when we have a machine that really reasons, feels and speaks like a normal human being. And then it'll say, "Actually I don't understand most of the things on my computer. I just use it for typing letters really ... "

My new credit card came with a sticker on it, giving the phone number to authorise the new account. I called up and was offered the option: "Press one to activate the card." This led me to a live person, who answered with her first name and the title "credit card activator".

As I got ready to give the requisite information, she interrupted me, asking, "How can I help you?"

ANGELA NOLA

Low on petrol, I pulled my van into a service station to fill up. As I was turning in, I spotted a petrol cap lying on the ground that looked like it might replace my missing one.

I hurriedly parked by the pump, jumped out of the van, ran over and picked up the cap. I was pleasantly surprised to find that it screwed easily into my tank. A perfect fit, I thought. Then I noticed the keyhole in the top of the cap.

BOB SJOSTRAND

Recently my wife was in a queue behind a car with three bumper stickers: "Don't be fooled by genetically engineered food – demand labels and safety testing"; "Eat for the health of it"; and "Support organic farmers".

The car was in front of her at a McDonald's drive-through restaurant.

B. MONK

New to the area, I was eager to meet people. So one day I struck up a conversation with another woman in the gym. Pointing to two men playing squash in a nearby court, I said to her, "There's my husband." Then I added, "The thin one – not the fat one."

After an uncomfortable silence she replied, "And that's my husband – the fat one."

NITYA RAMAKRISHNAN

SIGN LANGUAGE

On a plumbers truck:

"You don't have to sleep with that drip tonight."

C. WURST

My grandmother moved in with our family of five. As I was cleaning my teeth one morning, she rapped on the bathroom door.

"Is anyone in there?" she called.

I mumbled an answer, to which she replied, "Is that a yes or a no?"

ALEXI LEONDARITIS

I am full-figured, and when I eat in restaurants, I often find the chairs too small and uncomfortable. The last time I had a meal out, I filled in a comment card saying that while the food and service were wonderful, the chairs did not accommodate anyone over a size 14.

Several weeks later I received a note of apology – and a coupon for a free dessert.

PAT BALLARD

Several hours into a visit to my mother's house, she noticed I hadn't lit up a cigarette once. "Are you trying to kick the habit?"

"No," I replied, "I've got a cold and I don't smoke when I'm unwell."

"You know," she observed, "you'd probably live longer if you were sick more often."

IAN HAMMEL

My friend works in customer services for a travel company. One furious customer told her that something they'd eaten on holiday had made them ill and he demanded compensation.

After looking into his complaint, my friend informed him that the company did indeed pay compensation for food poisoning – but not on its self-catering breaks.

LYNSEY HAWKINS

For our honeymoon my fiancée and I chose a fashionable hotel known for its luxurious suites.

When I called to make reservations, the desk clerk inquired, **"Is this for a special occasion?"**

"Yes," I replied. **"It's our honeymoon."**

"And how many adults will there be?" she asked.

LARRY REEVES

My father and I belong to the religion of Sikhism. We both wear the traditional turban and often encounter strange comments and questions. Once, in a restaurant, a child stared with amazement at my father. She finally got the courage to ask, "Are you a genie?"

Her mother, caught off guard, turned red in the face and apologised for the remark. But my dad took no offence and decided to humour the child.

He replied, "Why, yes I am. I can grant you three wishes."

The child's mother blurted out, "Really?"

MANVIR KALS

The road by my house was in bad condition after a rough winter. Every day I dodged potholes on the way to work. So I was relieved to see a construction crew working on the road one morning.

Later, on my way home, I noticed no improvement. But where the construction crew had been working stood a new, bright-yellow sign with the words "Rough Road".

SARAH LIND

Over the years, my husband and I have usually managed to decode the gender signs they sometimes put on lavatory doors in restaurants ("Buoys & Gulls", "Laddies & Lassies" and so on), but occasionally we get stumped.

Recently my husband Dave wandered off in search of the men's room and found himself confronted by two marked doors, one labelled "Bronco" and the other "Cactus".

Completely baffled, he stopped a restaurant employee and asked which of the doors he should open.

"Actually, we'd prefer you to go there," the employee said, pointing to a door down the hall marked "Men". "'Bronco' and 'Cactus' are private dining rooms."

S. LEE

93

My colleagues and I received this e-mail from our facilities department: "Due to building work, your office may be either cooler or warmer than usual on Tuesday. Dress accordingly."

DEBRA DONAT

My friend was puzzled with the odd messages left on his answering machine. Day after day friends and family would talk and then say, "Beep."

He discovered the reason for the joke when he decided to listen to his greeting. "Hi," it said. "I'm not in right now, so please leave a beep after the message."

SHEEBA MATHEW

After a recent move, I made up a list of companies, agencies and services that needed to know my new address and phoned each to ask them to make the change.

Everything went smoothly until I made a call to one of my frequent-flier accounts. After I explained to her what I wanted to do, the woman I reached in customer service told me, "I'm sorry; we can't do that over the phone. You will have to fill out our change-of-address form."

"How do I get one of those?" I asked.

"We'd be happy to provide you with one," she said pleasantly. "Can I have your new address so I can post it to you?"

Bad weather had backed up all flights, and as a result our plane had been sitting on the runway for three hours. All attempts to placate the passengers weren't working.

Then the pilot came on the intercom to announce his umpteenth update: "Ladies and gentlemen, we'll be getting permission to take off, but I have to tell you that we're twenty-sixth in line for departure."

As a collective groan filled the aircraft, a flight attendant added, "Will all passengers please close your window shades. We will soon be showing our almost-in-flight hit movie, *Anger Management*."

STEVE NORTH

After booking my 90-year-old mother on a flight, I called the airline to go over her needs. The woman representative listened patiently as I requested a wheelchair and an attendant for my mother because of her arthritis and impaired vision. I also asked for a special meal and assistance in changing planes.

My apprehension lightened a bit when the woman assured me everything would be taken care of. I thanked her profusely.

"Why, you're welcome," she replied. I was about to hang up when she cheerfully asked, "And will your mother be needing a hire car?"

THOMAS CORBETT

No good deed goes unpunished. I had volunteered to tar the roof of my father's shed. I was about halfway through when I slipped and fell flat on my face, getting black gloop all over my shirt, trousers and even my hair.

Hearing the thud, Dad looked up. "What happened?" he asked.

I got up and began to say, "All I did was … " when my feet shot from under me and I flipped into the sticky mess again.

"You know," said Dad dryly, "you could have just told me."

JOHN CORNWELL

SIGN LANGUAGE

At a coffee shop a sign on the staff's tip box said **"Thanks a latte."**

On our first day at a resort, my wife and I headed to the beach. When I went back to our room to get something to drink, one of the hotel maids was making our bed.

I was on my way back out when I stopped at the door and asked, "Can we drink beer on the beach?"

"Of course," she said, "but I have to finish the rest of the rooms first."

L. ALLARD

95

I have a large scar on the left side of my face from a car accident. One night a customer walked into the petrol station where I work, and after glancing at me exclaimed, "My God, what happened to your face?"

I told the customer about the accident, hoping that would be the end of it, but he kept pressing for more information. Finally, he stopped his questioning and made his purchase. Just before walking away he said, "Don't worry: it's not that noticeable."

ROBERT GOEBEL

At 82 years old, my husband applied for his first passport. He was told he would need a birth certificate, but his birth had never been officially registered. When he explained his dilemma to the passport agent, the response was less than helpful.

"In lieu of a birth certificate," the agent said, "you can bring a notarised affidavit from the doctor who delivered you."

ELGARDA ASHLIMAN

One day my wife and I came home to find an answering-machine message from a friend of hers. It said she had applied for a job and had given my wife's name for a character reference – someone to verify she was honest and

"Of course, it's nothing serious, honey ... just a flooded engine."

trustworthy. She added that there was also a form for my wife to sign. "But I couldn't find you," the friend concluded, "so I forged your signature."

WILL PETERS

Approaching the cash machine at my bank, I noticed someone had left his card in the slot. Since it was a Friday evening, I thought the decent thing to do was to try to find the card's owner so he wouldn't have to spend the weekend without it.

Fortunately, I located the owner's unusual name in the phone book and

dialled the number. I told the man who answered that I'd found his bank card. He gave a sigh of relief then asked hopefully, "You didn't happen to find my sunglasses too, did you?"

G.D. PETERSON

My friend Ann and I had decided to have a meal at a Chinese restaurant. When a waiter set chopsticks at our places, Ann made a point of reaching into her handbag and pulling out her own pair. "As an environmentalist," she declared, "I don't approve of destroying bamboo forests for throwaway utensils."

The waiter inspected her chopsticks. "Very beautiful," he remarked politely. "Ivory."

ERICA CHRISTENSEN

I was working in my village shop when I noticed a customer had left his mobile phone on the counter. I scrolled through the saved numbers and found one titled "Mum". I dialled the number and, when the man's mother answered, I told her to let him know what had happened.

Five minutes later, the mobile rang. Before I could say anything, a woman said, "Martin, you've left your phone in the village shop."

ROBERT COOMBS

As manager of a supermarket, I noticed a customer trying to force a shopping trolley through the turnstiles at the entrance.

When I politely pointed out to her that it should be pushed through the adjacent plastic flaps, she grinned sheepishly, adding, **"How silly of me,"** and guided the vehicle through the flaps following it on all fours.

PAUL SMITH

My three sisters and I have weight problems and are always sharing diet tips. One day my oldest sister was showing us a low-fat cookbook and pointed out a chicken dish she had tried the night before. Reading the ingredients, I commented, "It looks like it would taste really bland."

"It did," she replied, "until I added cheese and sour cream."

PATRICIA LAANSMA

At the supermarket checkout, I refused a carrier bag from the cashier. "If everyone brought their own bag," I said smugly, popping my groceries into my rucksack, "there would be much less waste."

"You're quite right," she agreed before crumpling up the carrier bag and throwing it in the bin.

KALI TURIL

I was having a drink at a local restaurant with my friend Justin when he spotted an attractive woman sitting at the bar. After an hour of gathering his courage, he approached her and asked "Would you mind if I chatted with you for a while?"

She responded by yelling at the top of her lungs, "No, I won't come over to your place tonight!"

With everyone in the restaurant staring, Justin crept back to our table, puzzled and humiliated.

A few minutes later, the woman walked over to us and apologised.

"I'm sorry if I embarrassed you," she said, "but I'm a postgraduate student in psychology and I'm studying human reaction to embarrassing situations."

At the top of his lungs Justin responded, 'What do you mean, two hundred pounds?'

J. SMODISH

While away on business, a colleague and I decided to pay a visit to the local cinema.

As we approached it, we read the billboard above the entrance. It bore the name of the film followed by the numbers "7", "5" and "9". Assuming these were the programme times, we were a bit perplexed by their order. I went inside to ask about it. The box office attendant told me the next show began at eight. "But your display says there's one at seven, five then nine," I pointed out. "Right," she agreed. "That's 7.59. We've lost our number eight."

DIANE CLANCY

97

Dad is from the old school, where you keep your money under the mattress – only he kept his in the underwear drawer. One day I bought my dad an unusual personal safe – a can of spray paint with a false bottom – so he could keep his money in his workshop. Later I asked Mum if he was using it.

"Oh, yes," she replied, "he put his money in it the same day."

"No burglar would think to look on the work shelf!" I gloated.

"They won't have to," my mum replied. "He keeps the paint can in his underwear drawer."

J. MULVEY

My very pregnant sister-in-law had just returned from another disappointingly uneventful trip to the hospital when she went into true labour. With no time to make it back to the hospital, my brother called 999. In shock, he followed the telephone instructions of the operator to deliver the baby. He even tied the umbilical cord with a string.

The ambulance team arrived shortly thereafter, only to see an exhausted mother holding her beautiful daughter – with a tennis shoe dangling on the cord between them!

SABRINA FORD

There was a letter that appeared in my mail. It told me I was required to go to court as a witness against someone whose name I did not recognise. Calling for more information, I found out my notice was for reporting a dangerous driver – ten years ago when I had been driving a bus part-time.

The appearance date was the same time as my night class, so I called to see if my court appearance could be rescheduled. Two days later someone returned my call.

"We cannot push the date back," they said. The reason? "The accused is entitled to a speedy trial."

JANIS SMITH

Early one Saturday morning, the flashing lights of a police car appeared in my rear-view mirror.

After checking my licence, the officer asked, "Do you know why I pulled you over?"

"No," I responded.

"One of your brake lights is out," he said. "I'm going to issue you with a warning."

"Thank goodness," I said, without thinking. "I thought you'd pulled me over because my insurance had expired."

ANDREA SHIPPER

"He just sits there all day, waiting to chase the e-mail man."

Hoping to learn more about financial matters, I went to a book shop and grabbed a copy of *Personal Finance for Dummies*. A glance at the book's price sticker, however, revealed just how little credit the shop's management gave people like me.

It read: **"Publisher's list price: £16.95; our discount price: £17.99."**

NAOMI WELSH

The escalators were broken at our local cinema, so staff had put up signs pointing out that not only would you have to walk up them, but you could expect two-way traffic.

To help bring order to the predicted chaos, the staff had a system. The signs read, "Please walk on the left going up and on the right going down."

ALISON EFFENY

Standing on the sidelines during a game being played by my school's football team, I saw one of the players take a rather nasty knock. He tumbled to the ground and didn't move.

We grabbed our first-aid kit and rushed out on to the field. The team coach picked up the young man's hand and urged, "Son, can you hear me? Squeeze once for yes and twice for no."

RICHARD CORBIN

When we arrived at a popular restaurant, it was crowded. My wife went up to the manager and asked, "Will it be long?" The woman ignored her and kept writing in her book.

My wife repeated the question. The manager looked up and said the wait would be about ten minutes.

A short time later we heard an announcement over the loudspeaker: "Willette B. Long, your table is ready."

HERBERT KARP

Although I am of Chinese descent, I never really learned to speak Chinese. One evening, I came home boasting about a wonderful meal I'd had in Chinatown. Unfortunately, I couldn't remember the name of the restaurant, but was able to write the Chinese character that was on the door and show it to my mother.

"Do you know what it says?" Mum asked with a smile. "It says 'Pull'."

BARBARA MAO

TIMELESS HUMOUR

70s Our telephone had just been installed and Jennifer, my three-year-old daughter, asked if she could phone her friend Sally Anne who lives next door. I phoned my neighbour, explaining Jennifer's request, and Sally Anne was called to the phone. My daughter suddenly became dumbstruck. In desperation, I spoke to Sally Anne, imitating Jennifer. The answer was sweet and clear.

Later, I went to explain to my neighbour, but before I could do so, she said "Sorry, I couldn't get Sally Anne to say a word so I spoke to Jennifer in my best little girl voice. I hope I was convincing."

JOAN LONMON

99

When I was in junior school, I lost the sight in my right eye during a playground mishap. Fortunately, the accident had little effect on my life. When I reached my 40s, however, I needed to get glasses.

At the opticians, the optometrist's young assistant pointed to an eye chart. "Cover your right eye and read line three," she said.

"I'm blind in my right eye," I told her. "It's a glass eye."

"Okay," she responded. "In that case, cover your left eye."

BILL SLACK

My flight was delayed. Since the gate was needed for another flight, our aircraft was backed away from the terminal, and we were directed to a new gate. We all found the new gate, only to discover a third gate had been designated for our plane.

Finally, everyone got on board the right plane, and the flight attendant announced: "We apologise for the gate change. This flight is going to Washington, D.C. If your destination is not Washington, D.C., you should disembark at this time."

A moment later a red-faced pilot emerged from the cockpit, carrying his bags. "Sorry," he said, "wrong plane."

ROY SCHMIDT

Wandering in and out of tiny, cottage-like shops in a small village, my friend peered in through one window to see shelf-upon-shelf of interesting-looking books. She went inside.

A lady appeared through a bead curtain and asked, "Can I help you?"

"No, just browsing," said my friend.

"Fine," came the curt reply, "but it is usual to knock before entering someone's home."

JANE MURRAY

One evening my former boss was getting out of the shower when his wife called, asking him to turn off an iron she had mistakenly left on in the basement before she left for the weekend. Thinking no one would see him, he ran down the stairs into the dark basement without even a towel on.

As he flipped on the light switch, though, he was shocked to hear dozens of people yell "Surprise!" His wife had orchestrated the secret party to celebrate his 40th birthday.

JENNIFER JASEK

I began viola lessons as an adult. When I started, I called my mother to share my excitement. "Wonderful!" she exclaimed. "But I've never heard a viola. What does it sound like?"

Unable to give an apt description, I phoned my mother a few days later, after buying a CD of viola music. "Listen to this," I said as I placed the telephone receiver next to the stereo speaker, and turned the music on for about 30 seconds of a Schubert sonata. Then I picked up the receiver. "Well, Mum, what do you think?"

A moment of silence followed, then a question: "I'm speechless, Debbie. How many lessons have you had?"

DEBORAH HAYS

When I was seven months pregnant, I went shopping with my husband to a sports shop famous for its huge sales, and I caught the attention of a reporter covering the event. He asked what we were looking for and I patted my stomach and said we needed a tent to accommodate our growing family. The reporter asked my distracted husband: "Is this your first?"

"No," he replied, "we have another tent at home."

MARY ANN HAEFNER

I frequently receive calls from pollsters asking me to participate in telephone surveys. One woman began with a barrage of questions.

"Wait a moment," I interrupted. "Who are you and whom do you represent?"

She told me and immediately continued asking questions.

"What's the purpose of this survey?" I asked.

"Sir," she replied irritably, "I don't have time to answer your questions." Then she hung up.

HENRY SHEPPARD

My stepdad bought an autofocus camera on holiday and lined the family up for a photo beside the pool.

"I don't need any help; this camera is foolproof," he told us as he stepped backwards into the water.

CHARLOTTE JOSEPH

A steak fanatic, my father always picks out dishes that include a bone because he loves to nibble on it. One night Father and I were finishing our dinners at a restaurant, and I could tell he wanted to start gnawing on the bone. But he couldn't bear to do so in public.

"Excuse me," he said, calling the waitress over, "would you please wrap this bone up for my dog?" Father has never owned a dog in his life, but the white lie seemed a tactful solution to his dilemma.

A few minutes later the waitress returned to our table. "Here's your bone, sir," she said, handing over a large package. "And while I was in the kitchen, I grabbed a few more out of the scrap bucket."

KAREN FREEMAN

On a shopping trip, a friend and I nipped into a small café for lunch. After studying the daily specials on the blackboard, we went to order.

My friend fancied cheese on toast and asked what kind of cheese was used. This perplexed the young girl behind the counter.

However, after a few moments of intense consideration, her face lit up and she answered, "Grated."

OLIVIA WHITEHURST

Having just finished a load of washing after a long day at the office, I grabbed my teenage son and told him to go and hang it out on the line. "But Mum!" he complained. "It's raining."

"Use your initiative," I snapped. "Take an umbrella."

PADDY ALLEN

101

Turnip surprise

BLACKADDER'S LODGINGS

Breakfast time at Lord Blackadder's place. Percy and Blackadder are eating the Elizabethan equivalent of toast.

PERCY: I must say, Edmund, it was jolly nice of you to ask me to share your breakfast before the rigours of the day begin.

BLACKADDER: It is said, Percy, that civilized man seeks out good and intelligent company so that through learned discourse he may rise above the savage and [become] closer to God.

PERCY: (*Delighted*) Yes, I'd heard that.

BLACKADDER: Personally, however, I like to start the day with a total dickhead to remind me I'm best.

Blackadder rises and goes to sort out the mail.

PERCY: (*Laughing*) Beshrew me, Edmund, you're in good fooling this morning!

BLACKADDER: Don't say "beshrew me", Percy. Only stupid actors say "beshrew me".

PERCY: Oh, how I would love to be an actor. I had a great talent for it in my youth – I was the man of a thousand faces.

BLACKADDER: How did you come to choose the ugly mug you've got now, then?

Percy laughs

PERCY: Oh, tush, my lord.

BLACKADDER: And don't say "tush" either. It's only a short step from "tush" to "hey nonny nonny" and then I'm afraid I shall have to call the police.

He at last gets round to reading his letter. Immediately, his face lightens.

Well, God pats me on the head and says, "Good boy, Edmund."

PERCY: My lord?

BLACKADDER: My aunt and uncle, Lord and Lady Whiteadder, the two most fanatical puritans in England,

have invited themselves to dinner here, tonight.

PERCY: But aren't they the most frightful bores?

BLACKADDER: Yes, but they have one great redeeming feature: their wallets. More capacious than an elephant's scrotum and just as difficult to get your hands on. At least until now. For tonight they wish to "discuss my inheritance".

PERCY: Hey nonny nonny, my lord – good news!

BLACKADDER: *Baldrick!*

Baldrick enters with a piece of cheese hanging from his nose on a string.

Why have you got a piece of cheese tied to the end of your nose?

BALDRICK: To catch mice, my lord. I lie on the floor with my mouth open and hope they scurry in.

BLACKADDER: And do they?

BALDRICK: Not yet, my lord.

Richard Curtis and Ben Elton, *Blackadder II*

BLACKADDER: I'm not surprised. Your breath comes straight from Satan's bottom, Baldrick. The only sort of mouse you're going to catch is one without a nose.

BALDRICK: That's a pity because the nose is the best bit on a mouse.

BLACKADDER: Any bits of mouse will seem like luxury compared to what Percy and I must eat tonight. We are entertaining puritan vegetable folk, Balders, and that means no meat.

BALDRICK: In that case, I shall prepare my turnip surprise.

BLACKADDER: And the surprise is?

BALDRICK: There's nothing in it except the turnip.

BLACKADDER: So another word for turnip surprise would be a turnip.

BALDRICK: Oh, yes.

BLACKADDER: Good.

A knock on the door.

Get the door, Baldrick.

Baldrick obeys and exits.

PERCY: Well, my lord, if things go as planned tonight, it would seem congratulations are in order.

BLACKADDER: Nice try, Percy, but forget it: you're not getting a penny.

There is a loud crash and Baldrick enters, carrying the door.

Baldrick, I would advise you to make the explanation you are about to give phenomenally good.

BALDRICK: You said, "Get the door."

BLACKADDER: Not good enough. You're fired.

BALDRICK: But, my lord, I've been in your family since 1532.

BLACKADDER: So has syphilis. Now get out.

BALDRICK: Very well, my lord. Oh, by the way, there was a messenger outside when I got the door. Says the queen wants to see you. Lord Melchett is very sick.

BLACKADDER: (*Grinning*) Really?

BALDRICK: Yes. He's at death's door.

BLACKADDER: Well, my faithful old reinstated family retainer, let's go and open it for him then!

103

After his wife died, the uncle of one of my friends decided to plan ahead and order a gravesite marker for himself.

A week or so later he came home to find a message on his answering machine. It was from a young woman at the company where he'd placed his order.

"I don't know if it's good news or bad," she said, **"but your headstone is ready."**

OLIVIA VAZ

One of our friends was having problems with her car, so my wife volunteered my services as an amateur mechanic.

The starter was broken, the battery was dead and a spark plug needed replacing.

Days later I handed the keys back to our friend saying, "Your car is good for many more miles."

"Thanks," she said. "I just want it to run long enough to make it to the dealer. I'm trading it in tomorrow."

GEORGE MARSHALL

We purchased an old house from two elderly sisters. Winter was fast approaching, and I was concerned about the house's lack of insulation. "If they could live here all those years, so can we!" my husband confidently declared.

One November night the temperature plunged to below zero, and we woke up to find interior walls covered with frost. My husband called the sisters to ask how they had kept the house warm. After a brief conversation, he hung up. "For the past 30 years," he muttered, "they've gone away for the winter."

LINDA DOBSON

I was queueing at a souvenir stall at a Renaissance-themed fair when a man asked the cashier, "Do you sell sunglasses?"

"Alas, yeoman," she answered in her best sixteenth-century voice. "Coloured bits of glass suspended before the eyes were not invented until after the Renaissance, so those are not goods we purvey."

As he turned away, ye olde cashier added, "But we have baseball caps with our logo on them."

KATHY SHEEHAN

Learning new computer skills can be a challenge. An office manager in my software training class, taking nothing for granted, jotted down every word I said. During a recent session, I peeked over his shoulder and read what he'd written: "New Computer Training – password is first name ... Mine is Bob."

TIMOTHY FOUBERT

Looking for a particular species of poplar that has a lovely perfume, I went to the garden centre. Unfortunately, the one I went to didn't stock the plant, but the assistant suggested another type that apparently smelt almost as good, though she couldn't say for sure as she had no sense of smell.

"That must be a mixed blessing," I remarked.

"Well," she said, "it is and it isn't."

CAROL HILL

On holiday, I stopped at a small village Post Office and shop for some food and postcards.

"I'd like some stamps too, please," I told the shopkeeper.

"You'll have to go across to the Post Office for those," he said. Crossing the shop, he unlocked the post office counter and stood behind the grille.

"Six stamps, please," I asked again.

"Sorry," he replied. "I'm all out of stamps."

POLLY PUTT

QUOTABLE QUOTES

It's easy to get a reputation for wisdom. It's only necessary to live long, speak little and do less.

P.D. JAMES, A Certain Justice (Knopf)

You can't have everything. Where would you put it?

STEVEN WRIGHT

The one thing that unites all human beings, regardless of age, gender, religion or ethnic background, is that we all believe we are above-average drivers.

DAVE BARRY, Dave Barry Turns 50 (Crown)

I left the room with silent dignity, but caught my foot in the mat.

GEORGE GROSSMITH

When you don't know what you're talking about, it's hard to know when you're finished.

TOMMY SMOTHERS

There's a sucker born every minute.

PHINEAS T. BARNUM

Outside of a dog, a book is man's best friend; inside of a dog, it's too dark to read.

GROUCHO MARX

Before you criticize someone, you should walk a mile in their shoes. That way, when you criticize them, you're a mile away and you have their shoes.

Quoted in The Sisterhood of the Traveling Pants by Ann Brashares (Delacorte Press)

My husband and I were touring our friends' new home. Mr. and Mrs. Henry Curtis had put special touches everywhere. In the bathroom my husband leaned over to me and whispered, "They even have monogrammed taps."

PAT GNAU

One day I noticed my sister wasn't wearing a watch. When I asked her why, she replied that she didn't need one. "At home there's a clock in every room and in the car I have a clock on the dashboard," she explained.

Knowing my sister's an avid shopper, I enquired how she told the time when out on a spending spree.

"That's easy," she replied. "I buy something and look at the time printed on the receipt."

M. MCGOWAN

Although my father is good at playing golf, he always hooks his tee shots quite badly to the left. After not playing together for several years, we decided to play a round and I noticed that he was slicing the ball badly to the right. "I thought you had a problem with hooking to the left," I said.

"Yes," he replied. "I've cured that."

DAVID VAN DEN BERGH

"On Dasher, on Dancer, on Prancer and Vixen. On Comet, on Cupid, on Donner and Blitzen ... wait ... this can't be right."

I was in a queue at a restaurant. In front of me was a mother with her university-age son and his girlfriend. It was the middle of the dinner rush, and many customers were restless at the long wait, but the young couple, holding hands and kissing, were oblivious to everything around them. Although clearly not approving, the mother was silent, until one prolonged kiss when the young man had his face and hands buried in his girlfriend's long, curly locks.

"Do you have to do that here?" the embarrassed mother asked.

"I'm not doing anything, Mum," came her son's muffled voice. "My earring's caught in her hair."

KATHY GASTON

When our tumble dryer broke, my husband set to work. He found the problem quickly and, since he needed to replace the belt, decided to repair a cracked knob and broken hinge too. When he went to get the replacement parts, he told the assistant that he needed a belt, knob, hinge and a crescent-shaped wire he'd found inside the dryer. He didn't know where it belonged, but he confidently assured the assistant that he could figure it out once he got into the job.

"I have the other parts," the clerk said, "but for the wire you have to go to a lingerie shop. This is an underwire from your wife's bra."

BARBARA YEAGER

Our catering manager lacks certain social skills – like knowing when to keep her mouth shut. While discussing a christening party with a young couple, she told the mother, "You look as if you've lost most of your pregnancy weight."

"Thanks," came the clenched-teeth reply. "We adopted."

KIMBERLY MILO

I went to a vintage-car rally and noticed a name-the-car competition. I thought the vehicle looked cute so I guessed its name was **"Sarah"** and submitted my entry.

Later, the judge announced the answer over the loudspeaker. **"The car is not a Sarah, as one person thinks,"** he said, **"but is, of course, a Lotus Esprit."**

STEPHEN MITHAN

My mother had just finished taking a CPR class at a local college when she and I were in a shopping centre and saw a big crowd gathered around a still body. Suddenly my mother took off running at a speed I didn't know she could muster. "Everyone back," she yelled. "I know CPR!"

Just as she threw herself next to the body and was about to begin the procedure, a pair of strong hands pulled her to her feet.

"Madam," barked a policeman standing beside her, "we are trying to arrest this man."

TALEA TORRES

When I called my gas supplier concerning a minor problem with my grill, their automated telephone system put me on hold for more than 20 minutes.

As I waited, I was grateful my problem wasn't worse, especially when I heard a pre-recorded message advise, "If you smell gas, stay on the line."

H. GITLIN

My sisters and I stopped at a café for a late snack. Walking in, we smelt gas. When the waitress came to seat us, we urged her to tell someone there was a leak. She thanked us, saying she'd look into it straight away.

Then she asked in her most pleasant waitress voice, "Will that be smoking or non-smoking?"

SHARON SWEENE

Early in our romance, my fiancé and I were strolling on a beach. He stopped, drew a heart in the sand and inscribed our initials inside the heart. I was thoroughly charmed, and took a photo of his artwork. Later we used that same picture on our wedding invitations.

Seeing the photo, Emily, the pre-teen daughter of a friend, exclaimed, "Wow! How did you ever find one with your initials on it?"

C.G. SMITH

Dispatching her ten-year-old son to pick up a pizza, my sister handed him money and a two-pound coupon. Later he came home with the pizza, and the coupon.

When asked to explain, he replied, "Mum, I had enough money. I didn't need the coupon."

MARGARET MET

My cousin was on a plane that had just taken off when one of the flight attendants announced over the public-address system that the plane's lavatories were out of order.

She went on to apologise for any inconvenience, then finished cheerily with: "As compensation, free drinks will be served."

M. OAK

107

After an unusually heated argument with what he considered his overbearing parents, my brother announced that the minute he left school he intended to join the Navy. No more was said until a few days later, when he walked proudly into the house and declared that he was to report for duty the following morning.

"Why?" my mother asked tearfully.

"Because," he stormed, "I am sick and tired of taking orders!"

MRS. A.V. HEIGHES

Because our new refrigerator was taller than our old one, I told my wife I'd have to cut away part of an overhanging kitchen cabinet to make it fit. Not wanting to mess it up, I called a local radio DIY programme for advice. I was in the middle of getting the instructions when my wife burst into the room.

"You won't believe this," she said, "but there's a man from round here on the radio with exactly the same problem!"

GARY BRINGHURST

I sold an item through eBay, but it got lost in the post. So I popped in to my local post office and asked them to track it down.

"It's not that simple," the cashier scolded. "You have to fill in a mail-loss form before we can initiate a search."

"OK," I said. "I'll take one."

He rummaged under his counter and then went to some other cashiers, who did the same – only to return and inform me, "You'll have to come back later. We can't find the forms."

D. ROGERS

My husband, who is a car mechanic, received a repair order that read: "Check for clunking noise when going around corners." Taking the car out for a test drive, he made a right turn, and a moment later heard a clunk. He then made a

left turn and again heard a clunk. Back at the shop, he opened the boot and soon discovered the problem.

Promptly he returned the repair order to the service manager with this notation: "Remove bowling ball from boot."

K. TUTTLE

I spotted my neighbours on my way to the local shops. They excitedly told me that they had won a holiday and were rushing to buy a couple of last-minute items before jetting off.

"I hope you have a smashing time," I said. "By the way, where are you going?"

"We're off to the chemist!" they replied in unison.

RUTH SEGALL

Our house was for sale so when the doorbell rang one morning, we knew it would be someone to view the property. Because the place was in such a mess, my family panicked and we threw ourselves face down on the hall floor so that the viewers couldn't see us through the frosted-glass front door and would think we were out. Lying there on the carpet, we heard a key turning in the lock and the door opening. Our estate agents had given the viewers a key.

SARAH EMERY

Aging gracelessly

It happens to everyone eventually, but luckily growing older and growing up can be two very different things.

"That's strange. This suit wasn't a thong last year."

Our dear friend Trudy attended my husband's birthday party. Though she's been through a lot – including a double mastectomy and reconstructive surgery – Trudy was the life of the party as usual. Hugging her good-bye, I couldn't help noticing she had nothing on under her blouse.

"Trudy, you're not wearing a bra!" I whispered.

With a twinkle in her eye she replied, "I may be 70, honey, but they're only 15."

JUDITH KROL

The plane was only half-full. When an attractive young woman asked if the seat next to mine was free, my male ego soared. Soon we were chatting pleasantly, and she told me it was her first flight.

"Mum said to sit next to someone I thought I could trust," she confessed nervously, "and you look just like my dad."

ROY RAGSDALE

Rock concerts are a little different now than when I was younger. Recently, I went to a concert with some friends. As the band started to play a ballad, we instinctively raised our cigarette lighters, like all good rock fans I grew up with. But looking around me, I noticed that times had indeed changed.

The mostly under-25 crowd was swaying to the upraised glow of their mobile phones.

ANGELA STIMA

My brother and his wife started their family in their early 40s. One day my sister-in-law and I were commiserating about the effects of time marching on.

"I just got my first pair of glasses," she said, and paused as her two preschool boys thundered past her. "Now, if only my hearing would go."

IRENE PALM

After working for months to get in shape, my 42-year-old husband and I hiked to the bottom of the Grand Canyon. At the end of two gruelling days, we made it back to the canyon's rim. To celebrate, we each bought an "I hiked the canyon" T-shirt.

About a month later, while my husband was wearing his shirt, a young man approached him. "Did you really hike the Grand Canyon?" he asked.

My husband beamed with pride and answered, "Sure did!"

"No kidding!" the fellow said. "What year?"

CAROL LATKIEWICZ

I had arranged a reunion lunch with a friend I hadn't seen for many years, and arrived at the restaurant a little early. As she was not at the table I had reserved, I went to the ladies' cloackroom in an effort to disguise the effects of the intervening years. Busy with facial repairs, I glanced in the mirror to find myself face to face with my lunch date, who was also making hasy adjustments.

"Don't worry," she reassured me. "We'll pretend we haven't seen each other until we've finished."

N. SAMPSON

111

"Keep making that face and it's going to freeze that way," was what my mother used to say to us as kids.

I knew times had changed after she noticed my sister scowling recently and warned, **"Keep making that face and you're going to need Botox."**

MARY BOUCK

I was having trouble with the idea of turning thirty and was oversensitive to any signs of advancing age. When I found a prominent grey hair in my fringe, I pointed to my forehead.

"Have you seen this?" I indignantly asked my husband.

"What?" he asked. **"The wrinkles?"**

WENDY LILLIE

On my birthday I got a really funny card from a friend. It joked about how our bodies might be getting older, but our minds were still "tarp as shacks".

I wanted to thank the friend who sent the card, but I couldn't. She forgot to sign it.

MERIS MACK

The summer after university graduation, I was living at home, fishing in the daytime, spending nights with my friends – generally just hanging around. One afternoon my grandfather, who never went to university, stopped by.

Concerned with how I was spending my time, he asked about my future plans. I told him I was in no hurry to tie myself down to a career.

"Well," he replied, "you better start thinking about it. You'll be thirty before you know it."

"But I'm closer to twenty than to thirty," I protested. "I won't be thirty for eight more years."

"I see," he said, smiling. "And when will you be twenty again?"

MARSHALL ESSIG

My sister, Sharon, and I are close, and that allows us to be honest with each other. As I fidgeted in front of the mirror one evening before a date, I remarked, "I'm fat."

"No, you're not," she scolded.

"My hair is awful."

"It's lovely."

"I've never looked worse," I whined.

"Yes, you have," she replied.

PATRICIA SOUZA

When a woman I know turned 99 years old, I went to her birthday party and took some photos. A few days later, I brought the whole batch of prints to her so she could choose her favourite.

"Good Lord," she said as she was flipping through them, "I look like I'm a hundred."

HELEN MARROW

My 20 year school reunion was held at a hotel on the same night that another school's tenth-year reunion was taking place. While my friends and I were in the toilets talking, some unfamiliar women entered.

After their stares became uncomfortable, we turned toward them. One of the women said, "Don't mind us. We just wanted to see how we'd look in another ten years."

S. OLIVIERI

Out bicycling one day with my eight-year-old granddaughter, Carolyn, I suddenly became a little wistful. "In ten years," I said, "you'll want to be with your friends and you won't go walking, cycling and swimming with me like you do now."

Carolyn shrugged. "In ten years you'll be too old to do all those things anyway."

JAMES AHEARN

My fortieth birthday had arrived, so to make myself feel better about my aging appearance, I booked a cut and set at the hairdresser's.

All was fine and I was enjoying being pampered, until the salon assistant put me under the stand-up hairdryer.

"Would you like a magazine to read?" she asked gently. "Or would you prefer to have a little sleep?"

E. CORBY

I had been thinking about colouring my hair. One day while going through a magazine, I came across an ad for a hair-colouring product featuring a beautiful young model with hair a shade that I liked. Wanting a second opinion, I asked my husband, "How do you think this colour would look on a face with a few wrinkles?"

"I do stay in shape. This is the shape I stay in."

He looked at the picture, crumpled it up, straightened it out and studied it again. "Just great, my darling."

JOAN KEYSER

As my 40th birthday approached, my husband, who is a year younger, was doing his best to rub it in. Trying to figure out what all the teasing was about, our young daughter asked me, "How old is Daddy?"

"Thirty-nine," I told her. "And how old will you be?"

"Forty," I said sadly.

"But Mummy," she exclaimed, "you're winning!"

K. MARTINEZ

Both my fiancé and I are in our 40s. I thought it was both amusing and touching when he assumed the classic position to propose to me – down on one bended knee.

"Are you serious?" I asked, laughing.

"Of course I'm serious," he said. "I'm on my bad knee."

DEBORAH MASSEY

My friend and I were celebrating our 40th birthday the same year. As a gag gift, I gave her a CD by the band UB40.

For my birthday, she retaliated with a CD as well. The group? U2.

MONA TURRELL

113

I'm always relieved when someone delivers a eulogy and I realize I'm listening to it.

GEORGE CARLIN

I'm at the age where my back goes out more than I do.

PHYLLIS DILLER

Hair is the first thing. And teeth the second. A man's got those two things, he's got it all.

JAMES BROWN

Age is nothing at all ... unless you are a cheese.

BILLIE BURKE

The old believe everything: the middle-aged suspect everything: the young know everything.

OSCAR WILDE

I wear glasses, so I can look for things I keep losing.

BILL COSBY,
Time Files (Bantam Books)

It's not that I'm afraid to die: I just don't want to be there when it happens.

WOODY ALLEN

It's all right letting yourself go, as long as you can let yourself back.

MICK JAGGER

My mother always used to say, "The older you get, the better you get. Unless you're a banana."

LIZZY PHAN, as Betty White in "The Golden Girls"

114

For over 40 years my grandfather put in long hours at his job, so I was more than a little curious about the way he filled his days since his retirement.

"How has life changed?" I asked.

A man of few words, he replied, "Well I get up in the morning with nothing to do, and I go to bed at night with it half-done."

DENNIS LUNDBERG

My husband was bending over to tie my three-year-old's shoes.

That's when I noticed my son, Ben, staring at my husband's head. He gently touched the slightly thinning spot of hair and said in a concerned voice,

"Daddy, you have a hole in your head. Does it hurt?"

After a pause, I heard my husband's murmured reply: **"Not physically."**

L. GERHARDSTEIN

I was having some chest pains, but my doctor assured me nothing was wrong. Then I told him I was planning to go on a cruise and asked how I could avoid any discomfort.

"Have fun," he said with a straight face, "but don't go overboard."

LES WANDEL

When I was a 20-something university student, I became quite friendly with my study partner, a 64-year-old man, who had returned to finish his degree. He confessed he had once thought more than friendship might be a possibility.

"So what changed your mind?" I asked him.

"I went to my doctor and asked if he thought a 40-year age difference between a man and woman was insurmountable. He looked at my chart and said, 'You're interested in someone who's 104?'"

KELLY MOORE

My daughter and I were sitting in an almost-empty cinema, watching a very sexually explicit film with a title that did not warn us of its content.

Two elderly ladies were settled three rows behind us. After a while, one turned to the other and said very clearly, "Would you have come if you had known it was going to be about this sort of thing?"

There was a brief silence, then the other replied, "Oh, yes, definitely."

CHRISTABEL MILNER

My grandfather has a knack for looking on the bright side of life. Even after receiving the terrible diagnosis that he had Alzheimer's, he was philosophical.

"There's one good thing that'll come from this," he told my father.

"What's that?" asked Dad.

"Now I can hide my own Easter eggs."

CHRIS KERN

115

Mary Lou BEAUTICIAN

Patricia

"I wouldn't raise my hopes too high if I were you."

Just as she was celebrating her 80th birthday, our friend received a jury-duty notice. She called to remind the people at the court that she was exempt because of her age.

"You need to come in and fill out the exemption forms," they said. "I've already done that," replied my friend. "I did it last year."

"You have to do it every year," she was told.

"Why?" came the response. "Do you think I'm going to get younger?"

J. SIVLEY

As a carer for the elderly, I regularly visited a deaf old lady who did nothing but moan about family members who never came to visit.

One day, as she complained on in her chair, between bites of crab sticks, I asked her if her family didn't visit because they were selfish.

"What?" she replied.

"Are they selfish?" I repeated.

"EH?" she shouted.

"ARE THEY SELFISH?"

"NO, NO," she bellowed crossly. "THEY'RE CRAB STICKS."

ABIGAIL MARTIN

I sat there waiting for my new doctor to make his way through the file that contained my very extensive medical history.

After he finished all 17 pages, he looked up at me. "You look better in person than you do on paper."

CAROLYN BLANKENSHIP

"You mean the older I get, the older you get?"

Having just started using some cream that promised younger-looking skin, my sister was amazed at the result.

"Well, it worked," she told me over the phone. "I've now developed big, ugly spots, just like when I was a teenager."

BARBARA ROSE

As my father placed his purchases on the supermarket counter, the cashier smiled and asked, "A little late, aren't you?"

He didn't get what she was talking about at first – then he looked at the items he was buying: an inexpensive pair of reading glasses and a big bag of carrots.

NATALIE MILLER

Someone recommended a new dentist to me. On my second visit the dentist finished cleaning my teeth, and as I prepared to leave, I asked brightly, "And what is your name?"

"Patricia," she answered.

"I can remember that," I commented. "It's my sister's name."

Her reply: "That's what you said last time."

IRIS CRADDOCK

TIMELESS HUMOUR

70s One customer near me in the shoe shop was a steely haired, conservatively dressed grandmother. On impulse, she had tried on a pair of platform shoes in the wildest imaginable turquoise. The salesgirl and I were telling her how they suited her when her granddaughter came into the shop.

She groaned, "Oh no, Gran! You're not getting those!"

"I am," said Gran bravely.

The teenager tried to reason with her "Come on, Gran. What would you wear them with?"

"Defiance!" Gran replied.

BEE HARGROVE

At the checkout at the supermarket, I noticed the teenager helping to pack up the shopping eyeing my two adopted children. They often draw scrutiny, since my son's a blonde Russian, while my daughter has shiny black Haitian skin. The boy continued staring as I paid. Finally he asked, "Those your kids?"

"They sure are," I said with pride.

"They adopted?" "Yes," I replied.

"I thought so," he concluded. "I guessed you're too old to have kids that small."

CYNTHIA MEYER

Leading activities for the residents of an old people's home, I asked my group to complete well-known phrases. For example, I'd prompt them with, "Better safe ... " to which they would respond, "than sorry".

The game went as expected until I got to the phrase "Make love, not war". I had barely got out the first two words when a 90-year-old woman shouted from the back, "While you can!"

JANE KIEHL

I was middle-aged when I went back to university, which meant some of my classmates were 20 years younger. Still, many became my friends.

I ran into one of them recently in a restaurant he manages, and he, my husband and I all had a pleasant chat at the cashier's counter. As we said good-bye, my young friend explained to the couple behind us, "She and I were at university together." I noticed the confused look on their faces.

Later, I asked my husband, "What do you suppose they were thinking?"

"Either that he's had a very easy life," he replied, "or you've had a very hard one."

BARBARA LEE

One of the salespeople at a local stationery shop had to be a good sport to survive her 40th birthday. Not only did she have to put up with two large banners that announced: "Cathy is 40 today!" but she also had to spend the day with other saleswomen who wore tags saying: "I'm not Cathy."

HELEN BECOUVARAKIS

117

"Higher."

Easy does it

In a boat, I have always noticed that it is the fixed idea of each member of the crew that he is doing everything. Harris's notion was that it was he alone who had been working, and that both George and I had been imposing upon him. George, on the other hand, ridiculed the idea of Harris's having done anything more than eat and sleep, and had a cast-iron opinion that it was he – George himself – who had done all the labour worth speaking of.

He said he had never been out with such a couple of lazy skulks as Harris and I.

That amused Harris.

"Fancy old George talking about work!" he laughed; "why, about half an hour of it would kill him. Have you ever seen George work?" he added, turning to me.

I agreed with Harris that I never had – most certainly not since we had started on this trip.

"Well, I don't see how *you* can know much about it, one way or the other," George retorted to Harris;

"for I'm blest if you haven't been asleep half the time. Have you ever seen Harris fully awake, except at meal-times?" asked George addressing me.

Truth compelled me to support George. Harris had been very little good in the boat, so far as helping was concerned, from the beginning.

"Well, hang it all, I've done more than old J., anyhow," rejoined Harris.

"Well, you couldn't very well have done less," added George.

"I suppose J. thinks he is the passenger," continued Harris.

And that was their gratitude to me for having brought them and their wretched old boat all the way up from Kingston, and for having

Jerome K Jerome, *Three Men in a Boat*

superintended and managed everything for them, and taken care of them, and slaved for them. It is the way of the world.

We settled the present difficulty by arranging that Harris and George should scull up past Reading, and that I should tow the boat on from there. Pulling a heavy boat against a strong stream has few attractions for me now. There was a time, long ago, when I used to clamour for the hard work: now I like to give the youngsters a chance.

I notice that most of the old river hands are similarly retiring, whenever there is any stiff pulling to be done. You can always tell the old river hand by the way in which he stretches himself out upon the cushions at the bottom of the boat, and encourages the rowers by telling them anecdotes about the marvelous feats he performed last season.

"Call what you're doing hard work?" he drawls, between his contented whiffs, addressing the two perspiring novices, who have been grinding away steadily up-stream for the last hour and a half;

"why, Jim Biffles and Jack and I, last season, pulled up from Marlow to Goring in one afternoon – never stopped once. Do you remember that, Jack?"

Jack, who has made himself a bed, in the prow, of all the rugs and coats he can collect, and who has been lying there asleep for the last two hours, partially wakes up on being thus appealed to, and recollects all about the matter, and also remembers that there was an unusually strong stream against them all the way – likewise a stiff wind.

"About thirty-four miles, I suppose, it must have been," adds the first speaker, reaching down another cushion to put under his head.

"No – no; don't exaggerate, Tom," murmurs Jack, reprovingly; "thirty-three at the outside."

And Jack and Tom, quite exhausted by this conversational effort, drop off to sleep once more. And the two simple-minded youngsters at the sculls feel quite proud of being allowed to row such wonderful oarsmen as Jack and Tom, and strain away harder than ever.

When I was a young man, I used to listen to these tales from my elders, and take them in, and swallow them, and digest every word of them, and then come up for more; but the new generation do not seem to have the simple faith of the old times. We – George, Harris, and myself – took a "raw 'un" up with us last season, and we plied him with the customary stretchers about the wonderful things we had done all the way up.

We gave him all the regular ones – the time-honoured lies that have done duty up the river with every boating man for years past – and added seven entirely original ones that we had invented for ourselves, including a really quite likely story, founded, to a certain extent, on an all but true episode, which had actually happened in a modified degree some years ago to friends of ours – a story that a mere child could have believed without injuring itself much.

And that young man mocked at them all, and wanted us to repeat the feats then and there, and to bet us ten to one that we didn't.

119

When I was a university professor, I taught during the day and did research at night. I would usually take a break around nine, calling up the strategy game Warcraft on the Internet and playing with an online team.

One night I was paired with a veteran of the game who was a master strategist. With him at the helm, our troops crushed opponent after opponent, and after six games we were undefeated. Suddenly, my fearless leader informed me his mum wanted him to go to bed.

"How old are you?" I typed.

"Twelve," he replied. "How old are you?"

Feeling my face redden, I answered, "Eight."

T. S.

My hearing had become worse, and ultimately I was faced with a decision: buy a boat, which I could enjoy all summer, or get a hearing aid. The choice was obvious – to me at least. However, my sisters did not approve of the boat.

One day during lunch with them, I was having trouble following the conversation. Finally I leaned over to one of my sisters and asked what had just been said.

"You should have brought along your boat," she replied.

B. HENDRICK

"Empty-nesters. They're hoping to sell before the flock tries to move back in?"

My wife and I stopped for a drink at a country pub which was empty except for three old men in a corner contemplating their pints. The silence was broken by a group of young people who burst in laughing and then continued to talk loudly, generally destroying the ambience. Finally, one of the old men rose from his seat, ambled across to the group and tapped a newcomer on the shoulder. "You're wanted outside," he said quietly.

"Oh, by whom?" came the reply.

"Everybody in here," answered the old man, already half-way back to his seat.

COLIN BLOMELEY

We had our ten-year-old daughter late in life, long after our two boys were born. My husband is self-conscious about being an older father and jokingly tells people that by the time she graduates, he'll be in a nursing home.

One day she asked, "Mum, you know how Dad always says he'll be in a home when I graduate?" I nodded, expecting some sad question about mortality.

"Can I have the car then?"

T. GRAY

Residents of a local nursing home loved our karate school's demonstration. We could tell because they gave us a big hand at the end. After the applause died down, everyone stayed seated, so we showed off a few more moves. When our encore ended and again no one budged, we launched into our second encore.

"I didn't expect karate to be so popular here," I said to one resident.

"It's not," she said with a kindly smile. "We're waiting for you to leave so we can get on with the bingo."

D. MERCADO

Korey, my granddaughter, came to spend a few weeks with me, and I decided to teach her how to sew.

After I had gone through a lengthy demonstration of how to thread the machine, Korey stepped back and put her hands on her hips. **"You mean you can do all that,"** she said in disbelief, **"but you can't operate my Game Boy?"**

NELL BARON

I've been considering a face-lift, but it's very expensive, so I've seesawed back and forth. One day my husband and I discussed it yet again when I asked, "What if I drop dead three months later? Then what would you do?"

After a moment of reflection he offered, "I guess we'd have an open casket."

CAROL FUGERE

During a visit with a friend at an old people's home, I was invited to stay for lunch. As we entered the cafeteria, she leaned towards me and whispered, "They have two queues here. We call them cane and able."

MARTHA LEONARD

At his 103rd birthday party, my grandfather was asked if he thought that he'd be around for his 104th.

"I certainly do," he replied. "Statistics show that very few people die between the ages of 103 and 104."

HARRY COLEMAN

My wife and I stood watching a bird across the mudflats for a long time, but our aging eyes couldn't agree whether it was a heron or an ibis.

Finally, we plucked up the courage to ask a bystander with binoculars. "Oh, that's a polythene bag," he answered.

G. MCINTOSH

While my friend Emily was visiting her mother, they went for a walk and bumped into an old family acquaintance. "Is this your daughter?" the woman asked. "Oh, I remember her when she was this high. How old is she now?"

Without pausing, Emily's mother said, "Twenty-four." Emily, 35, nearly fainted on the spot.

After everyone had said their good-byes, Emily asked her mother why she'd told such a whopper.

"Well," she replied, "I've been lying about my age for so long, it suddenly dawned on me that I'd have to start lying about yours too."

ROBERT WHITMIRE

"Not those! At our age, we need all the preservatives we can get."

121

After a shopping expedition, my friend Gina and I stopped in a local bar for a drink. We hadn't been seated long when she leaned over and said that four young men at the next table were watching us. Since we're both thirty-something, married with children, we found the situation flattering. We sat a little straighter and tried to look slimmer and younger.

In a few minutes, one of the men got up and came toward our table. "Excuse me," he said. Then he reached over our heads to turn up the volume on the televised football game.

SANDRA LYONS

On a recent visit to see my parents, I discovered that my father, who is 98 and has been clean-shaven all his life, was sporting a white beard.

My mother took me to one side and implored me to have a word with him. "Will you please convince your father to shave off that blasted beard?" she asked. "It makes him look old."

JIM HOUSTON

While having a drink in the pub, I heard three mature ladies discussing the effects of aging.

"I have to say, I've still got the figure I had at 20," said one. Then, after a moment's reflection, she continued. "Trouble is, everything's four inches lower."

WILLIAM BOND

I was feeling old and out of shape, so I joined an aerobics class for the over-50s. I bent, twisted, gyrated, jumped up and down and perspired for an hour. But by the time I got my leotard on, the class was over.

REGINA LALLY

As I cleaned his carpet, a client began to tell me what a wonderful woman his recently deceased wife was. "Bless her soul,

"Dad?!"

we had 35 happy years together," he said, pausing to reminisce.

Looking up, he added, "That isn't too bad out of 50."

STEPHEN PRYJDA

My husband is perfectly fit but worries about his heart. After strenuously digging the garden one day his hands took on a bluish tinge. Fearing that his efforts had brought on a circulation disorder, we telephoned the doctor who said he'd better go to the surgery right away. Now really worried, my husband visited the bathroom before setting off and, on washing his hands, rinsed away the blue dye from his gardening gloves.

CATHERINE YORKE

While on maternity leave, a woman from our office brought in her new bundle of joy. She also had her seven-year-old son with her. Everyone gathered around the baby, and the little boy asked, "Mummy, can I have some money to buy a drink?"

"What do you say?" she said.

Respectfully, the boy replied, "You're thin and beautiful."

The woman reached in her purse and gave her son the money.

M. NICKSE

Leisure pursuits

Getting in tune

I am having my cello lesson. Bliss. One hour's escape from the daily drear. I rush upstairs for some money to pay Teacher, but what is wrong with my mother? She has her hands clapped over her ears, is wailing loudly and wearing a look of pain.

"You're not to pay her!" she roars, incensed that Teacher is to be rewarded for her part in the ghastly cello playing. But Teacher and I ignore this critique. We know that I will never be Jacquline du Pré. My practice is minimal, the tone often grating and growling, the tuning wambly, but sometimes, just sometimes, I manage a few pleasant bars, which makes my years of struggle worth it.

If only I had learnt this divine instrument decades ago, instead of now, with the elderly stick fingers, failing eyesight and the brain stymied by the tenor clef. But my dream is to play, before I peg out, in a small orchestra. And another dream – to play Fats Domino-style piano, accompanied by anyone else who cares to join in. Quick, before we all get arthritis.

This is the big cloud hanging over my plan. Decreptitude and incapacity may catch up with me before I make it. How many baroque gems will I never have time to play or even hear? How fluent will my sight-reading never be, now that the Last Big Deadline is looming. So I must practise like billy-o, despite fierce opposition.

Last week in the broiling heat, I practised the cello with the French windows open. Daughter, sunbathing in the garden with chums, begged me to shut the door, or practise the piano instead. So I did. More wailing from my mother upstairs.

But their suffering and my efforts are paying off. Last week I played in a small orchestra, easy bits only, but what a divine interlude. Join an orchestra, forget the world.

How sensible of me to have forced Daughter to learn the violin as a child. She can now play it. We try some simple duets. Soon we hear the dreaded rumbling of my mother's stairlift. She descends, she glares, and then – surprise of the century – she applauds! "First time I've heard you sound nice," says she. But I mustn't be bitter. She is *being positive* – a new skill! We can all have one, even at ninety-seven. Next week – "Blueberry Hill".

Hide and seek

The other day someone asked Olivia what she did. "I look for things," she said, because that's what she spends most of her life doing. Olivia spent the whole of Saturday looking for £60, which she had stuck down the side of her shoe, which she thought would be more sensible than putting it down somewhere, forgetting where she'd put it, and then having to look for it.

Michele Hanson, *Living with Mother*

She couldn't put it in her purse because she didn't know where her purse was, and didn't have time to find it.

Anyway, the £60 disappeared. It must have fallen out of her shoe. Olivia searched everywhere she thought she'd been with the shoe on and, as she had tidied the front garden, she had to look indoors, outdoors and through all the garden rubbish, but she never found it.

I suspect Olivia has too much on her plate: gruelling job, new grandchild, the house being decorated, the extra shopping in fifty-acre furniture warehouses. When one is exhausted, in demand, overworked and over fifty, things tend to get lost, then we have to look for them in this room, that room, upstairs, downstairs and under all the piles of crapola that have mushroomed, because there isn't the time to tidy them, because we are spending the bulk of our lives looking for things.

Poor Fielding once spent thirty-six hours looking for a Van Morrison ticket, which he had placed in a book for safe-keeping. He searched every page of every book he owned, hurled his books about, wrecked his house, found long-lost bills, O-level and birth certificates, but no ticket. Three months too late he found it in a Martin Amis.

Last night I lost a letter, my mother's TV guide, the cello rosin, my reading glasses and my mind, because there is only so much searching, grovelling and screaming one can do before one is hot and faint with fatigue and rage and ready to crack up.

"This is why retired people live in bungalows," says Rosemary. But even in her flat she is still forever losing her purse, keys and phone numbers on bits of paper. This week, *chez nous*, we lost the peeler, strainer, bottle opener, Daughter's glasses, keys, cash card and passport. But at least I found last night's letter. It was stuck under the dinner tray, hiding. With what remained of my mind.

125

Shortly after my father's death, my 90-year-old grandmother insisted that my mother have a complete physical. After some debate, my mother reluctantly made an appointment. The doctor not only gave her a clean bill of health, but remarked that she'd probably live to be 110.

To our surprise, my grandmother did not seem entirely pleased by the good report. She sat quietly for a few minutes, then said with a sigh, "And just what am I going to do with a 110-year-old daughter?"

B.L.M.

When my husband worked at a prison, we only had one car, so I used to roll out of bed at 5am, drive him to work, then come home and go back to sleep. One day while talking to some colleagues, my husband took out his wallet and showed them pictures of me and my daughter. One of the photos of me was a "glamour shot" that I had posed for at a shopping centre.

"Wow," a colleague remarked. "Who's that?"

"My wife," my husband proudly replied.

"Oh," his friend responded, looking puzzled. "Then who's that woman who drops you off in the mornings?"

LISA PROCTOR

A friend spent more than two hours in the hairdressers getting her hair coloured, cut and blow-dried. After all that, was it too much to ask to be treated like Cinderella?

Yet when she went to the desk to pay, the receptionist said to her, "Hello, who is your appointment with today?"

PETER CROMPTON

Heading off to university at the age of 40, I was a bit self-conscious about my advancing years. One morning I complained to my husband that I was the oldest student in my class.

"Even the teacher is younger than I am," I said.

"Yeah, but look at it from my point of view," he said smiling. "I thought my days of going out with college girls were over."

BRENDA MCMILLEN

My grandfather's aunt passed away, and he went to pay his respects. At the funeral home, he overheard two women as they peered into the open casket.

"She looks wonderful," said one. "I've never seen her look so good. Why, she looks better than I do!"

"You're right," the other replied. "But remember, you have the flu."

SARAH SHORT

I was hospitalized with an awful sinus infection that caused the entire left side of my face to swell. On the third day, the nurse led me to believe that I was finally recovering when she announced excitedly, "Look, your wrinkles are coming back!"

FRANCES KRUEGER

"It's definitely hereditary. It's called aging."

few years ago, I opened the invitation to my cousin's 100th birthday party. On the front – in bold letters – it screamed, "If he's heard it once, he's heard it a hundred times. Happy Birthday, Sam!"

LOUIS GLICKMAN

My four-year-old nephew had drawn a picture for his grandmother, and was anxious to show it to her. Finding the door to her bathroom unlocked, he burst inside just as she was stepping out of the shower, soaking wet and without a towel.

He looked her up and down for a moment, then stated quite matter-of-factly, "Grandma, you look better with your glasses on."

Turning 50 two years ago, I took a lot of good-natured ribbing from family and friends. So as my wife's 50th birthday approached, I decided to get in some needling of my own. I sat her down, looked deep into her eyes, then said I had never made love to anyone who was over 50 years old.

"Oh, well, I have," she deadpanned. "It's not that great."

BOB MORELAND

I had laryngitis and finally decided to go to the doctor.

After the nurse called for me, she asked my age. **"Forty-nine,"** I whispered.

"Don't worry," she whispered back. "I won't tell anyone."

L. BELL

A student in my maths course I taught at university, developed a severe case of tendinitis. Since she couldn't write, she brought a video camera to tape my lectures. After three or four classes, I asked her if she found the method satisfactory. She said it was working quite well, even better than note-taking.

"Actually," she confessed, "I have another reason for doing this. When I told my mother you were a widower, she wanted to see what you look like."

G. WHEELER

Approaching 40, my frugal husband yearned for a boat. Frugality won out until the day he came across the obituary of an old school mate, Ted. Certain this was a sign that life was too short, my husband purchased a boat that weekend.

Days later, a former classmate called. "Sure was a sad thing, wasn't it?" he said. "You know, Ted's boating accident and all."

CHRISTINE CRAIG

I was having lunch with several thirty-something friends when talk turned to the dismal prospect of our growing older.

"Well, judging by my mother," I said, "at least my hearing will improve. My mother can hear my biological clock ticking from 200 miles away."

SHERRY YATES

127

Since they hadn't reserved a table at a busy restaurant, my elderly neighbour and his wife were told that there would be a 45-minute wait before they could be seated.

"Young man," the husband told the waiter. "We're both 90 years old. We may not have 45 minutes."

They were seated immediately.

R. KALISH

The 3 stages of man.

Paul was in his mid-60s and had just retired. He was planning to landscape his yard and was trying to find some small shrubs or trees. Burleigh, a 90-year-old from across the road, offered Paul some white-ash saplings that were about two feet tall.

Paul asked, "How long will it take them to be full grown?"

"Twenty years or so," replied Burleigh.

"No good for me, then," said Paul. "I won't be around that long."

The 90-year-old shook his head and replied, "We'll miss you!"

CLYDENE SAVAGE

Listening to the radio, I heard the disc jockey announce, "This next record is for Pete Malloy, who is 111 years old." There was a pause, and then, "My goodness, that is old, isn't it!"

Another pause. "Oh, I'm sorry. I got that wrong. This next record is for Pete Malloy, who is ill."

VALERIE BALL

My friend Brad, whose youthful looks belied his actual age and experience, flew charter flights in Florida. One day he was assigned to take an elderly woman across the Everglades. She studied him carefully as he helped her with her seat belt.

Once airborne, with nothing but water and swamp below, she cleared her throat and said apprehensively, "You seem awfully young. How long have you been flying?"

Brad flashed his most charming grin. "You mean counting today?" he answered.

BOB WHITE

Having fought the battle of the bulge most of my life, I found the battle getting even harder as I approached middle age.

One evening, after trying on trousers that were too tight, I said to my husband, "I'll be so glad when we become grandparents. After all, who cares if grandmothers are fat?"

His prompt reply: "Grandfathers."

IRIS CAVIN

My energetic 78-year-old mother hurt her shoulder at keep-fit, so I advised her to make some allowances for her age. "All right'" she said after a pause for thought, "I'll start using that shampoo for women over 40."

B. ROBERTS

I recently ran into the woman who used to clean our house and was surprised to hear that she was still at it, despite her advanced age.

"How do you manage it?" I asked.

She explained her secret: "I just keep clients who can't see the dirt any better than I can."

MALCOLM CAMPELL

129

One of the English classes I taught at school consisted of a particularly well-motivated group of pupils, who felt free to ask questions on any subject that concerned them.

One afternoon a girl raised her hand and asked me to explain all the talk about a woman's "biological clock". After I'd finished, there was a moment of silence, and then another hand shot up.

"Mrs. Woodard," a student asked, "is your clock still ticking, or has the alarm gone off?"

LINDA WOODARD

My father, at age 93, had only the most basic needs and very few wants. Last autumn, my sister-in-law, hoping to get a little help in choosing a suitable birthday gift for him, asked, "Dad, what would you like for your birthday this year?"

"Nothing," he replied.

"But, Dad," she kidded, "that's what we gave you last year."

"Well," he answered, "I'm still using it."

L. COUILLARD

Widowed for the second time, my grandmother told me she would probably not remarry.

"You're still young," I said. "Why not?"

"When I married your dad's father, I became a Smith," she replied. "Then I married your Grandpa Ernie and became Schmidt. I'm afraid of what'll happen next."

SARA SMITH

To celebrate his 40th birthday, my boss, who is battling middle-age spread, bought a new convertible sports car. As a finishing touch, he put on a vanity plate with the inscription "18 Again". The wind was let out of his sails, however, when a salesman entered our office the following week.

"Hey," he called out, "who owns the car with the plate 'I ate again'?"

CINDY GILLIS

Venus and Mars

Despite thousands of years of practice, men and women still don't always see eye to eye. But it's fun to watch them try!

"My son's into extreme sports, my daughter's into extreme makeover, and my husband's into extreme denial."

The escalator was broken and the only way out of the airport was up a flight of stairs. I had a big suitcase and a sore knee.

I began dragging my bag and was making a loud thud on every step when a man behind me grabbed the suitcase and carried it to the top.

"That was so chivalrous," I gushed.

"Chivalry had nothing to do with it," he said. "I've got a splitting headache."

MEGAN SICLARI

Before going out for the evening with my husband, I had my hair cut and restyled. As we were leaving, we met in the hall and he said nothing. I complained that he had not even noticed my hair. "You used to pay attention to every little thing and now you take me for granted!"

My partner stood there rubbing his face as he let me rant and rave. Then it hit me: he'd shaved off his six-month-old beard.

M. ANDERSON

While I was having a meal at a restaurant with my wife, we heard the couple sitting at the next table furiously rowing. "You are a disgusting pig," said the wife. "A miserable excuse for a man!"

"Quite right, darling," said the husband, realizing the whole restaurant was listening. "And what else did you tell him?"

RON BIRD

Out shopping, I narrowly avoided bumping into a pedestrian. As he stepped to his right, I stepped to my left. As I moved to my right, he moved to his left. He stood still, put his hands out and said, "I'll only do this once more then I have to go."

IRENE ABBOTT

As part of our regular service, members of the congregation are allowed to make announcements or requests for prayers. One man, Bob, mentioned his forthcoming 37th wedding anniversary. At the obvious nudging of his wife, he quickly corrected that to 38.

As the chuckling died down, heard from the back of the church was, "I'd like to offer a prayer for Bob."

JUDITH LENSINK

Standing in line waiting to pay, I watched as the woman ahead of me handed over her credit card. The customer waited for a long time while the saleswoman went to verify the account. When she finally returned, the assistant said, "I'm sorry, but this card is in your husband's name, and we can't accept it because the records show he is deceased."

With that, the woman turned to her spouse and asked, "Does this mean I don't have to make lunch for you today?"

MARILYN ARNOPOL

For my fourth Caesarian section I opted for a bikini incision, which, along with the previous scars, would form an arrow on my tummy. "Honey," my husband joked when I told him, "after 13 years and 4 kids, I hardly need directions."

P. CECIL

133

TIMELESS HUMOUR

50s A husband-and-wife photography team we know shoot their pictures together, do their developing and printing together – in fact, they're together 24 hours of the day. We wondered how they managed to keep up such good working relations.

"Well, frankly," the wife said, "it wouldn't work out if one of us didn't have a good disposition."

"Which one?" we asked.

"Oh," she laughed, "we take turns."

ELIZABETH JETER

My daughter had absent-mindedly left her trainers on our kitchen table. "That's disgusting," my husband grumbled. "Doesn't she realise we eat off that table?" Then he went outside to work on the car.

I cleaned the table and left to do my grocery shopping. When I came home I couldn't set my bags down anywhere. Sitting in the middle of the kitchen table was a car silencer.

KATHERINE HORGAN

After the birth of my son, a woman from the records department visited my hospital room to get information for his birth certificate. "Father's date of birth?" she asked. When I told her, she said, "Do you realise that his birthday is exactly nine months before your son's birth?"

"No, I hadn't thought about it," I responded, "but now that you mention it, I have a daughter who turned two a couple days before the same date."

After she finished taking down all the data, she patted my hand and said, "Maybe you should start buying your husband a tie for his birthday."

M. PIGOTT

"Romance has nothing to do with it. Dan and I are renewing our marriage vows because he has forgotten them."

When my parents run the dishwasher, they let each other know the dishes are clean by placing the box of detergent on the counter. When Mum got home from work one day, she was surprised to find the box on the worktop because she had emptied the dishwasher the night before. She couldn't understand why my dad had used the dishwasher again – until she opened it and found the top tray full of golf balls.

MICHELE FERGUSON

Surfing the internet, I came across a film poster of a man and woman kissing passionately in the pouring rain. I called my husband over. "How come you never kiss me like that?"

He studied the sodden couple. "We haven't had that much rain."

SERENA S.

After a massive row, my husband and I ended up not talking to each other for ages. Finally, on the third day, he asked me where a shirt of his was.

"I see," I said, "now you're speaking to me." He looked really confused. "What do you mean?"

I asked if he'd noticed I hadn't spoken to him for three days.

"Oh," he replied. "I just thought we were getting along."

BETH DORIA

TIMELESS HUMOUR

60s On the day of my uncle's retirement my aunt received a sympathy card from a group of friends. She was puzzled until she noted that every signatory was the wife of a man who had already retired.

MRS. M. ALBRIGHT

Curious when I found two black-and-white negatives in a drawer, I had them made into prints. I was pleasantly surprised to see they were of a younger, slimmer me taken on one of my first dates with my husband.

When I showed him the photographs, his face lit up. "Wow! It's my old Plymouth."

DONNA MARTIN

It seemed that all our appliances had broken in the same week, and repairs were straining our budget. So when I picked up the kids from school and our Jeep started making rattling sounds, I decided that rather than burden my husband, I'd deal with it. I hadn't reckoned on my little tell-tales, however. They rushed into the house with the news: "Daddy, the Jeep was breaking down, but Mummy made the noise stop!"

Impressed, my husband asked, "How did you fix it?"

"I turned up the volume on the radio," I confessed.

RUTH TEN VEEN

One morning a customer entered my flower shop and ordered a bouquet for his wife. "No card is necessary," he instructed us. "She'll know who sent them."

The delivery van hadn't even returned to the shop when the phone rang. It was the customer's wife. "Who sent the flowers?" she asked.

After explaining that the customer had requested that no card be included, I considered the matter closed – but not so. A bit later, she came rushing in.

"You've got to tell me who sent the flowers," she demanded, "before my husband gets home."

LINDA COUCH

135

At my brother's wedding, my mother managed not to cry – until she glanced at my grandparents. My grandmother had reached over to my grandfather's wheelchair and gently touched his hand. That was all it took to start my mother's tears.

After the wedding, Mum went over to my grandmother and told her how that tender gesture had triggered her outburst. "Well, I'm sorry to ruin your moment, dear," Grandmother replied. "But I was just checking to see if he was still awake."

MARK SAMPLE

"You realise, of course, there's a five-day cooling-off period on sports car loans."

After his marriage broke up, my manager became very philosophical. "I guess it was in our stars," he sighed.

"What do you mean?" I asked.

"Her astrological sign is the one for earth. Mine is the one for water. Together we made mud."

L. PHILLIPS

The first time I met my wife, she was an intense aerobics instructor at my health club and I was an out-of-shape new member. After one gruelling workout, I gasped, "This is really helping me get toned."

She looked me up and down. Feeling self-conscious, I added, "Big men run in my family."

She raised an eyebrow. "Apparently not enough."

JOHN PARKER

y mum had always wanted to learn to play the piano, so Dad bought her one for her birthday. A few weeks later, I called and asked how she was doing. "We returned the piano," said Dad. "I persuaded her to switch to a clarinet."

"Why?" I asked.

"Because," he explained, "with a clarinet, she can't sing along."

DON FOSTER

When my friend got a job, her husband agreed to share the housework. He was stunned by the amount of effort involved in keeping a house clean with small boys to pick up after, and insisted that he and his wife shop for a new vacuum cleaner.

The salesman gave them a demonstration of the latest model. "It comes equipped with all the newest features," he assured them.

The husband was not convinced. "Don't you have a ride-on one?" he asked.

PAT MONTGOMERY

His aching back made it difficult for my friend's husband to get a decent night's sleep on their lumpy mattress. "Until I feel better, I'm going to sleep on the sofa," he announced.

Ordinarily a spouse moving out of the bedroom isn't a good sign for the marriage, so his wife couldn't resist: "Okay, but as soon as we have an argument you're back in our bed."

ANNA GUTHRIE

Going into a stationery shop, I bought a sign that read "I'm the Boss", and stuck it on my office door. When I returned from lunch, there was a yellow Post-it note beneath the notice. "Your wife called," it said. "She wants her sign back."

KARL ZOLLINGER

"God may have forgiven you, George, but I haven't."

QUOTABLE QUOTES

Mobile phones are the only subject on which men boast about who's got the smallest.

NEIL KINNOCK

No matter what kind of backgrounds two men are from, if you go, "Hey, man, women are crazy," you've got a friend.

CHRIS ROCK

Love is the answer, but while you're waiting for the answer, sex raises some pretty good questions.

WOODY ALLEN

Instead of getting married again, I'm going to find a woman I don't like and just give her a house.

ROD STEWART

Men want the same thing from their underwear that they want from women: a little bit of support, and a little bit of freedom.

JERRY SEINFELD

Behind every great man is a woman rolling her eyes.

JIM CARREY
in "Bruce Almighty"

137

When you're in love, it's the most glorious two-and-a-half minutes of your life.

RICHARD LEWIS

Here's the secret to a happy marriage: Do what your wife tells you.

DENZEL WASHINGTON

Wedding belles

When Charlie Deshler announced that he was going to marry Dorothy, someone said he would lose his mind posthaste. "No," said a wit who knew them both, "post hoc." Dorothy had begun, when she was quite young, to finish sentences for people. Sometimes she finished them wrongly, which annoyed the person who was speaking, and sometimes she finished them correctly, which annoyed the speaker even more.

"When William Howard Taft was–" some guest in Dorothy's family home would begin.

"President!" Dorothy would pipe up. The speaker may have meant to say "President" or he may have meant to say "young", or "Chief Justice of the Supreme Court of the United States". In any case, he would shortly put on his hat and go home. Like most parents, Dorothy's parents did not seem to be conscious that her mannerism was a nuisance. Very likely they thought that it was cute, or even

bright. It is even probable that when Dorothy's mother first said "Come, Dorothy, eat your–" and Dorothy said "Spinach, dear," the former telephoned Dorothy's father at the office and told him about it, and he told everybody he met that day about it – and the next day and the day after.

When Dorothy grew up she became quite pretty and so even more of a menace. Gentlemen became attracted to her and then attached to her. Emotionally she stirred them, but mentally she soon began to wear them down. Even in her late teens she began correcting their English. "Not 'was', Arthur," she would say, "'were'. 'Were prepared'. See?" Most of her admirers tolerated this habit because of their interest in her lovely person, but, as time went on and her interest in them remained more instructive than sentimental, they slower drifted away to less captious, if dumber, girls.

Charlie Deshler, however, was an impetuous man, of the

sweep-them-off-their-feet persuasion, and he became engaged to Dorothy so quickly and married her in so short a time that, being deaf to the warnings of friends, whose concern he regarded as mere jealousy, he really didn't know anything about Dorothy except that she was pretty and bright-eyed and (to him) desirable.

Dorothy as a wife came, of course, into her great flowering: she took to correcting Charlie's stories. He had traveled widely and experienced greatly and was a truly excellent *raconteur*. Dorothy was, during their courtship, genuinely interested in him and in his stories, and since she had never shared any of the adventures he told about, she could not know when he made mistakes in time or in place or in identities. Beyond suggesting a change here and there in the number of a verb, she more or less let him alone. Charlie spoke rather good English, anyway, – he knew when to say "were" and when to say "was" after "if" – and this was

James Thurber, *The Secret Life of Walter Mitty and Other Pieces*

another reason he didn't find Dorothy out.

I didn't call on them for quite a while after they were married, because I liked Charlie and I knew I would feel low if I saw him coming out of the anaesthetic of her charms and beginning to feel the first pains of reality. When I did finally call, conditions were, of course, all that I had feared. Charlie began to tell, at dinner, about a motor trip the two

had made to this town and that – I never found out for sure what towns, because Dorothy denied almost everything that Charlie said. "The next day," he would say, "we got an early start and drove two hundred miles to Fairview–" "Well," Dorothy would say, "I wouldn't call it *early*. It wasn't as early as the first day we set out, when we got up about *seven*. And we only drove a hundred and eighty

miles, because I remember looking at that mileage thing when we started."

"Anyway, when we got to Fairview–" Charlie would go on. But Dorothy would stop him. "Was it Fairview that day, darling?" she would ask. Dorothy often interrupted Charlie by asking him if he were right, instead of telling him that he was wrong, but it amounted to the same thing, for if he would reply: "Yes, I'm sure it was Fairview," she would say: "But it *wasn't*, darling," and then go on with the story herself. (She called everybody that she differed from "darling".)

Once or twice, when I called on them or they called on me, Dorothy would let Charlie get almost to the climax of some interesting account of a happening and then, like a tackler from behind, throw him just as he was about to cross the goal-line. There is nothing in life more shocking to the nerves and to the mind than this. Some husbands will sit back amiably – almost it seems, proudly – when their wives interrupt, and let them go on with the story, but these are beaten husbands. Charlie did not become beaten. But his wife's tackles knocked the wind out of him, and he began to realize that he would have to do something. What he did was rather ingenious. At the end of the second year of their marriage, when you visited the Deshlers, Charlie would begin some outlandish story about a dream he had had, knowing that Dorothy could not correct him on his own dreams. They became the only life he had that was his own.

"I thought I was running an airplane," he would say, "made out of telephone wires and pieces of old leather. I was trying to make it fly to the moon, taking off from my bedroom. About half-way up to the moon, however, a man who looked like Santa Claus, only he was dressed in the uniform of a customs officer, waved at me to stop – he was in a plane made of telephone wires, too. So I pulled over to a cloud. 'Here,' he said to me, 'You can't go to the moon, if you are the man who invented these wedding cookies.' Then he showed me a cookie made in the shape of a man and woman being married – little images of a man and a woman and a minister, made of dough and fastened firmly to a round, crisp cookie base." So he would go on.

Any psychiatrist will tell you that at the end of the way Charlie was going lies madness in the form of monomania. You can't live in a fantastic dream world, night in and night out and then day in and day out, and remain sane. The substance began to die slowly out of Charlie's life, and he began to live entirely in shadow. And since monomania of this sort is likely to lead in the end to the reiteration of one particular story, Charlie's invention began to grow thin and he eventually took to telling, over and over again, the first dream he had ever described – the story of his curious flight toward the moon in an airplane made of telephone wires. It was extremely painful. It saddened us all.

After a month or two, Charlie finally had to be sent to an asylum. I was out of town when they took him away, but Joe Fultz, who went with him, wrote me about it. "He seemed to like it up here right away," Joe wrote. "He's calmer and his eyes look better." (Charlie had developed a wild, hunted look.) "Of course," concluded Joe, "he's finally got away from that woman."

It was a couple of weeks later that I drove up to the asylum to see Charlie. He was lying on a cot on a big screened-in porch, looking wan and thin. Dorothy was sitting on a chair beside his bed, bright-eyed and eager. I was somehow surprised to see her there, having figured that Charlie had, at least, won sanctuary from his wife. He looked quite mad. He began at once to tell me the story of his trip to the moon. He got to the part where the man who looked like Santa Claus waved at him to stop. "He was in a plane made of telephone wires, too," said Charlie. "So I pulled over to a kerb–"

"No. You pulled over to a *cloud*," said Dorothy. "There aren't any kerbs in the *sky*. There *couldn't* be. You pulled over to a cloud."

Charlie sighed and turned slightly in his bed and looked at me. Dorothy looked at me, too, with her pretty smile.

"He always gets that story wrong," she said.

A train was just pulling out of the station when an elderly couple rushed on to the platform where I was waiting. Out of breath, they sat down beside me and started berating each other. "If you hadn't dawdled with your shopping," said the man, "we'd have caught the train."

"And if you hadn't run so fast," retorted the woman, " we wouldn't have to wait so long for the next one."

ALBRECHT TOEPPER

My mother-in-law enjoys cooking, and my father-in-law loves gardening. One day in autumn, she needed some onions and went to the string bag he had hung near the back door. The resultant dish was different, but tasty.

Next morning, as he reached for the string bag, Dad announced that he had better plant the tulip bulbs before it rained.

T. BURNS

Driving into a crowded carpark, I rolled down the car windows to make sure my labrador retriever had fresh air. She was stretched out on the back seat, and I wanted to impress upon her that she must remain there. I walked to the kerb backwards, pointing my finger at the car and saying emphatically, "Now you stay. Do you hear me? Stay!"

The driver of a near-by car gave me a startled look. "I don't know about you," he said incredulously, "but I usually just put the handbreak on."

PATRICIA GAY

Working for a pest-control company, my husband likes to confirm his appointments the night before. One evening, he called a customer and said to the man who answered, "Hello. This is Gary from the pest-control company. Your wife telephoned us."

There was silence for a moment and then my husband heard the man say, "Darling, someone wants to speak to you about your relatives."

WENDY KENNY

Upset over a newlywed squabble with my husband, I went to my parents' house to complain. Trying to console me, my dad said that men weren't like this all the time. "Rubbish," I said. "Men are only good for one thing!"

"Yes," my mother interjected, "but how often do you have to parallel park?"

JENNIFER LEE

I was in my boss's office when my boyfriend telephoned. My boss disapproves of personal calls at

"Better get two dozen. She won't be able to hit you as hard with both arms full."

work, so I gave short, vague replies. My boyfriend soon clicked. "All right, darling," he said, "just answer yes or no. How much milk should I put in mashed potatoes?"

NATHALIE LANNIER

Just before my sister and her husband left on a three-hour car journey with their two small children, my sister had worked a night shift and was functioning on two hours' sleep. "However," she said upon arrival at our house, "I was only short with the children for one moment."

"Yes," her husband replied, "from the moment we left until the moment we arrived."

PEGGY HEINCKE

My husband is wonderful with our baby daughter, but often turns to me for advice. Recently I was in the shower when he poked his head in to ask, "What should I feed Lily for lunch?"

"That's up to you," I replied. "There's all kinds of food. Why don't you pretend I'm not home?"

A few minutes later, my mobile phone rang. I answered it to hear my husband saying, "Yeah, hi, darling. Uh ... what should I feed Lily for lunch?"

JULIE BALL

While waiting to register at a hotel, I overheard the couple ahead of me asking for a room with a double bed. The receptionist apologized and said that the only rooms available had twin beds. Disappointed the man remarked, " I don't know. We've been sharing the same bed for 44 years."

"Could you possibly put them close together?" the wife asked. Several people near by smiled, and someone commented "How romantic."

Then the woman finished with, "Because if he snores, I want to be able to punch him."

POLLY SITTERLEY

My wife-to-be and I were at the registrar's office for our marriage licence.

After recording the vital information – names, dates of birth, etc – the clerk handed me our licence and deadpanned, **"No refunds, no exchanges, no guarantees."**

ALBERT CAMPBELL

"I'm going to Venus. He's going to Mars."

Some newly married friends were visiting when the topic of children came up.

The bride said she wanted three, while the young husband said two would be enough. They discussed this discrepancy for a few minutes, until the husband said boldly, "After our second, I'll just have a vasectomy."

"Well," his partner retorted, "I hope you'll love the third one as if it's your own."

LISA MONGAN

My husband, an exercise enthusiast who spends an hour and a half at an athletics club every morning before work, encouraged a middle-aged and quite overweight friend to join him for his morning sessions. The colleague decided not to tell his wife about his project until after he had shed the pounds, and he faithfully began meeting my husband at 6am every day.

At the end of the first week, the friend's wife rolled over in bed and offered this parting advice: "I don't know where you're going, dear, or what you are doing. But just remember: you aren't used to it."

DEBBIE BEAUCHAMP

To our shock and horror, my sister-in-law and I realised we had each been married nearly 50 years. "That's a long time," I observed.

"A long, long time," she agreed. Then she smiled. "Something just occurred to me."

"What's that?"

"If I had killed your brother the first time I felt like it, I'd be out of jail by now."

BARBARA MASON

Rushing to a bridge tournament, I was pulled over for doing 43 in a 35mph. zone. "What'll I tell my husband?" I worried, explaining to the police officer that he was a self-described "perfect" driver.

The officer took a second look at the name and address on my licence. "Did your husband take the car out this morning?" he asked.

Baffled, I answered, "Yes."

"I stopped him for doing 47."

ANN DUNN

I was wandering aimlessly through the supermarket. Because I am elderly, a concerned young man asked if I was looking for something.

"Yes," I said. "Have you seen my wife?'

"Well, I don't know her," he replied.

"Have you seen a beautiful, tall girl with a wonderful smile, long legs and a miniskirt?"

He looked at me in disbelief. "No."

"It's just that I was distracted by her and now I've lost my wife."

L. JEFFRIES

When, by means of an at-home early pregnancy test, my wife discovered she was pregnant, she tried to get in touch with me at work. I was out, so she left a message. Later, I found a note on my desk: "E. P. T. – phone home."

JON RISING

When my younger brother and his wife celebrated their first anniversary, they invited the rest of the family to join them for dinner. The conversation focused on the newlyweds and how they happened to meet. Caught up in the romance of the story, one by one the men related how we had met our wives. Eventually everyone had told his story except for my youngest brother.

All eyes were on him when he said, "Oh, Cindy and I met at university. We were matched up by a computer according to compatibility."

143

"That's the whole story?" my wife asked incredulously.

"Oh, no," he replied with a grin. "They've fixed the computer since then."

JOHN MORRISSEY

"They said he has a real fear of intimacy."

One night my friend John and I were sitting at a bar where he used to work, when an attractive woman, a former colleague, came in and sat next to him. She told him she had just had a fight with her husband, a police officer, and needed to get out of the house for a while.

They had been talking for a few minutes when, as a joke, I leaned over to John. "Don't look now," I whispered, "but a guy about six foot five just walked in. And he's got a gun."

Without hesitating, John turned to me. "Quick, Ed," he said, "kiss me on the lips."

E.J. KRAMER

On my day off work, I shed the corporate uniform and dressed scruffily, with rollers in my hair. Glancing out of the window, I saw a van blocking my drive. Incensed, I flew to the door and told the driver to move it immediately.

About an hour later, dressed for shopping, I was reversing my car on to the road and noticed the driver standing on the pavement. Slightly embarrassed, I nodded hello.

"Madam," he said to me, "I hope your grandmother is only visiting. She is one tough old woman."

JEAN HENRY

Driving my friend Steve and his girlfriend to the airport, we passed a billboard showing a beautiful slim woman in a bikini holding a can of beer.

Steve's girlfriend glanced up at the poster and announced, "I suppose if I drank a six-pack of that brand, I'd look like her."

"No," Steve corrected. "If I drank a six-pack, you'd look like her."

JOHN BOYD

My boyfriend and I went to pick up his 19-year-old niece to take her to a weekend music festival.

When we arrived at her house, she appeared in tasteful, but very cropped, shorts and a little top with spaghetti straps. A debate then ensued about whether she was appropriately dressed or not. I took the girl's side, recalling that when I first started to see my boyfriend, I wore the same sort of clothes.

"Yes," said my boyfriend sternly, "and I said something about it, didn't I?"

Everyone looked at me. "You certainly did," I replied. "You asked me for my phone number."

C. WATSON

For our anniversary, my husband and I holidayed in Hawaii, where we went snorkelling. After an hour in the water everyone got back on the boat, except for me and one handsome young man.

As I continued my under-water exploring, I noticed that everywhere I swam, he swam. I snorkelled for another 40 minutes. So did he. I climbed back in the boat. So did he.

I felt very flattered and, as I took off my fins, asked him coyly why he had stayed in the water for so long.

"I'm the lifeguard," he replied matter-of-factly. "I couldn't get out until you did."

SHARON FORGUE

One morning I found a beautiful long-stemmed rose lying by the kitchen sink and thought how lovely it was that even after all these years of marriage, my husband could still make such a wonderful romantic gesture.

Going over to the flower, I noticed a love note lying next to it. "Dear Sue," it read. "Don't touch the rose. I'm using the stem to unclog the drain."

SUZAN WIENER

My wife and her friend Karen were talking about their labour-saving devices as they pulled into our driveway. Karen said, "I love my new garage-door opener."

"I love mine too," my wife replied, and honked the horn three times. That was the signal for me to come out and open the garage.

G. WARD

My husband knows the pitfalls of trying to communicate with the opposite sex. For instance, I recently tried on a pair of trousers and needed a second opinion about how they looked. "Do I look too fat in these?" I asked.

"No," he said, pausing, obviously worried about his response. "You look ... just fat enough."

KATHY SEUFERT

For years my sister's husband tried unsuccessfully to persuade her to get a hearing aid. "How much do they cost?" she asked one day after he had pitched the idea to her again. "They're usually about £1000," he said.

"Okay, well, if you say something worth £1000," she replied, "I'll get one."

EDWIN REINAGEL

At my granddaughter's wedding, the DJ polled the guests to see who had been married the longest. Since it turned out to be my husband and me, the DJ asked us, "What advice would you give to the newly married couple?"

I said, "The three most important words in a marriage are, 'You're probably right.'"

Everyone looked at my husband for a retort. "She's probably right," he said.

BARBARA HANCOCK

145

One wintry evening, my husband and I were snuggled on the floor watching TV. During a commercial break, he reached over and gave my foot a gentle squeeze.

"Mmm," I said. "You're very sweet."

"Actually," he replied, "I thought that was the remote."

STEPHANIE EELE

When I was first married, I didn't know how to cook and failed badly in my attempt at lasagne. Fifteen years later, I tried again. My husband came to the table and glanced at the food.

"What!" he exclaimed. "Surely not lasagne again?"

IRENE MUNIZ

When a woman in my office became engaged, a colleague offered her some advice.

"The first ten years are the hardest," she said.

"How long have you been married?" I asked.

"Ten years," she replied.

T. WINTER

In the frozen-food section of our local shop, I noticed a man shopping with his son. As I walked past he ticked something off his list and I heard him whisper conspiratorially to the child, "You know, if we really mess this up, we'll never have to do it again."

JANET CAMPBELL

At the end of a frantic afternoon of chores, I walked into the living room to find my husband reclining in his chair. He was looking at our new puppy, who was napping. "If I'd wanted to look at something lying around sleeping all day," he complained, "I would have bought a cat."

"Or a mirror," I said.

TRACEY SMITH

I met a friend in a bar and noticed two pretty girls looking at me. "Nine," I heard one of them whisper when I passed. Feeling chuffed, I swaggered up to my friend and told him that the girls had just rated me a nine out of ten.

"I don't want to ruin it for you," he replied, "but when I walked past them, they were speaking German."

RICHARD MOGRIDGE

While working in a remote village in Sierra Leone, I befriended Alpha, who was one of the local men on our building team. Alpha was impressed with my tool kit and amazed to find a woman working in construction. He would bring extra rice and greens for lunch and we would sit and talk. When he enquired about my husband, I explained that I wasn't married. Alpha said he wanted to have children and would marry soon. He wondered if I was going to stay in his country, and then surprised me by saying he had an important question to ask. I was rather nervous, but the next day Alpha was solemn as he asked if I was ready to answer his question. I nodded.

"When you go back home," he said, "may I have your trowel?"

CAROL HUMBYRD

"Our credit card was stolen, but I've decided not to report it. The thief is spending less than you did!"

Our dentist recently hired a beautiful young dental hygienist. We exchanged small talk as she cleaned my teeth and I gazed at her adoringly.

When she had finished, she smiled and told me, "You have the most perfect mouth." My heart skipped a beat. Then she looked at me with her lovely pale-blue eyes and continued: "Usually I have a lot of trouble when I have to reach people's wisdom teeth. But your mouth is so big, I can get both hands in easily."

PHILLIP MURRAY

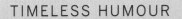

TIMELESS HUMOUR

50s The bus was crowded and I could not help overhearing a couple amiably pursuing a rambling argument about some domestic triviality. The husband, I thought, had rather the better of it. But as he completed a statement that seemed to settle the matter, his wife calmly captured game and set. "Now look, George," she said firmly, "I already know what I think – so don't try to confuse me with a lot of facts."

J.H. LONG

While in the checkout line at my local hardware shop I overheard one man say to another, "My wife has been after me to paint our shed. But I let it go for so long she got cross and did it herself."

His friend nodded. "I like women who get cross like that."

C.V. MAYNARD

I realised that the ups and downs of the stock market had become too big a part of our life one night as my husband and I prepared for bed. As we slid beneath the covers, I snuggled up to him and told him I loved him.

Drifting off to sleep, he drowsily whispered back, "Your dividend growth fund went up three days this week."

SHIRLEY DILLON

My wife and I attended the reunion of my university year. As I looked around, I became aware of the other men with their expensive suits and bulging stomachs. Proud of the fact that I weighed just five pounds more than I did at university, I said to my wife, "I'm the only man here who can wear the suit he graduated in."

She glanced at the group, then back at me and said, "You're the only one who has to."

GEORGE CRENSHAW

At the airport check-in counter, I overheard a woman ask for window seats for her and her husband. The clerk pointed out that this would prevent them from sitting together.

"Sweetie," the woman replied. "I just spent ten days of quality time in a budget hire car with this man. I know what I'm requesting."

CAROL GORES

My sister's lack of sports knowledge recently became evident when we went to an ice hockey game. After the home team scored, the crowd erupted and the monitors around the rink flashed: "G O A L".

After cheering wildly, my sister turned and asked: Who's Al?"

KAREN KELLY

147

One evening my husband's golfing buddy drove his secretary home after she had imbibed a little too much at an office reception. Although this was an innocent gesture, he decided not to mention it to his wife, who tended to get jealous easily.

Later that night my husband's friend and his wife were driving to a restaurant. Suddenly he looked down and spotted a high-heel shoe half hidden under the passenger seat. Not wanting to be conspicuous, he waited until his wife was looking out her window before he scooped up the shoe and tossed it out of the car. With a sigh of relief, he pulled into the carpark. That's when he noticed his wife squirming around in her seat.

"Sweetheart," she asked, "have you seen my other shoe?"

JOAN FELDMAN

My husband, Mike, and I had several stressful months of financial difficulties. So one evening I was touched to see him gazing at the diamond wedding ring that symbolised our marriage.

"With this ring ... " I began romantically.

"We could pay off Visa," he responded.

DAWN HILL

Soon after we were married, my husband, Paul, stopped wearing his wedding ring.

"Why don't you ever wear your ring?" I asked.

"It cuts off my circulation," Paul replied.

"I know," I said. "It's supposed to."

MARILYN WARE

I spent an afternoon helping my boyfriend move into a new home. In one box I found a slow-cooker, with an odd-looking and very dirty metal lid. Later I ushered my boyfriend into the kitchen and asked why he hadn't mentioned this perfectly good pot.

He stared at it, then replied, "Well, after I broke the lid I never thought of replacing it with a hubcap."

CAROLINE JONES

After I had taken on a few too many projects, my responsibilities began piling up on me. To keep my forgetfulness to a minimum, I started a daily reminder list, ticking off items as I completed them. About two weeks later I bragged to my husband, Clarence, "Thanks to that list I have never once overlooked a single important detail."

Not long afterward I returned home from a late-night meeting and picked up my list to check on the next day's activities. There, in my husband's handwriting, wedged between "1:30 hair appointment" and "Clean the airing cupboard," was the note: "Seduce Clarence."

MARY HOWELL

For a while my husband and I had opposite schedules. He worked during the day and I worked at night. One morning I noticed he had left a note to himself on the kitchen counter that said "STAMPS" in large letters. As a helpful surprise, I bought him some at the post office and put them on the counter before going to work.

The next morning I found the same note. "STAMPS" was crossed out. Underneath he had written, "ONE MILLION POUNDS".

STEPHANIE SHELLEY

"I guess I thought if we came to France,
you wouldn't still be, you know, you!"

149

My wife, a registered nurse, once fussed over every pain or mishap that came my way. Recently, however, I got an indication that the honeymoon is over.

I was about to fix the attic fan, and as I lifted myself from the ladder into the attic, I scratched my forehead on a crossbeam. Crawling along, I picked up splinters in both hands, and I cut one hand replacing the fan belt. On the way down the ladder, I missed the last two rungs and turned my ankle.

When I limped into the kitchen, my wife took one look and said, "Are those your good trousers?"

RICHARD SCHWIETERMAN

I was examining cantaloupe melons at the supermarket and turned to a shop assistant who was refilling the section.

"Choosing a cantaloupe is a bit like picking a mate for marriage," I observed. "A person has no idea what he's getting until it's too late."

When the man did not comment, I wasn't sure he'd heard me.

After a thoughtful pause he lifted his head and turned to me. "I know," he said. "I've had three cantaloupes."

GLORIA WEGENER

"No one's winning. It's ballet."

As a single, never-married woman in my 40s, I have been questioned endlessly about my status by friends, relatives and colleagues. Over the years I've noticed a subtle change in the nature of their inquiries.

In my teens, friends would ask, "Who are you going out with this weekend?"

In my 20s, relatives would say, "Who are you dating?"

In my 30s, co-workers might inquire, "So, are you dating anyone?"

Now people ask, "Where did you get that adorable handbag?"

MARY ELDER

Birdwatching is a passion of mine, and my wife has always been impressed by my ability to identify each species solely by its song. To help her learn a little bit about birds, I bought a novelty kitchen clock that sounds a different bird call for each hour. We were relaxing in our garden when a bird started singing. "What's that?" I challenged.

She listened closely. "It's three o'clock."

RICH PERSHEY

150

TIMELESS HUMOUR

70s Neighbours of ours had a terrible disagreement over a patio they wanted for their garden. The wife had rather grand ideas, while the husband wanted costs kept to a minimum. The wife won out, and the construction bill climbed higher and higher.

I dropped by one day, when the patio was near completion, and was surprised to find the husband smiling from ear to ear as the workmen smoothed over the surface. I remarked how nice it was to see a grin replace the frown he had been wearing lately.

"You see where they're smoothing that cement?" he replied. "I just threw my wife's credit cards in there."

R. HORN

A woman in my office, recently divorced after years of marriage, signed up for a refresher CPR course.

"Is it hard to learn?" someone asked.

"Not at all," she replied. "Basically you're asked to breathe life into a dummy. I don't expect to have any problem. I did that for 32 years."

P. BROOKS

Recently engaged, my brother-in-law Jeff brought his fiancée home to meet the family. When asked if she was enjoying herself, she politely replied yes.

"She would say that," Jeff interjected. "She's not the type to say no."

"I see," my husband said after a brief silence. "And that explains the engagement."

ALLISON BEVANS

My wife had to rush to hospital and asked me to bring in a few belongings from home.

One of the specified items was "comfortable underwear".

Worried I'd bring the wrong garments, I asked how I would know which ones to pick.

"Hold them up and imagine them on me," she said. "If you smile, put them back."

ROBERT KERCHER

On my way home from a long and stressful day at the office, the phone rang. It was my husband. "Will you be joining me in the whirlpool bath tonight?" he asked.

What a lovely way to spend an evening, I thought. I was about to tell him how considerate he was when he continued, "Because if you're not, I need to start adding more water to the tub."

SUSAN NELSON

Trying to impress a young lady I was dating, I cooked her a meal. As I served it, I told her bashfully, "Don't expect too much. It's probably not fit for the dog."

She tried a bit and, in an effort to reassure me, said, "You're too modest. It is fit for the dog."

GORDON WALLACE

"Don't ask questions, Ralph. Just tell me who you'd rather look like – Sean Connery or Robert Redford."

151

A guy knows he's in love when he loses interest in his car for a couple of days.

TIM ALLEN

My husband is so confident that when he watches sports on television, he thinks that if he concentrates he can help his team. If the team is in trouble, he coaches the players from our living room, and if they're really in trouble, I have to get off the phone in case they call him.

RITA RUDNER

Love is like the measles; we all have to go through it.

JEROME K. JEROME

Three words strike fear into the hearts of men: Pop the question.

ROXANNE HAWN
in The Denver Post

According to Modern Bride magazine, the average bride spends 150 hours planning her wedding. The average groom spends 150 hours going, "Yeah, sounds good."

JAY LENO

Women don't want to hear what you think. Women want to hear what they think, in a deeper voice.

BILL COSBY

Women and elephants never forget an injury.

SAKI

A man in love is incomplete until he has married. Then he's finished.

ZSA ZSA GABOR

My wife and I were comparing notes the other day. "I have a higher IQ, did better on my exams and make more money than you," she pointed out.

"Yeah, but when you step back and look at the big picture, I'm still ahead," I said.

She looked mystified. "How do you figure?"

"I married better," I replied.

LOUIS RODOLICO

A friend and her husband were participating in a blood drive, and as part of the prescreening process, an elderly volunteer was asking some questions. "Have you ever paid for sex?" the woman asked my friend's husband sweetly.

Glancing wearily over at his wife, trying to calm a new baby and tend to several other children milling around her, he sighed, "Every time."

W. WOOLF

Every year on their wedding anniversary, my boss Woody and his wife celebrate by staying at the same hotel.

On their twenty-fifth anniversary they booked their usual room, but when the hotel head porter escorted them upstairs, they got a surprise.

"There must be some mistake," Woody said. "This looks like the bridal suite."

"It's OK," reassured the porter. "If I put you in the ballroom, that doesn't mean you have to dance."

CONNIE SELLERS

I was about to leave the house on an errand, and my husband was getting ready for a dental appointment. "I wish we could trade places," I said, knowing how much he dreaded the coming ordeal.

He watched as I gathered our newborn onto my left arm and picked up a package with that hand. I flung a nappy bag and my handbag over my right shoulder, grabbed our two-year-old

with my free hand and wrestled the car keys from him.

My husband shook his head. "No, thanks," he said. "At least where I'm going they give you anaesthesia."

LINDA CHIARA

While at a marine-supply shop stocking up on equipment for my boat, I also purchased an inflatable life preserver. "It was my wife's idea," I explained to the salesman at the counter. "She's buying it for me as a present."

"Lucky you," he said as he started to write up the order. "My wife got me a length of chain and a cement block."

THOMAS FRONCEK

153

TIMELESS HUMOUR

50s Friends of a man who was known for his inability to think of anything to say to women were amazed when, the morning after the shy one met a girl at a dance, it was announced that he had become engaged. One inquired as to how it happened. "Well," said the bashful man, "I danced with her three times, and I couldn't think of anything else to say."

DAN BENNETT

All those years of marriage and they still get emotional on Valentines Day!

I was bending over to wipe up a spill on the kitchen floor when my wife walked into the room behind me. **"See anything you like?"** I asked suggestively. **"Yeah,"** she said. **"You doing housework."**

MICHAEL SHOCKLEY

One day my housework-challenged husband decided to wash his sweatshirt. Seconds after he stepped into the laundry room, he shouted to me, "What setting do I use on the washing machine?"

"It depends," I replied. "What does it say on your sweatshirt?"

"University of Edinburgh," he yelled back.

J. BOYER

The birth of our second child, a daughter, came after a long and difficult labour. But it was definitely worth it when our beautiful little girl emerged, perfect in every way. Later, in my room, my husband looked at her tenderly, with tears in his eyes.

Then as he glanced up at me, I expected him to utter something truly poetic. Instead he asked, "What's her name again?"

CHRISTINA MILLER

I accompanied my husband when he went to get a haircut. Reading a magazine, I found a hairstyle I liked for myself, so I asked the receptionist if I could take the magazine next door to make a copy of the photo.

"Leave some ID – a driver's licence or credit card," she said.

"But my husband is here getting a haircut," I explained.

"Yes," she replied. "But I need something you'll come back for."

MELISSA ANDERSON

As I was stepping into the shower after an afternoon of gardening, my wife walked into the bathroom. "What do you think the neighbours would say if I cut the grass dressed like this?" I asked.

Giving me a casual glance, she replied, "They'd say I married you for your money."

JOHN BUCO

After four years of separation, my wife and I finally divorced amicably. I wanted to date again, but had no idea of how to start, so I decided to look in the personals column of the local newspaper. After reading through all the listings, I circled three that seemed possible in terms of age and interests, but I put off calling them.

Two days later, there was a message on my answering machine from my ex-wife: "I came over to your house to borrow some tools today and saw the ads you circled in the paper. Don't call the one in the second column. It's me."

NELSON WORKMAN

"How do you know when you're in love? I don't know. Go ask your mother."

Humour in uniform

The trials and tribulations of our sons, daughters, parents
and friends in the military.

"Remember, men, our motto is leap before you look."

Going over our weekly training schedule one morning at our small Army garrison, we noticed that our annual trip to the rifle range had been canceled for the second time, but that our semi-annual physical-fitness test was still on as planned. "Does it bother anyone else," one soldier asked, "that the Army doesn't seem concerned with how well we can shoot, yet is extremely interested in how fast we can run?"

THOMAS HAMMOND

The colonel who served as inspector general in our command paid particular attention to how personnel wore their uniforms. On one occasion he spotted a junior airman with a violation. "Airman," he bellowed, "what do you do when a shirt pocket is unbuttoned?"

The startled airman replied, "Button it, sir!"

The colonel looked him in the eye and said, "Well?"

At that, the airman nervously reached over and buttoned the colonel's shirt pocket.

G. DEARING

When my husband visited our son, Michael, at training camp, he found him marching smartly with his unit. Michael's father proudly approached the soldiers and began to snap photo after photo. Embarrassed and worried about getting into trouble, Michael looked straight ahead and didn't change his expression.

Suddenly his drill sergeant barked, "Comito, give me 25 push-ups. And the next time your father wants your picture, you smile!"

E. COMITO

During basic training, our drill sergeant asked for a show of hands of all Jewish personnel. Six of us tentatively raised our hands. Much to our relief, we were given the day off for Rosh Hashanah.

A few days later in anticipation of Yom Kippur, the drill sergeant again asked for all Jewish personnel to ID themselves. This time, every soldier raised his hand. "Only the personnel who were Jewish last week can be Jewish this week," declared the sergeant.

ALLEN ISRAEL

I had just married a navy lieutenant. As we came out of the church doors, I turned to him for those precious words with which to start our marriage. "You're out of step," he said.

MRS RALPH WEISS

TIMELESS HUMOUR

60s A newly commissioned air force officer and his beautiful young bride had the cottage next to ours one summer. He left early each morning for the near-by airfield, and exactly one hour later she would leave the cottage carrying a large, white bathing towel and go for a walk on the beach.

My husband and I wondered about her solitary walks until one morning when she returned convulsed with laughter. She told us that her husband flew over the beach on his way to patrol the coastal waters. When he saw the white towel waving, he would either dip his left wing to say "I'm on duty all night and won't be home," or dip his right wing to say "In eight hours I'll be holding you in my arms." This morning he had led a formation out. As he passed overhead, he had slowly dipped his left wing. Before she'd had time to feel disappointed that he would not be home, the rest of the formation flew over, and each pilot smartly lowered his right wing.

M.V

157

Spotted on T-shirts in support of the Coastguard:

"Support Your Local Coastguard ... Get Lost."

G. BARCK

I spent several years as a submariner, and while at sea we would have a celebration half-way through a patrol.

One such night, the captain, who was serving dinner to the crew, tried to put some vegetables on a recruit's plate. The young seaman wouldn't take them. "With all due respect, sir," the recruit said, "I don't eat them for my mother, and she outranks you."

MARK WILDMAN

After joining the Navy, my husband underwent a physical. During the exam, it was discovered that, due to an abnormality, he couldn't fully extend his arms above his head. Perplexed, the doctor conferred with another doctor.

"Let him pass," said the second doctor. "I don't see any problems unless he has to surrender."

B. LEE

Safety is job one in the Air Force. Overstating the obvious is job two, as I discovered when crawling into my military-issue sleeping bag. The label read: "In case of an emergency, unzip and exit through the top."

KEITH WALTERS

My daughter, Emily, told a friend that her brother, Chris, was training to become a Navy submariner. The friend, who'd just been assigned to a Navy destroyer, good-naturedly called Chris a Bubblehead.

Later I related the story to Chris and asked if he'd heard the term. He said he had, and added, "We also have a name for people who work on destroyers."

"What is it?" I asked.

"Targets."

JO BARKER

CAMOUFLAGE PAINT

TIMELESS HUMOUR

50s Booked on an early morning plane, I was delayed at a railwaycrossing halfway to the airfield. Arriving just in time to see my plane taxiing down the runway, I grabbed my brief-case and started running after the plane, shouting and gesturing, coat-tails flying in the breeze.

Then from the tower loud-speaker came these instructions: "You're cleared for take-off, Commander."

Lieutenant-Commander
A.O. CLOUSE

Serving as a recruiter, I found a young man who met all the requirements and was ready to enlist. I explained the importance of being truthful on the application, and he began filling out his paperwork. But when he got to the question "Do you own any foreign property or have any foreign financial interests?" he looked up at me with a worried expression.

"Well," he confessed, "I do own a Toyota."

We enlisted him the next day.

PATRICK JACKS

Having helped prepare the annual budget for my unit of the Seventh Army Special Troops in Heidelberg, Germany, I took the report to the office of the adjutant, who signs all official papers. The adjutant was not in, but his assistant, a young lieutenant, was.

He gasped as I handed him the huge sheaf of charts, figures and explanations. "What am I supposed to do with this?" he asked.

"You have to sign it, sir."

"Thank goodness," he said, sighing with relief. "I thought I had to read it."

TIMOTHY QUINN

To post a big package of cookies to my two Air Force sons, both of whom were serving in Saudi Arabia, I was required to attach a label describing the contents. I carefully marked the box "Cookies" and sent it off, but after a month my sons said they had yet to receive my package.

Suspicious, I baked another batch, only this time I labelled the contents "Health Food". Within a week my sons reported they had received the goodies.

W. HAMEISTER

After being at sea in the Persian Gulf for 90 straight days, I went to the squadron command master chief to complain. "Chief, I joined the Navy to see the world," I said, "but for the past three months all I've seen is water."

"Lieutenant," he replied, "three-quarters of the earth is covered with water, and the Navy has been showing you that. If you wanted to see the other quarter, you should have joined the Army."

PAUL NEWMAN

**"That's Admiral Blackly.
He drowned in a sea of red tape."**

159

"He's our most decorated general,
although he obviously lost the Battle of the Bulge."

Our commanding officer was at a briefing that relied on projectors to show maps of Norway with symbols for military units. The captain giving the briefing explained what each image represented. Our CO spotted a narrow racetrack-shaped image at the top of the screen and asked what it stood for.

The captain stopped, looked at his notes and replied ,"Sir, that's a paper clip."

G. MANDIS

My son, Barry, came home from a three-month deployment aboard his submarine, and told us that one of the ways the sailors kept up morale was to make wooden cars out of kits and have car races.

"What do you do for a ramp?'" my husband inquired.

"Don't need one," Barry said. "We just put the cars on the floor and then tilt the sub."

MARY RYAN

When I was an infantry platoon commander, my Marines trained regularly for night-time reconnaissance patrol. As we moved along, each of us would whisper the name of any obstacle to the person behind so that no one would be surprised and utter a cry that would disclose our position.

During one exercise, the lead man in the formation occasionally turned around and whispered to me "Log" or "Rock", which I would pass along. Suddenly there was a crash ahead of me and, from several feet down, I heard a single whispered word – "Hole".

MIKE ROBBINS

Some months after joining the RAF, my son decide to grow a moustache. He was proud of its progress, until on parade one day his sergeant commented: "What's this, laddie? One of your eyebrows come down for a drink?"

MRS J.W.

Notice seen on the bulletin board of an air base:

"The following enlisted men will pick up their Good Conduct medals in the supply room this afternoon. Failure to comply with this order will result in disciplinary action."

MYRA HAYES

My brother and I arrived at training camp together. On the first morning, our unit was dragged out of bed by our drill sergeant and made to assemble outside. "My name's Sergeant Jackson," he snarled. "Is there anyone here who thinks he can whip me?"

My six-foot-three, 20 stone brother raised his hand and said, "Yes, sir, I do."

Our sergeant grabbed him by the arm and led him out in front of the group. "Men," he said, "this is my new assistant. Now, is there anyone here who thinks he can whip both of us?"

ROBERT NORRIS

During basic training we had a very tough sergeant. As well as having a bellowing voice and a mean face, he carried a little black book in which he entered every mistake we made. Decisions about duty rosters, requests for three-day passes, and kitchen duty were made only after the sergeant had carefully studied the notebook.

One day he ordered me to clean his quarters. The black book lay on a table. I could not resist a desire to see what was in it. The notebook was completely blank.

C.W.R

In disguise

CHURCH HALL

The rear two ranks are marking time.

WILSON: Quick march. Left, right, etc. (*The front rank march in*) Halt! (*They halt*) Turn left! (*They do so*)

MAINWARING: Excellent turn out, men, don't you think so, Wilson?

WILSON: Yes, absolutely first class, sir.

Mainwaring stops in front of the first man, he is covered from head to foot in hay.

MAINWARING: (*Aside to Wilson*) Who's this, Wilson?

WILSON: I haven't the faintest idea, sir.

Walker pulls aside the hay and pokes his head through.

WALKER: It's me, sir. I'm a small haystack.

MAINWARING: Good gracious that's good.

WILSON: Awfully good, sir.

Suddenly there is a terrific sneeze from young Pike who is standing beside Walker. He sneezes again, his eyes are running and he is in a terrible state.

MAINWARING: What on earth's the matter with you, boy?

PIKE: I can't stand it, sir, it's my hay fever.

MAINWARING: Well, don't stand next to him then, move to the end of the line.

PIKE: Yes, sir.

He moves to the end of the line. Mainwaring moves on to Godfrey who is wearing a beekeeper's mask and veil which is full of holes, he is also wearing a lei of flowers round his neck.

MAINWARING: What's this supposed to be, Godfrey?

GODFREY: Well, I tried several things on, sir, and none of them really seemed to suit me.

MAINWARING: But you're supposed to break up your outline.

GODFREY: I thought it looked pretty broken up as it is, sir.

MAINWARING: What's that you've got round your face?

GODFREY: It's my apiaristic mask, sir.

MAINWARING: Your what?

GODFREY: Bee keeping.

MAINWARING: But it's full of holes.

GODFREY: It's all right, my bees are quite friendly.

MAINWARING: (*Touching the 'lei'*) But why this? It looks as if you're going on a cruise to the South Seas.

GODFREY: Well, I got the idea from a film I saw at the Odeon last week, it was called "South of Pago-Pago", it had Dorothy Lamour and Victor Mature in it.

FRAZER: Was it good?

Jimmy Perry and David Croft, *Dad's Army*

GODFREY: Well, I liked it, but my sisters thought Miss Lamour was rather fast.

MAINWARING: What's that got to do with camouflage?

GODFREY: I don't know really, sir, I just thought it looked rather er ... open air.

MAINWARING: I see. (*He moves on*)

WILSON: He's right you know, sir, it does look open air.

Mainwaring gives him a glare and stops in front of Frazer. He has a battered top hat on his head and a tatty bit of white sheeting round his shoulders like a cloak.

MAINWARING: What have you been to see? The Phantom of the Opera?

FRAZER: No, this is winter camouflage, sir, you wear it in the snow.

He crouches down, and turns the sheet so that it falls in front of him. It has three black buttons painted on it. On the back of his head he has a snowman mask which he turns round, he replaces top hat and sticks a pipe in his mouth.

MAINWARING: Well done, Frazer. (*He passes on to Jones who is wearing his butcher's outfit, straw hat and apron*) Why aren't you wearing camouflage, Jones?

JONES: I am sir, I'm camouflaged as a butcher.

MAINWARING: But you are a butcher.

JONES: I know that and you know that, but Jerry doesn't, sir. Well, sir, I'm standing outside my shop, right. (*Mainwaring nods*) A Jerry soldier comes along, he don't know I'm in the Home Guard, he thinks I'm a butcher, right. (*Mainwaring nods*) Then when he's not looking, whop! Right up with the old cold steel. And that's one thing they don't like, you know, sir.

MAINWARING: Yes, thank you, Jones. I'm well aware of that fact.

He passes on to Pike who is wearing his uniform and no camouflage.

MAINWARING: What's the meaning of this, Pike?

PIKE: I've got a note for you, Mr Mainwaring, it's from my mum. (*He hands Mainwaring note, Mainwaring takes it and moves down with Wilson*)

MAINWARING: (*Reads*) "I'm not having our Frank covered in a lot of damp leaves, it will only set his chest again." Right, this is the finish, Wilson, I want to speak to you in my office as soon as the parade's over.

163

We had just moved to an Army post from an Air Force base and my young son, an avid fan of GI Joe toys, was excited to see the troops marching in formation. An even bigger thrill came when he passed the motor pool with its tanks, jeeps and trucks.

"Look!" he squealed with delight. "They have the whole collection!"

JEREMY THORNTON

My Army troop was learning how to parachute from a plane. At 12,000 feet, our drill instructor shouted out instructions for surviving a jump from above the clouds at more than 200mph. A recruit raised his hand and asked, "Once we jump out, how much time do we have to pull the cord?"

The instructor looked back, smiled and said, "The rest of your life."

KEVIN HENDRICK

Reservists like myself always had a hard time parking on base, as most spaces were set aside for the brass. My wife never had this problem. I finally found out why after she drove me to the base and parked in a space marked "Reserved".

"See?" she said. "Just look at all the spaces they've set aside for you Reserves."

JAMES KLEEMAN

"This one is for fighting off defence spending cuts."

My unit was detailed with guard duty. However, since live ammunition was reserved for sensitive locations, our rifles were issued with unloaded magazines. One day while we stood at attention for inspection, the officer in charge confronted a private and barked, "What is the maximum effective range of your M-16, soldier?"

The hapless private glanced down at his empty rifle and replied, "As far as I can throw it, sir."

JAN GETTING

Our personnel officer, annoyed by the report from his secretary that troops and members of the staff were using the new copying machine for personal documents, posted this notice on the machine: "Troops are not to tamper with the secretary's reproduction equipment without approval of the officer in charge."

FLOYD SEAY

I was learning to fly light aircraft for the Army. One day I made a perfectly smooth landing – at last. To my horror, when I stepped on the brakes, nothing at all happened.

I shouted to my instructor. "The brakes failed!"

"I'm not surprised," he growled. "We're still two feet in the air."

D. ADAMS

Whenever I begin to feel a bit smug, I recall my first week at naval officer candidate school. I learned quickly, I thought, and was getting adept at giving commands like, "To the rear ... ", "March" and "Company ... Halt."

There is a procedure for stacking rifles in which they end up looking like a small tepee. My bubble of pride was burst when I realised during a drill that I hadn't the faintest idea what the command to stack rifles should be.

With all the dignity I could summon, I called out, "Rifles in little bunches ... Put!"

WILLIAM DUTSON

My wife never quite got the hang of the 24-hour military clock. One day she called the orderly room and asked to speak with me. The person who answered told her to call me at the extension in the band rehearsal hall. "He can be reached at 4700, madam," the soldier advised.

With a sigh of exasperation, my wife responded, "And just what time is that?"

ERIC ERICKSON

One young officer's extreme keenness in demanding strict adherence to official regulations was causing problems. Eventually I took him aside for a chat on "man-management", suggesting that the regulations should be taken as a guide and were not meant to be strictly applied.

"Where in the regulations," he asked briskly "is that stated?"

LIEUTENANT-COLONEL DAWSON

In helicopter training, I heard a radio transmission between an instructor and his student pilot. They were practicing hovering, a tricky manoeuvre.

"See if you can keep your helicopter inside the concrete boundary," the instructor said.

A few minutes later, he revised his request. "Hell, Candidate," he shouted, "just try to keep it in this county."

ANTHONY LONG

I was attending a committee meeting at an RAF station during which several complaints wre raised about the high temperatures in the living quarters. A young airman suggested circulating cold water through the central heating system, but the station engineering officer immediately dismissed the idea, saying it was impossible. The airman meekly replied, "Begging your pardon, sir, but you did manage to do it most of last winter."

GEOFF LIDDLE

165

The crew of a fast frigate was practicing the man overboard drill by "rescuing" a bright orange fluorescent dummy dubbed Oscar. The captain watched as a young lieutenant nervously stopped the ship, turned it and manoeuvered into place. Unfortunately, he ran right over Oscar.

Surveying the remains of Oscar scattered around the ship, the captain told the lieutenant, "Son, do me a favour. If I ever fall overboard, just drop anchor and I'll swim to you."

ANTHONY WATSON

Newly married, I was en route to join my husband, a recently commissioned second lieutenant. I arrived at the gate and was motioned in. Gripping a map he had given me, I drove on, looking for the signs for where to go.

After turning onto one road, I heard a siren and was startled to see two airmen in a jeep, motioning me over. One got out and ran toward me. "Please follow us," he said.

"Why?" I asked.

"Well, ma'am," he politely replied, "that plane down there would like to take off."

DIANE SMITH

As a department head stationed on a Navy vessel, I was concerned about one of my senior enlisted men. He was a superb technician, but he had a problem taking orders. One day I took him aside and suggested he try something that had worked for me. "Whenever an officer gives you a directive that you think is stupid," I told him, "just say, 'Yes, sir.' But in your mind, think, 'You're an idiot!' Will this work for you?"

He smiled at me and replied, "Yes, sir!"

LEO KING

Serving as an air force instructor pilot, I was on duty one day as landing supervisor at an auxiliary field where flying cadets were performing their initial solo flights. One student pilot was having trouble getting his aircraft on the ground. When he had made four unsuccessful attempts at landing, I decided he needed some reassurance and advice. I asked on the radio for the pilot who had just made his fourth approach.

"There's no pilot in this aircraft," came back the high-pitched reply. "I'm up here by myself."

E.J.O.

What's up, Doc?

Packed with hilarious tales about our doctors, our bodies and our ongoing attempts to get healthy, this will have you in stitches!

Patricia

"The other foot, too, Mrs. Zipsky."

A man walked into a chemist and headed to the counter to speak with the pharmacist. "Do you have anything for hiccups?" he asked.

Without warning, the pharmacist reached over and smacked the man on the shoulder. "Did that help?" he asked.

"I don't know," the startled man replied. "I'll have to ask my wife. She's waiting in the car."

NANCY MACMILLAN

My husband was at the doctor's for an examination. When asked if he's had any problems since his last visit, he thought for a while. Then he answered, "Now that you mention it, I did have a flat tyre a couple of weeks ago."

B. BISHOP

"I think my wife's going deaf," Joe told their doctor.

"Try testing her hearing and let me know how bad it is," the doctor said.

So that evening, when his wife was preparing dinner, Joe stood 15 feet behind her and said, "What's for dinner, darling?" No response. He moved to ten feet behind her and asked again. No response. Then he stood five feet behind her and tried again but still got no answer.

Finally, he stood directly behind her and asked, "What's for supper?"

She turned round. "For the fourth time – I said chicken."

GORDON BAYLISS

During a CPR training class, we were paired up to practice the Heimlich manoeuvre. The instructor set the scene by saying, "Imagine you're at a dinner party with your partner and he or she starts choking."

He then reminded us not to do anything to people who were coughing, because they'd probably dislodge the obstruction on their own. We were to calm such victims with quiet talk and encourage them to continue coughing.

When the role playing began, one woman moved close to her coughing "husband". She placed a hand on his shoulder and whispered, "Darling, did you post your life insurance premium cheque yesterday.

TOM CLEVELAND

I recently enquired of my daughter, "Darling, I think my painkillers might be affecting my memory. Would you ask your doctor friends whether I should stop taking them?"

"Stop taking them, Dad," she replied. "You asked me that last week."

ARTHUR COLBURN

A colleague told me about the day he went to his school reunion: "My wife and I walked through the door, and a man I didn't recognise started hugging me, saying how happy he was to see me. When I confessed that I didn't know him, he said 'I don't know you either, but until you came I was the baldest man here.'"

R. WILLOUGHBY

169

TIMELESS HUMOUR

50s I was waiting in the office of our lone, overworked doctor when a local repairman, father of seven children, dashed in looking worried and distraught.

To the nurse he explained, "My kids are all sick with some kind of bug. I know that the doc is too busy for me to bring them all in here, but I wondered if I could bring in one for a sample?"

NANCY CURRY

Walking to work one day, my husband was hit by a car. It was a minor accident and the driver apologised, adding, **"You certainly are lucky. We're right next to a doctor's surgery."**

"I don't know how lucky that is," my husband replied. **"I'm the doctor."**

SANDRA MARCHAND

In the Lamaze childbirth classes I teach, the first hour is a lecture. During the second hour, the couples get on the floor to practice breathing and relaxation techniques. The lecture one evening was "Sex During Pregnancy".

When I finished presenting the material, I asked if there were any questions. After waiting a moment, I tried to proceed – only to be interrupted when the class burst out laughing. It took me a few seconds to realise what I'd said: "Okay, if there are no questions about sex during pregnancy, let's get down on the floor and practice."

NANCY ROMANS

Our house is on the route of a triathlon. Every year my parents invite friends over to sit in the garden and cheer the athletes.

Last year one older runner impressed my father. The man ran by and Dad called out, "I admire your courage!"

Glancing at Dad sitting comfortably in the front garden, the man shouted back, "I admire your wisdom!"

JUDY HALL

When I dislodged two discs in my lower back doing the housework, my friends rallied round and my washing, ironing and cooking were all taken care of. A few days later a friend who is a busy mum came to visit. Surveying all the activity going on around us she leaned towards me and whispered thoughtfully, "Now tell me once again – exactly how were you bending when you tried to move the washing maching?"

CELIA BURROWS

"I know you're a recent graduate, Griswold, but around patients it's advisable to say 'major surgery' – not 'the jackpot'."

An elderly woman in the hospital where I am a nurse managed to keep up her spirits by engaging in friendly banter with the staff. One day while her family was visiting, she looked at the attending nurse and said, "I wonder if one of those fine young men from X-ray came up here and spent the night with me whether it would help my recovery."

The family froze in embarrassment, but the nurse immediately countered, "It probably would, dear – but I doubt your insurance would cover it."

CARY MUNDY

My 60-year-old mother-in-law, completing two years of wearing orthodontic braces, was in the office having them adjusted. As she sat in one of the waiting-room chairs, the teenager next to her looked at my mother-in-law in astonishment. "Wow," he said. "How long have you been coming here?"

DAVID REEVES

As a dentist, I recently tried out a new chocolate-flavoured pumice toothpaste on my patients. No one liked it except for a six-year-old boy. While I polished his teeth, he continued to smile and lick his lips. "You must really like this new flavour," I said.

"I'm prescribing a squiggly line, two slanted loops, and something that looks like a P or a J."

"Yep," he replied, nodding with satisfaction. "It tastes just like the time I dropped my chocolate bar in the sandpit."

JEFFERY LEIBFORTH

After my wife had an ultrascan, I asked my mother-in-law to guess the sex of the twins her daughter was carrying.

"Two boys," she said.

I shook my head.

"It must be two girls," she offered. Again I told her no.

"Well, then," she asked, "what are they?"

F. WATESKA

One of our regular patients at the counselling centre had complained of hearing voices. So the doctor gave him medication. When the man came back for a follow-up, I asked if the prescription helped.

"I don't know," he said. "Now I'm having hallucinations."

"Well, make sure to tell the doctor so he can change the medication."

"I don't know if I want to change," he joked. "Finally, I get to see who's talking to me."

BARBARA ALLEN

My friend was getting increasingly deaf. One day, to my relief, he turned up in a pair of headphones with a large brass microphone attached to the waistcoat. "Do you find it a help?" I bellowed at him.

"Oh yes," he replied, and then added with a knowing look "there are no batteries in, mind you, but when people see it they all speak up."

REVEREND JACKSON

171

Suffering from chest pains, I went to the hospital to have an ECG. After the test I asked the nurse if everything seemed OK, but she said she didn't know and that I'd have to wait for the doctor. "But surely you must have some idea," I insisted.

"All I know," she told me, "is that if there's a straight line, we're in trouble."

RONALD PEARCE

One day at the office of the orthopaedic specialist I work for, we had to make arrangements for an elderly patient with spinal arthritis to have a special injection. We said we would phone him with the information.

Two days later, the patient called us, concerned that he had missed our call because of his poor hearing. "I can barely hear, barely see and barely walk," he told me.

Then he added cheerfully, "Things could be worse, though. At least I can still drive."

ALEX AVALLON

While on duty as a nurse in the obstetrics department at the hospital, I was checking a young mother-to-be. "Is this your first baby?" I asked her.

"Yes," she answered calmly.

"Are you having any contractions or pressure?" I continued.

"No," she stated.

"Are you having any discomfort?"

Again the response was no. Laying my equipment aside, I said, "May I ask you why you're here?"

"Today is my due date!" she replied happily.

SUSAN HOLLIS

At the doctor's office, my mother had to fill out a questionnaire. One question was, **"What kind of exercise do you do?"**

"None," she wrote. The next question read, **"How often do you do it?"** She quickly filled in, **"Every day."**

MELISSA FETTERMAN

"It's a deal – two more years, then we let ourselves go."

One afternoon in the hospital operating theatre where I am a nurse, I heard one of our anaesthetists trying to put a patient to sleep. "Now I want you to breathe in and out," she intoned. "In and out, slowly in and out."

The patient opened her eyes and said, "Is there any other way?"

ANN QUEZADA

When I became a licensed chiropractor, I moved back to my home town and soon had a thriving practice. One morning I saw a new patient whom I recognised as my old headmaster.

"Gosh," I said nervously, "I'm a little surprised to see you here."

"Why?" he replied. "You certainly spent a great deal of time in my office."

D. REGITZ

Standing outside my office during a cigarette break, I was approached by a small boy who asked for a cigarette. He looked no more than 11, so I told him that he wasn't old enough to smoke.

"I'm 16!" he protested.

"You don't look it," I replied. "You're too small."

"It's all the smoking," he persisted. "It's stunted my growth."

KARLA MORRIS

"Great news, Mr. Hopwood. We got it all!"

A friend of mine had resisted efforts to get him to run with our jogging group until his doctor told him he had to exercise. Soon thereafter, he reluctantly joined us for our 5.30am jogs on Mondays, Wednesdays, and Fridays.

After a month of running, we decided that my friend might be hooked, especially when he said he had discovered what "runner's euphoria," was. "Runner's euphoria," he explained, "is what I feel at 5:30 on Tuesdays, Thursdays, and Saturdays."

NEIL BUDGE

For several years, my job was to answer all viewer phone calls and mail concerning the daytime television soap operas our company produced. One day a woman called wanting medical advice from an actor who portrayed a doctor on one of our shows. I explained that

"I'm prescribing a low-carb diet for your diabetes, a high-carb diet for your colon, a low-fat diet for your heart and a high-fat diet for your nerves."

the man wasn't a real doctor and couldn't help her.

After a moment of shocked silence, the woman replied indignantly, "Well, no wonder it takes his patients months to recover!"

SANDY GRANT

At the salon where I was a hairdresser, the conversation turned to smoking and its ill effects on our bodies. Even after hearing one woman reveal that she had survived cancer of the uterus, another customer lit up a cigarette. "Aren't you afraid of getting cancer of the uterus?" she was asked.

"Oh, no, dear," the smoker replied, without batting an eye. "I don't inhale that far down."

MARY ARTERBURNU

With today's focus on exercising, I've been trying to talk my husband into joining me in a 20-minute walk each night. One evening after reading an article called "Brighten Your Sex Life", I felt I had a new argument to present.

I told my husband that, according to what I read, if he just walked 20 minutes a day it would improve his sex life.

He replied, "Who do I know that lives 20 minutes away?"

BONNIE SHORTT

TIMELESS HUMOUR

70s Several months ago, my daughter and I had similar virus symptoms. She decided to consult a doctor so as not to lose any more time from her job. "I'll see the doctor," she said, "and then tell you what's wrong with us."

The next day she called to say, "Guess what, Mum. We're pregnant!"

HOPE SULLIVAN

I was watching a new workout video to prepare myself for an exercise session the next morning.

My husband stuck his head in the room, looked around, and said, **"That would probably work a lot better if you actually did the exercises."**

J. ASHLYNN

As a dental hygienist, I try to relieve my patients' anxiety by going over the procedures before starting. After talking to one patient, a police officer, I asked him if he had any questions.

I must have been a little too graphic in my description, because he replied, "I have just one. I've never given you a ticket, have I?"

W. CRUMPLER

The orthopaedic surgeon I work for was moving to a new consulting room, and his staff was helping transport many of the items. I sat the display skeleton in the front of my car, his bony arm across the back of my seat. I hadn't considered the drive across town.

At one traffic light, the stares of the people in the car beside me became obvious, and I looked across and explained, "I'm delivering him to my doctor's surgery."

The other driver leaned out of his window. "I hate to tell you, madam," he said, "but I think it's too late!"

TRUDY VINEYARD

When an increased patient load began to overwhelm our hospital's emergency department, we initiated a triage system to ensure that the most critical people were treated first. However, some of the less seriously ill patients occasionally had to wait as long as several hours before they could be seen. Complaints were common.

One day, trauma cases abounded, and the wait was particularly long. A police officer came in and approached the reception. "I hate to tell you this," he said apologetically, "but we just got a 999 call from your waiting room."

J. KARGER

When one of my patients came to me complaining of ear trouble, I looked around for the appropriate instrument with which to examine him. Unable to find it, I buzzed my receptionist and asked, "Have you seen my auriscope?"

"No," came the reply. "What sign do you come under?"

J. MANN

175

"I'm going to prescribe something that works like aspirin but costs much, much more."

If anything is sacred the human body is sacred.

WALT WHITMAN

"Vegetarian" is an old Indian word for "doesn't hunt well."

PAUL HARVEY

It's time to diet and exercise when you accept the fact that you can fool some of the people all of the time and all of the people some of the time – but not while you're wearing a bathing suit.

GENE PERRET

I think I have a disease called spontaneous disclosure. I need to tell everyone my life story instantaneously.

KELLY RIPA

Life is one long process of getting tired.

SAMUEL BUTLER

Be careful about reading health books. You may die of a misprint.

MARK TWAIN

Not all chemicals are bad. Without hydrogen and oxygen, for example, there would be no way to make water, a vital ingredient in beer.

DAVE BARRY in The Miami Herald

Housework can't kill you, but why take a chance?

PHYLLIS DILLER

A colleague was planning a trip to my business office and asked if I could find him a hotel with exercise facilities. I called several hotels, with no luck.

Finally I thought I had found one. I asked the receptionist if the hotel had a weight room.

"No," she replied, "but we have a lobby and you can wait there."

SUE GIBSON

One rainy morning, my mother went for her daily run. As she returned to the house, she slipped and fell, hitting her head on the driveway. I called for an ambulance. When they arrived, they asked my mum some questions to determine her coherency. "What is today?" inquired one man.

Without hesitation, Mum replied, "Rubbish day."

J. SWART

I sat in the bus shelter with tears streaming down my face and my eyes red and puffy. An old lady came over and gave me a tissue. Then she sat down beside me.

"He's probably not worth it," she said, putting her arm round my shoulder. "If he's messing you about, you should give him what for." Her bus arrived and, as she got up, she looked me deep in the eyes and said sincerely, "Take care now." She

waved as the bus drove off. I waved back. Then reached into my bag for my hay-fever spray.

PATRICIA SMITH

I often get worried mums bringing babies with rashes into my GP's surgery. On one occasion, the mother told me that the rash appeared most mornings but had usually gone by the afternoon.

I examined the baby and found the problem – a horrible, raised crusted-yellow group of markings. I was about to consult a textbook when a thought came to me. Much

to the mother's horror, I picked off one of the bumps and sniffed it.

The diagnosis was clear. These ugly scaly lesions were, in fact ... Rice Krispies.

DR S. PLUMB

As a new patient, I had to fill out an information form for the GP's files. The receptionist noticed my unusual name. "How do you pronounce it?" she asked.

"Na-le-Y-ko," I said, proud of my Ukranian heritage.

"That sounds really nice," she said, smiling.

"Yes, it's melodious," I agreed.

"So," she enquired sweetly, "what part of Melodia is your family from?"

ANN NALYWAJKO

177

Because of a medical condition, I have to take antibiotics before having dental work done. When my husband and I wanted to start a family, I cancelled my dentist's appointment to avoid any risk the medication might pose.

Weeks later, the dentist's receptionist telephoned me to make another appointment. Unsure of how to tell her my reason for not coming in, I explained, "Well, you see, I'm trying to get pregnant and–"

"Oh, I'm sorry!" she interrupted. "I'll call back later."

ELISABETH SOUTHERN

My friend Kimberly announced that she had started a diet to lose some pounds she had put on recently.

"Good!" I exclaimed. **"I'm ready to start a diet too. We can be dieting buddies and help each other out. When I feel the urge to go out and get a burger and french fries, I'll call you first."**

"Great!" she replied. **"I'll come with you."**

K. FISHER

Immediately after my husband's company built a weightlifting facility for its employees, he and a colleague of his named Jamie joined the programme. Although Jamie dropped out of the programme, my husband continued faithfully.

Several months later, a colleague came up to him and expressed interest in weight training. My husband was flattered that someone had noticed the results of his dedicated effort, until the man exclaimed, "Yeah, I just saw Jamie – and he looks great."

KARLA HANSEN

I'm never very comfortable with any kind of physical test or procedure, but when I was referred to a doctor for a breast exam, I agreed to see him. I don't know the doctor, and he doesn't know me, I told myself. It is no big deal.

On the day of the appointment, I was a little nervous. But the exam went smoothly, and I breathed a sigh of relief when the doctor told me he was finished.

Just as I was about to step out of the office, however, his voice stopped me in my tracks. "By the way," said the doctor, "I really enjoyed your performance at the symphony concert last week!"

MARY KEEZER

My husband met me at the doctor's surgery for my routine checkup, and from there we decided to go out to eat. Since we had driven in separate cars, I arrived at the restaurant first.

"One for dinner?" asked the hostess.

"No," I replied. "There will be two of us in just a minute."

When I saw the panicky look on the hostess's face, I realised I had forgotten about my appearance. Anybody could see that I was at least 8 ½ months pregnant.

L. BURKE

Recovering from knee surgery and the extraction of impacted wisdom teeth, I was lying on the sofa with an ice pack on my leg and hot-water bottles against both cheeks.

From the kitchen I heard my mother cry out in pain. Through a mouth stuffed with gauze I asked her what had happened.

"You know," she replied, "there's nothing worse than a paper cut."

LISA APPLEBAUM

Traditional Chinese drugstores are always filled with bizarre remedies for everyday ailments. So while travelling in the Far East, I couldn't resist going into one to look around. There were rows and rows of jars filled with dried herbs, powders, and exotic oils. But one jar really caught my attention. The label said it was a guaranteed cure for stomach-ache.

The jar was filled with chocolate chip cookies.

F. FLORES

178

"I'm sorry, I thought I could save him, but there was too much paperwork."

A client of our optician's business was jubilant after I replaced the scratched, dirty lenses in his glasses with new ones. "This is great!" he said. "I just gained two hours of daylight."

STEPHANIE BAJOR

While attending a laser seminar for obstetric and gynaecologic surgeons, I found a booth where the doctors were encouraged to practice their laser skills on animal tissues. One young house officer used an excellent technique dissecting a membrane.

"Where did you learn that?" I asked her. "Labs? Seminars? Conferences?"

"No," she replied. "Nintendo!"

ANDY LOPREATO

DOES IT *HURT* WHEN I DO *THIS?*

PHYSIO

The note on the drinks machine in our coffee area warned: "Diet coke isn't working." Beneath that, someone else had written: "Try exercise and a low-carbohydrate diet."

PAUL COOPER

I was in my ninth month of pregnancy and feeling very uncomfortable. On top of everything, my pleas for sympathy seemed to go unnoticed by my husband.

One day I told him, "I hope in your next life you get to be pregnant!"

He replied, "I hope in your next life you get to be married to someone who's pregnant!"

P. COOK

A friend had been working out hard, guided by her Buns of Steel exercise video. When she asked her husband if he thought she was showing any results from all her effort, he wrapped his arms around her, gave a squeeze, and replied, "Sure, honey. You're up to aluminium."

JUDY COUT

For the second time in six weeks I had fallen off my horse and broken some ribs. The doctor in emergency was the same one I had seen previously. As I was about to leave, I jokingly asked, "Is there anything you can recommend for my horse?"

"Another rider," he replied.

CATHERINE LINFIELD

A fellow doctor came up to a nurse I was working with and said "I need to revise the death certificate I just handed you."

"What's wrong?" she asked.

"It's a little embarrassing," he said. Then, pulling her aside, he whispered, "I was in a hurry when I signed it and I accidentally wrote my name under 'Cause of Death'."

LAUREANO AGBISIT

My dad couldn't be more satisfied with his new pacemaker. In fact, he was so happy he insisted on showing me the information sheet about it. Pointing to one particular paragraph, he said excitedly, "Look! It has a lifetime guarantee!"

JIM KRAFT

Seen on a car parked outside a gynaecologist's consulting room: **"PUUUSH."**

CAROLE GROMADZKI

I went to the hospital for an electrocardiogram. While the technician was lining up her machine, I told her I have dextrocardia. "What's that?" she asked.

"It means my heart is on the right side of my chest rather than on the left," I answered. "So you should probably set up your machine to accommodate that."

As she attached the wires, she asked casually, "Tell me, have you had that for long?"

DAWN MCKEAG

A friend had just qualified as a dentist. His first duty at the dental hospital was to carry out routine checks on patients requiring general anaesthetics. After taking a medical history from a very attractive young woman, he asked her to go behind a screen and remove her shirt so that he could listen to her heart and lungs.

When he put his head round the curtain, he found her sitting naked from the waist up. Shy and flustered, he put the stethoscope on one or two places hastily and said, "You're done, you can put your clothes back on."

"Thanks," she replied. "But don't you need to put those things in your ears before you can hear anything?"

VAHEH AVANESSIAN

The minute I walked into the casualty department in my local hospital, I could see the place was packed with patients. The nurses and doctors seemed frazzled. Just how frazzled I discovered when a doctor came into the room, pulled out his light, pointed it in my ear and instructed, "Say, 'Ah'."

KRISTIN EGERTON

A couple we know were in Lamaze class, where they had an activity requiring the husband to wear a bag of sand – to give him an idea of what it feels like to be pregnant. The husband stood up and shrugged, saying, "This doesn't feel so bad."

The teacher then dropped a pen and asked him to pick it up.

"You want me to pick up the pen as if I were pregnant?" he asked.

"Exactly," replied the instructor.

To the delight of the other husbands, he turned to his wife and said, "Sweetie, pick up that pen for me."

S. BOWLING

One evening I was commenting on my bad exercise habits and tight clothes. Whenever I criticise myself, my four-year-old son always has something charming to say.

Using a new word this time, he smiled and said, "Oh, no, Mummy! You look flabulous!"

J. BAILEY

"There are some things they don't teach you in medical school. I think you've got one of those things.

After I warned the nurse taking blood that it would be very hard to find a vein on me, she said, "Don't worry. We've seen worse. Last year we had a girl come in to get a blood test and we had to stick her six times in four places before we got anything."

"Yes, I know," I said. "That was me!"

CONNIE DOWN

While walking through an airport, my dentist ran into a group of people he knew. Among them was one of his patients.

When he said hello, she gave him a curious stare, saying he looked familiar but she could not quite place him. "Lean back and look up at me," my dentist suggested. She did. "Oh! Mr Harrison!"

GEORGE JUST

When my wife called a friend on our touch-tone phone, the line was busy. She tried several more times, but without success. Watching her, I asked why she wasn't using the redial button.

"Darling," she answered, "I need the exercise."

HENRY POLITZER

Does it hurt?

It's sort of a shooting pain.

Reynolds

I was lying on my sofa, burning up with a fever, when my husband said I should go to bed. At three o'clock the next morning, I woke up soaked from head to toe. When my husband heard me stirring, he said that my fever must have broken.

I decided to spend the rest of the night back on the sofa so as not to disturb him any further. But then, three hours later, he appeared in the living room soaking wet. "Your fever didn't break," he said, still dripping. "The water bed did."

SUSAN BARR

There is a woman at my health club who always begins her workout with sit-ups and leg-lifts. One afternoon she entered the exercise room and, as usual, lay down on the slant board as if she were about to do sit-ups. This time, though, she did none. Instead, she turned around on the board and positioned herself for leg-lifts.

Again she stayed there for several moments without doing a single exercise. Finally she got up and headed out of the room. As she walked past me, she said, "Thinking about it was enough for today."

STEPHEN CAUBLE

Throughout her pregnancy, my sister Joanne insisted that she wanted no medication during labour. When the big day came, though, she wondered if she had made the right decision.

Knowing my sister's stance on drugs, the midwife did everything else to ease Joanne's pain. "You look uncomfortable," she said at one point. "Would you like to change positions?"

"Yes," Joanne replied. "I want to be the midwife!"

REBECCA WOODWORTH

I was queueing up in the cafeteria of the hospital where I work when I overheard a doctor ask an anaesthetist how his day was. **"Good,"** came the response. **"Everyone's woken up so far."**

JENNA GALAZEN

Panicking when her two-year-old swallowed a tiny magnet, my friend Phyllis rushed him to casualty.

"He'll be fine," the doctor promised. "The magnet will pass through his system in a day or two."

"How will I be sure?" she pressed.

"Well," the doctor suggested, "you could stick him on the fridge and when he falls off, you'll know."

MARIE THIBODEAU

My father is an early riser who likes to keep in shape. Every morning he sprints from our house to the bus stop.

One evening he overheard a man in the pub telling a friend, "There's a chap in our road who has to run for the bus every morning. He'd save himself a lot of trouble if he just got out of bed five minutes earlier."

BRUCE MACDONALD

I love the e-mail exchanges I have with our medical-transcription trainees from India. They use such beautiful, flowery language.

"With God's grace and you at the helm, I will endeavour to succeed on the road to perfection," wrote one man when he sent in his work.

I responded with a thank-you and three pages of corrections, which elicited another e-mail from him. "I see the road to perfection is longer than anticipated."

KATHRYN MOORE

While my friend Cheryl was working as a receptionist for a private eye surgeon, a very angry woman stormed up to her desk. She complained that someone had stolen her wig while she had been undergoing surgery the previous day. The doctor came out and tried to calm her down. He assured her that no one on the staff would have done such a thing and asked why she thought the wig had been taken from the clinic. The woman said that after the operation she noticed the wig she had on looked ugly and cheap.

"I think," explained the surgeon gently, "that means your cataract operation was a success."

RAHEELA SHAIKH

Sitting in the doctor's surgery, I noticed one of the receptionists licking and sealing a large stack of envelopes. Two of her colleagues were doing their best to persuade her to use a damp sponge instead. One woman said that she could get a paper cut. Another suggested that it might make her sick. However, she insisted on doing it her own way.

As I was leaving, I mentioned to the receptionist that there was a tenth of a calorie in the glue of one envelope. Then I saw her rummaging round for the sponge.

DOROTHY MCDANIEL

183

TIMELESS HUMOUR

60s My daughter, a lover of rich foods, is on a strenuous reducing diet. While shopping with her recently, I noticed her staring admiringly at a woman who was all skin and bones.

"Gosh, I'd like to have a figure like that!" my daughter exclaimed.

"Oh no!" I said. "You wouldn't want to be that skinny."

"No, but it would be wonderful to start with that and eat it up to a good figure."

J.W.

Miracle cures

One Tuesday in May the general's widow, Martha Pechonkina, who has been a practising homeopath for ten years, is seeing patients in her surgery. On the table in front of her is a box of homeopathic remedies, a medical dictionary, and some bills from a homeopathic chemist. On the wall hang letters from a certain Petersburg homeopath who, in Pechonkina's opinion, is a great and noteworthy man. Patients sit and wait in the vestibule. Most of them are peasants, and all but two or three are barefoot, as the widow Pechonkin has made them leave their stinking boots outside.

The door opens, and into the surgery comes the lady's neighbour, an impoverished landowner named Kuzma Kuzmich Zamukhrishin. He is a little old man with sour eyes and a cap under his arm. He stands his stick in the corner, walks up to the lady, and without a word falls on one knee before her.

"Kuzma Kuzmich, what on earth are you doing?" she exclaims in alarm, "For goodness sake!"

"I'll not rise while I live," says Zamukhrishin, pressing his forehead to her hand. "Let the world see me on my knees, my guardian angel. I'll do more than kneel for you, the good fairy who has shown me the true path and shone her light on my unbelief – I'll go through fire. Because I'm well again. You have resurrected me."

"Well, I'm ... very glad," mumbles the lady, blushing with pleasure. "Do sit down. You were quite ill last Tuesday."

"I was so sick, it's terrible to recall," says Zamukhrishin, taking a seat. "Rheumatism in every organ of my body. It's been eight years of torture. I've been to doctors, I went to professors in Kazan. I've taken mud-baths and drunk waters. But doctors did me nothing but harm. They drove the sickness inwards, but with all their know-how they couldn't drive it out. I'd be in my grave now if it weren't for you. I looked at those granules you gave me last Tuesday and thought:

'What's the use of them?' But I took one – and straight away it was as if I'd never been ill. My wife couldn't believe her eyes. 'Is that you?' she said. 'Yes, me,' said I."

Zamukhrishin wipes his eyes with his sleeve, and looks ready to go back down on his knees – but the lady stops him.

"Don't thank me," she says. "I am just the obedient instrument. But it really is miraculous – eight years of rheumatism, and just one granule."

"Actually you gave me three granules. The first I took at lunch – and straight away! I took the second that evening, and the last one the next day. Not a twinge since! Last Tuesday I could barely walk and now I could race a hare! Only thing is: what good is health if you have nothing to live on? Poverty is even more burdensome than illness. I mean, I should be sowing oats now, but there's no money for seed ... "

"I'll give you oats, Kuzma Kuzmich. You have made me so

Anton Chekhov, *Malingerers*

happy, I should be thanking you."

"That the Lord should send us such a blessing. You should rejoice in your own goodness, dear lady. As for us sinners, we have no call to rejoice. I mean, our homes are a farce – the roof leaks and we can't afford to buy planks to repair it .... "

"I'll give you some planks, Kuzma Kuzmich."

In addition, Zamukhrishin extracts the promise of a cow, and a letter of recommendation for his daughter, who is off to boarding school. Touched by the widow's generosity, he reaches into his pocket for his handkerchief. She sees a red slip of paper come out with the handkerchief, and fall silently to the floor. " ... I'll never forget this. I'll make my children remember it, and my children's children ... "

After seeing her patient out, the general's widow – her eyes full of tears – takes a moment to look around at the box, the dictionary, the bills, the chair in which the man she saved from death was just sitting. Then her gaze falls on the paper he dropped. She picks it up, unfolds it, and sees three granules – the very ones she gave him last Tuesday. "He didn't even unwrap it ... "

And for the first time in ten years, an element of doubt enters Martha's soul. As she treats her other patients, she notices something that hitherto has always passed her by. All of them praise her medical wisdom to the skies, curse doctors in general, and then – as soon as she is blushing with excitement – they put in their requests: a bit of land to plough, some wood, permission to hunt in her forests ... A new truth begins to gnaw at the lady's soul, a cruel, hard truth.

People are such liars.

My friend Esther told me about her son's career day, where the children were asked, "Who knows what a psychiatrist does?"

Esther's son replied, "That's someone who asks you to lie down on a couch and then blames everything on your mother."

CARLA GATES

Following a big storm, my husband worked long hours clearing the jumble of trees that littered our property. The longer he worked, however, the more painful it became for him to move his right arm.

He ignored my pleas to see the doctor until one night he yelped, "Ow! This is getting serious." As I turned to him in concern, he added, "Now it hurts to push buttons on the remote control!"

WENDY CLAY

The clinic where I work promoted a colleague to head the payroll department, or Payment Management Systems. The title on his door now reads "PMS Director".

MARILYN PEARSALL

While I was a nurse on a geriatric ward I contacted laryngitis and completely lost my voice. As many of my patients were

"You're looking well."

deaf this caused some difficulty.

I wanted one old lady to change her position so she didn't get bed sores. After numerous failed attempts at verbal communication, I wrote her a note: "Please roll over." She glanced at it and said, "You'll have to read it to me, dear, I haven't got my glasses on."

AUDREY MCCLELLAND

During a visit to see my mother in hospital, I popped into the cafeteria for breakfast. I set a piece of bread on the moving toaster rack and waited for it to return golden brown. Instead, it got stuck all the way at the back. When I couldn't reach it, the woman in line next to me took control of the situation. Seizing a pair of tongs, she reached in and deftly fished out the piece of

toast. "You must be an emergency-department worker," I joked.

"No," she said, "an obstetrician."

DONALD GEISER

During the year that my husband, Bob, was undergoing expensive dental reconstruction, he got to know everyone in the dentist's surgery. When a couple of members of staff teased him about his garbled speech after he got a mouth-numbing anaesthetic, Bob replied, "Well, it's hard to talk with £3000 in your mouth."

MARY MATHIS

TIMELESS HUMOUR

60s Resting in the hospital after the birth of our third child, I thought I would finally get a chance to finish reading Boris Pasternak's famous novel, Doctor Zhivago, and had it handy on my bedside table.

When the student nurse came in, it caught her eye and she looked at it sceptically. "If you want the real low-down on baby care," she said confidentially, "you can't beat Doctor Spock."

MRS. DAVID LYCHE

Since maternity patients at the small hospital where I work must travel 50 miles to another hospital for the actual delivery, they often check with us first to verify that they are, indeed, in labour.

One morning, a pregnant woman walked in, and we confirmed that delivery was definitely imminent. So a nurse called her husband at home, getting him out of bed. "Your wife's about to give birth," she told him. "You need to go to the hospital."

"Okay," he said groggily. "I'll wake her up and tell her."

ROSALIE DEAN

Employed as a dental receptionist, I was on duty when an extremely nervous patient came in for root-canal surgery. He was brought into the examining room and made comfortable in the reclining dental chair. The dentist then injected a numbing agent around the patient's tooth, and left the room for a few minutes while the medication took hold.

When the dentist returned, the patient was standing next to a tray of dental equipment. "What are you doing by the surgical instruments?" asked the surprised dentist.

Focused on his task, the patient replied, "I'm taking out the ones I don't like."

PAULA FONTAINE

As we left the gym after our first real workout in years, my husband and I both felt energised. "Let's renew our commitment to do it three times a week," I said.

"Absolutely," my husband agreed, "three times as a minimum."

"And no whining," I said. "No excuses."

"No, we'll do it with energy and enthusiasm."

"And on my late night, we can just meet here at the gym."

"The gym?" my husband said, crestfallen. "I thought we were talking about sex!"

LINDA JOHNSON

A friend of mine was working as a nurse in a West Australian coastal town when a tourist came into the medical centre with a fishhook lodged deep in his hand. Since it was the weekend, my friend had to summon the doctor from home.

The tourist was dismayed to see that the doctor was young, had long hair and wore sandals and a very casual shirt. "You don't look much like a doctor to me," he said dubiously.

The doctor examined the hook in the tourist's hand and responded, "And you don't look much like a fish to me."

MARION O'LEARY

**"You are in a deep, deep sleep.
When you awaken you will feel sweaty and exhausted."**

"I'm afraid you have ... Oh, what's that thing called
when you can't remember stuff ... "

A member of a diet club bemoaned her lack of will-power. She'd made her family's favourite cake over the weekend, she explained, and they'd eaten half of it. The next day, however, the uneaten half beckoned. She cut herself a slice. Then another, and another. By the time she'd polished off the cake, she knew her husband would be disappointed.

"What did he say when he found out?" one club member asked.

"He never found out," she said. "I made another cake and ate half."

HUSAIN ALI

Butch, our boxer, hated taking his medicine. After a lot of trial and error my father eventually figured out the simplest way to get it into him: blow it down Butch's throat with something called a pill tube. So Dad put the large tablet in one end of the tube, forced the reluctant dog's jaws open, and poked the other end into his mouth.

Then, just as my father inhaled to blow, Butch coughed. A startled look appeared on Dad's face. He opened his eyes wide and swallowed hard. "I think I've just been de-wormed," he gasped.

JOHN ROBERTSON

One of our patients wasn't taking any chances. Prior to her operation, she stuck cautionary notes all over her body for the surgeon: "Take your time", "Don't cut yourself", "No need to rush", "Wash your hands", etc.

As I helped her back into her bed after surgery, we discovered a new note stuck to her, this one from the surgeon: "Has anyone seen my watch?"

A. ALLEN

During her time as a student nurse, my wife was lucky enough to work with an eminent surgeon. Halfway through one operation, and completely engrossed in what was going on, she realised the surgeon was talking to her. "Nurse, would you please answer my pager," he growled. "It's beeped twice now."

Slightly flustered, she began patting up and down the front of his gown to retrieve it, much to the amusement of the theatre staff. As she groped around his waist in embarrassment, the great man stopped what he was doing and glared down. "Nurse," he said, "Loathe as I am to stop you, my pager is on the table."

CHRIS GRIFFITHS

Hypochondriac that I am, I constantly log on to the Internet to self-diagnose my latest ailment. But even I knew it was time to lighten up the day I searched using the key words liver disorders.

This led me to a medical website. With growing alarm, I realised I had each of the first seven symptoms. Then I came to the eighth and suddenly felt much better: "Feeling of lethargy. No longer enjoys romping and wagging tail."

DEBORA DAWSON

Although I was only a few pounds overweight, my wife was harping on at me to diet. One evening we took a brisk walk, and I surprised her by jumping over a parking meter, leapfrog style. Pleased with myself, I said, "How many fat men do you know who can do that?"

"One," she retorted.

R. MCLAURY

Hoping to lose some weight, my wife told me she wanted to get an exercise bicycle. I reminded her that she had a very nice and rather expensive bike in the garage. She explained that she wanted a stationary one.

"Your bicycle has been stationary," I remarked. "That's why you need to lose weight."

JIM WHITE

It had been a long time – seven years to be exact – since my friend Brian had been to see his doctor. So the nurse told him that if he wanted to make an appointment, he would have to be reprocessed as a new patient.

"Okay," said Brian, "reprocess me."

"I'm sorry," she told him. "We're not accepting any new patients."

BARBARA SAMPSON

A vet sent one of his employees to get a flat tyre repaired in the tyre store that I own. When I asked which tyre needed to be fixed, he replied, "Hind left."

GLENN RYE

My friend read her son's horoscope and thought it quite appropriate. "You've spent the last few weeks looking for escape," it said. "But now it's time to get on with your life."

She had just given birth to him that morning.

SUYEE KAOR

189

"The good news is we're pretty sure we're going to name this disease after you."

We took our newborn son to the paediatrician for his first check-up. As he finished, the doctor told us, "You have a cute baby."

Smiling, I said, "I bet you say that to all new parents."

"No," he replied, "just to those whose babies really are good-looking."

"So what do you say to the others?" I asked.

"He looks just like you."

MATT SLOT

My mother and my wife – both nurses – were shopping together when a woman in a nearby dressing room fell unconscious. Mum discovered that the woman wasn't breathing, so she and my wife started CPR and revived the shopper just as paramedics arrived.

They loaded the woman onto a gurney and were rolling her out of the shop when she yelled, "Stop!" My mother and my wife thought maybe she wanted to thank them, but instead she said, "I still want to buy those dresses."

JOSEPH O'CONNOR

My husband bought an exercise machine to help him shed a few pounds. He set it up in the basement but didn't use it much, so he moved it to the bedroom. It gathered dust there, too, so he put it in the living room.

Weeks later I asked how it was going. "I was right," he said. "I do get more exercise now. Every time I close the curtains, I have to walk around the machine."

P. OLSON

Although I knew I had put on a few pounds, I didn't consider myself overweight until the day I decided to clean my refrigerator. I sat on a chair in front of the appliance and reached in to wipe the back wall.

While I was in this position, my teenage son came into the kitchen.

"Hi Mum," he said. "Whatcha doin', having lunch?" I started my diet that day.

B. STROHM

I am a sister in a hospital. A woman bedecked in expensive jewellery came into my ward for surgery. Before her operation I itemised the rings, necklaces and bracelets and locked them in our safe. After the woman was discharged, she came into my office to collect the valuables. Tipping them all on to my desk, I checked off the items against my list, but found one gold earring was not mentioned.

"Do you only wear one earring?" I asked the woman as she looked on silently.

"That, my dear," answered the woman, "is a drawing pin."

JENNY CUNNINGHAM

At the hospital where my wife is an X-ray technician, patients hit the "call light" to get a nurse's attention. To underline the need to respond rapidly, a snappy catchphrase was created and printed on badges.

But the campaign came to an abrupt halt. The staff feared that patients might misunderstand if nurses entered their rooms wearing a button that read "Go to the Light!"

JAMES PARK

190

191

To confirm her suspicions, my sister needed to purchase a pregnancy test. Since I was going to the chemist, she asked me to pick one up. I didn't stop to think how I appeared to the shop assistant when I waddled up – nine months pregnant – to pay for the kit.

"Well," she said, "I can save you money right now. You're definitely going to have a baby."

ESTHER ERBLICH

My diminutive aunt Flora, just four feet nine inches tall, accepted an offer to visit a health club for a free session. After being greeted heartily, she was shown where she could change and told an instructor would soon be with her.

Having changed her clothes, Aunt Flora went back to the exercise area. Along one wall she noticed a silver bar that was not in use, and decided to try her hand at chin-ups while she waited. She jumped up, barely reaching the bar, and managed to strain through two chin-ups before the instructor came to her side.

Smiling politely, the instructor said, "If you want to let go of the coat rack and follow me, I'll be glad to help you get started."

M. MCQUEEN

I discussed peer pressure and cigarettes with my 12-year-old daughter. Having struggled for years to quit, I described how I had started smoking to "be cool".

As I outlined the arguments kids might make to tempt her to try it, she stopped me mid-lecture, saying, "Hey, I'll just tell them my mum smokes. How cool can it be?"

JUDI MOORE

During a visit to my doctor for a routine medical, I was impressed by his thoroughness. As the medical came to an end he asked me if I had a problem with my back. When I replied that I did not, he said "Good. You can bend down

and pull those weighing scales out from under the desk. My back is killing me."

PETER MARSHALL

"Don't you hate it when there are parts left over?"

Nearing 40 and woefully out of shape, I resolved to buy a bicycle and begin an exercise regime. As I browsed in the bike shop, a young, athletic-looking assistant approached. "What do you have for a fat old lady with a big, tender posterior who hasn't ridden in years?" I asked.

He didn't even blink. "Well, why don't you bring her in, and we'll see what we can do," he said, clinching the sale.

KAREN BATEMAN

With five kids at home and one more on the way, I wasn't quite sure what to think when I was assigned the following password for my computer at work: "iud4u."

CAROLYN THOMAS

When a woman called 999 complaining of difficulty breathing, my husband, Glenn, and his partner – both ambulancemen – rushed to her home. Glenn placed a sensor on her finger to measure her pulse and blood oxygen. Then he began to gather her information. "What's your age?" he asked.

"Fifty-eight," answered the patient, eyeing the beeping device on her finger. "What does that do?"

"It's a lie detector," said Glenn with a straight face. "Now, what did you say your age was?"

"Sixty-seven," answered the woman sheepishly.

SARAH SCHAFER

As a lawyer in a major law firm, I have many colleagues who work long hours. However, the reputation of one of my partners' workaholic ways even extended beyond the office. He not only had to leave work early one day because of a medical problem, but was also told by his doctor to stay home until the end of the week. My colleague grudgingly agreed to comply.

In the middle of the week, our receptionist received a call for him. She announced that the partner was out of the office until Friday. "Good," the caller said. "That's all I wanted to know."

It was my partner's doctor.

D. D.

While on duty in the maternity ward, I had a patient who had to undergo a Caesarean section.

After the operation I gave the patient her child and told her she had a healthy baby boy. Still groggy from the anaesthetic, she replied, "Great. What's his name?"

WENDY REYNOLDS

After noticing how trim my husband had become, a friend asked me how I had persuaded him to diet. It was then I shared my dark secret: "I put our teenage son's pants in his underwear drawer."

RUTH LUHRS

Television remote controls encourage couch potatoes to exercise their options while broadening their base.

WILLIAM ARTHUR WARD

Happiness is good health and a bad memory.

INGRID BERGMAN

I don't work out. If God wanted us to bend over, he'd put diamonds on the floor.

JOAN RIVERS

Time is the great physician.

BENJAMIN DISRAELI

The problem with the gene pool is there's no lifeguard.

STEVEN WRIGHT

For sleep, riches and health to be truly enjoyed, they must be interrupted.

JEAN PAUL RICHTER

The only way to keep your health is to eat what you don't want, drink what you don't like, and do what you'd druther not.

MARK TWAIN

When my generation was your age, we took crazy risks. The wildest thing was – prepare to be shocked – we deliberately ingested carbohydrates!

DAVE BARRY

Pregnant with our second child, I was determined to ride my exercise bike at least two miles a day. Late one night, having put it off all day, I climbed aboard the noisy contraption in our bedroom, where my husband was reading a book.

After about 20 minutes of listening to the squeaky machine, he glanced up, somewhat annoyed. "Don't you think it's time you turned around and headed for home?" he asked.

MARGARET KOCH

I was in a department store when I heard on the public-address system that the optical department was offering free ice cream. I headed down the escalator to take advantage of the offer, trying to decide on vanilla or chocolate. I was nearly drooling when I got to the optical section and said to the assistant, "I'm here for my ice cream."

"Ice cream?" came the reply. "Sorry. What we have is a free eye screening."

ROSEANNE BARNETT

Needing to shed a few pounds, my husband and I went on a diet that had specific recipes for each meal of the day. I followed the instructions closely, dividing the finished recipe in half for our individual plates. We felt terrific and thought the diet was wonderful – we never felt hungry!

But when we realised we were gaining weight, not losing it, I checked the recipes again. There, in fine print, was "Serves 6".

BARBARA CURRIE

As a nurse, I was accompanying a surgeon while he visited his hospital patients. One of the patients we checked on had a hernia operation three days earlier. The doctor asked the man why he hadn't yet got out of bed.

"I'm sore," was the reply. "You don't know how it feels."

"I know exactly how it feels," the doctor answered briskly. "I had the same treatment last month, and I was back at work two days later. There's no difference in our operations."

"Yes, there is," replied the patient. "You had a different surgeon."

B. CLEMENTZ

ANXIETY CLINIC

ONE THING   THE OTHER

A friend got into a hospital lift with a porter who was wheeling an elaborate machine. The device had several pipes, dials and gauges. My friend remarked that she would hate to be connected to such a machine.

"So would I," replied the porter. "It's a carpet shampooer."

CHARLES BARRON

As a dental hygienist, I had a family come in one day for cleanings. By the time I was ready for the father, he informed me I had a lot to live up to. His six-year-old daughter kept commenting that a "very smart lady" was cleaning their teeth today.

The father said she kept going on about my intelligence until he finally had to ask what she was basing her opinion on.

The little girl replied, "I heard people in here call her the Dental High Genius."

BARBARA GIVENS

At the age of 64 my uncle had to have a wisdom tooth removed. What was supposed to be a simple extraction proved to be a four-hour ordeal.

As my uncle, pale and a bit unsteady, prepared to leave the dentist's surgery, the attractive young receptionist expressed her concern. "Would you like me to walk home with you?" she asked.

He considered the offer carefully. "Not today," he said, "but maybe sometime when I'm feeling better."

WILLIAM HARTMAN

In an attempt to keep our rowdy class focused, our teacher was giving us random facts about the body's ability to burn calories. "Kissing," she said, "can burn up to 45 calories."

"Hey," a boy called out, "any of you girls want to lose weight?"

STEPHANIE FEIST

As an X-ray technician, I always ask female patients of childbearing age if they are pregnant before I proceed. I've received many responses, but my favourite was when a young woman looked at me with a straight face and replied, "If I am, it isn't mine!"

K. DARRELL

On a recent visit to my brother's, I witnessed conclusive proof that the sick male of the species can be a very self-indulgent sort.

My brother had a cold and was lying on the sofa while his wife saw to his every need. At one point she made him a rather weak hot toddy.

After taking a big gulp, he fixed her with a steely look. "Sweetheart," he said, as he reached for the brandy bottle, "I'm much sicker than that."

ALISTAIR DODD

My daughter couldn't muster the willpower to lose weight. One day, watching a svelte friend walking up our driveway, she lamented, "Linda's so skinny it makes me sick."

"If it bothers you," I suggested gently, "why don't you do something about it?"

"Good idea," she replied. Turning back, she called out, "Hey Linda, do you want some chocolate cake?"

D. FLETCHER

SIGN LANGUAGE

A Navy dentist's licence plate:

"TOP GUM."

Our local newspaper ran several stories about a study that tied male obesity to a virus. One evening my brother came in exhausted from a long day at work. **"Did you read the paper?"** he asked. **"I won't be going in to work tomorrow. I'm calling in fat."**

MARY LEANDERTS

Mother and I were discussing our mutual weight problem one evening, when I challenged her to a contest. If I lost the most weight in the next month, I wouldn't have to pay her the money that I owed her. If she lost the most weight, I would have to pay up. Anything for an incentive!

"All right," said Mother happily. "But let's wait two weeks before we start. There are some things I have to eat first."

IRENE LANE

While I waited in our school nurse's office, I overheard another student explain to the nurse how badly his eyes hurt. "My head is spinning," he moaned, "and I can't see straight."

After listening to his ailments for ten minutes, even the often-sceptical nurse was convinced. "I am calling your mother to come and pick you up," she said, dialling the telephone.

"Oh, that won't be necessary," the student instantly replied. "I can drive myself home."

L. BATEMAN

"Chest pains? Have you tried loosening your belt?"

The new phone book arrived with a handy blank emergency-number form attached to the front page. I guess everyone's notion of an emergency is different. The categories for phone numbers were listed in this order: 1. Pizza, 2. Takeaway Restaurants, 3. Taxi, 4. Poison Control, 5. Doctor.

MEGHAN HUNSAKER

198

Customer-service reps repeat the same tired phrases so often that we can do the job in our sleep. We hear a beep telling us a customer's on the line and we're away.

I never knew how this humdrum routine affected us until a colleague had heart surgery. She was coming to after her operation when she heard the beep of the heart monitor. In her anaesthetised stupor, she groggily said, "This is Sue. Can I help you?"

S.B.

A customer walked into my pharmacy asking for a particular nasal spray. "You know, that brand is very addictive," I warned her. "If it's used for a prolonged period of time, your congestion can come back worse than before, prompting even further use."

"That's ridiculous," scoffed the woman. "I've been using it every day for years."

CHARLES FREED

The orthodontist and his assistants were removing my ten-year-old son's brace.

Because it was cemented to his upper teeth, they had to use some pressure to release it.

When it finally popped out, three of his baby teeth came out as well. My boy was horrified when he saw the gaps. "Oh dear," he said to the staff gathered around him, "who do I see about getting dentures?"

KIM JAWORSKI

We were on our way to the hospital where our 15-year-old daughter was scheduled to undergo a tonsillectomy. During the drive we talked about how the procedure would be performed. "Dad," our teenager asked, "how are they going to keep my mouth open during the surgery?"

"They're going to give you a phone," my husband replied.

VALERIE HUGHES

The voice-dictation programme a doctor friend of mine purchased for his computer often misinterpreted words. Once, my friend dictated, "Recommend CAT scan if symptoms persist."

The program typed out, "Recommend casket if symptoms persist."

JASON SUROW

All creatures great and small

We live with them and we love them, even when they are up to no good.
Here are those funny moments when animals and humans cross paths.

A man is standing on the kerb, getting ready to cross the street. As soon as he steps down from the pavement, a car comes screaming down the road, heading straight towards him. The man picks up speed, but so does the car. So the man turns around and dashes back, but the car changes lanes and keeps coming. Now the vehicle is really close and the pedestrian is so scared that he freezes in the middle of the road. The car bears down on him, then swerves at the last possible moment and screeches to a halt.

The driver rolls down the window. Behind the wheel is a squirrel. "See," sneers the squirrel, "it's not as easy as it looks, is it?"

In good weather, my friend Mark always let his yellow-naped Amazon parrot, Nicky, sit on the balcony of his tenth-floor flat. One morning, Nicky flew away, much to Mark's dismay. He searched and called for the bird, with no luck.

The next day when Mark returned from work, the phone rang. "Is this Mark?" the caller asked. "You're going to think this is crazy, but there's a bird outside on my balcony saying, 'Hello, this is Mark.' Then it recites this phone number and says, 'I can't come to the phone right now, but if you will leave a message at the tone, I will call you back.'"

Nicky's cage had been kept in the same room as Mark's answering machine.

ANNE NEILSON

One beautiful morning, my husband and I decided to go for a drive in the country. Unfortunately, no matter which road we took, we kept seeing dead rabbits lying on the verge and in the road.

After several miles of this, my husband turned to me and said, "Now I think I know the answer to the age-old question 'Why did the chicken cross the road?'"

"What is it?" I asked.

"Well," he replied, "it was to prove to the rabbits that it could be done."

J. PAGE

My father's secretary was visibly distraught one morning when she arrived at the office and explained that her children's parrot had escaped from his cage and flown out an open window. Of all the dangers the tame bird would face outdoors alone, she seemed most concerned about what would happen if the bird started talking.

Confused, my father asked what the parrot could say.

"Well," she explained, "he mostly says, 'Here, kitty, kitty.'"

TERRY WALKER

When my daughter and I caught only one fish on our fishing trip – not enough for even a modest lunch – we decided to feed it to her two cats. She put our catch in their dish and watched as the two pampered pets sniffed at the fish but refused to eat it.

Thinking quickly, my daughter then picked up the dish, walked over to the electric can opener, ran it for a few seconds, then put the fish back down. The cats dug right in.

SUSAN WARD

201

Once while on the bus to work, I noticed a man at a stop enjoying a cup of coffee. As we approached the stop, he finished drinking and put the cup on the ground. This negligence surprised me, since it seemed to be a good ceramic cup.

Days later I saw the same man again drinking his coffee at the bus stop. Once again, he placed the cup on the ground before boarding. When the bus pulled away, I looked back in time to see a dog carefully carrying the cup in his mouth as he headed for home.

VALERIE HUEBNER

At a workshop on dog temperament, the instructor noted that a test for a canine's disposition was for an owner to fall down and act hurt. A dog with poor temperament would try to bite the person, whereas a good dog would lick his owner's face or show concern.

Once, while eating pizza in the living room, I decided to try out this theory on my two dogs. I stood up, clutched my heart, let out a scream and collapsed on the floor.

The dogs looked at me, glanced at each other and raced to the coffee table for my pizza.

SUSAN MOTTICE

A snake slithers into a bar and the bartender says, **"Sorry, buddy. I can't serve you."**

"Why not?" the snake asks.

"Because you can't hold your liquor."

L. LEATHERMAN

202

"I wasn't chewing it, I was editing it."

"George! NO! Your cholesterol."

"Have someone force one of these down your throat every six hours."

Reaching the end of a stay with my friend in South Africa, I called South African Airways to confirm my flight back to the UK.

During the conversation I was asked for my phone number, but I didn't know it and since I was alone in the house, had no one to ask.

"Hang on," I said, suddenly remembering that the telephone number was written on my friend's dog's collar. "I'll just go and get the dog." I returned to the phone to sounds of laughter.

"What did the dog say?" asked the telephonist.

DUNCAN COADE

Working at an animal rescue centre, I received a phone call from a pensioner who said she had found a baby hedgehog that appeared to be ill and needed picking up. I told her to encourage it to drink water and keep it warm until I arrived. When I got to the woman's house, she handed over a shoe box with the creature inside. The woman was very worried because she'd tried to give it some water but it didn't seem interested.

I looked in the box and saw a small brown shape wrapped in a tea towel with a saucer of water next to it. I thanked the lady and took the box away without ever telling her that she had lovingly rescued a conker.

EMMA SPICER

A man walks into a pub with a salamander on his shoulder and takes a seat at the bar.

"Nice pet," the bartender says. "What's his name?"

"I call him Tiny," the man replies.

"Why's that?"

"Because he's my newt."

BARNEY WELLS

A woman and a dog that was clearly out of control hurtled into our vet's surgery. Spotting a training video that we sell, the dog's owner wisely decided to buy one.

"How does it work?" she asked me. "Do I just make him watch it?"

BRANDI CHYTKA

SIGN LANGUAGE

Seen in a local paper:
"Ferret, likes kids, nice pet, but chewed the guinea pig's ear off.
Also, partially deaf guinea pig."

BILL PORTER

A lorry shot through a red light, almost sideswiping our car.

As my husband veered away, he threw his arm across me, protecting me from a possible collision.

I was ready to plant a big kiss on my hero's cheek when he apologised. In his haste, he admitted, he had forgotten it was me in the front seat and not our black Labrador, Checkers.

APRIL COLE

I worked at a boarding kennel where people leave their dogs and cats while on holiday. One morning I had taken a cat out of his cage, and after playing with him and replenishing his food and water, I put him back in.

A few minutes later, I was surprised to see the feline at my feet, since the cage doors lock automatically when they're shut. I couldn't figure out how the cat escaped, until I bent down to pick him up and spied his nametag: "Houdini".

BARBARA ROHRSSEN

Sitting in the vet's waiting room with my dog on my lap, I noticed that his tail was slapping the man sitting next to me.

"I'm sorry," I apologised, "there must be a bit of a greyhound in him." Just then the waiting room door opened and a person with a rabbit came in.

"Looks like we're about to find out for sure," commented the man.

ELIZABETH SIMPSON

In his younger days our golden retriever, Catcher, often ran away when he had the chance. The vet's surgery was about a mile down the road, and Catcher would usually end up there. The surgery staff knew him well and would call me to come pick him up.

One day I called the vet to make an appointment for Catcher's yearly injection. "Will you be bringing him?" asked the receptionist. "Or will he be coming on his own?"

LAURA STASZAK

205

"How can I ever live up to all this hype?"

If dogs could talk, it would take a lot of fun out of owning one.

ANDREW A. ROONEY, from "Not That You Asked" (Random House)

I feel strongly that the visual arts are of vast importance. Of course I could be prejudiced. I am a visual art.

KERMIT THE FROG

You know why fish are so thin? They eat fish.

JERRY SEINFELD

A racehorse is an animal that can take several thousand people for a ride at the same time.

MARJORIE JOHNSON

Does it ever amaze and delight you that of all the places in the world – cold grassy nests under hedgerows, warm patches of sun on a carpet – the cat chooses to sit on your lap?

NEVADA BARR, Seeking Enlightenment (Putnam)

The cat could very well be man's best friend but would never stoop to admitting it.

DOUG LARSON, United Feature Syndicate

Man is the only animal that blushes. Or needs to.

MARK TWAIN

The turkey is living proof that an animal can survive with no intelligence at all.

HARVEY D. COMSTOCK

At the end of a visit to Amsterdam, a friend borrowed an old suitcase from his hosts to carry home his souvenirs. At the airport, however, a customs officer subjected our friend's luggage to a thorough search and even sent for a drug-sniffing dog. Sure enough, the dog entered the area, headed straight for the borrowed bag and went into a frenzy. The customs officer now intensified his search, but ultimately he found nothing.

After arriving home, the young man immediately phoned his hosts and told them how puzzled he'd been by the dog's behaviour.

"Perhaps," the owner of the suitcase said, "it was because that's the bag our cat usually sleeps in."

J. RIETDIJK-SHEPHERD

I like hunting fossils, a hobby that isn't exactly my wife's favourite. On one excursion, I found the petrified bones of a squirrel-like mammal. When I brought them home and told my wife what they were, she squelched my excitement.

"I've heard of many a squirrel bringing a nut home," she remarked, "but this is the first time I've heard of a nut bringing a squirrel home."

J.H. HILL

One night while I was cat-sitting my daughter's indoor feline, it escaped outside. When it failed to return the following morning, I found the beast clinging to a branch about 30 feet up in a spindly tree. Unable to lure it down, I called the emergency services.

"We don't do that any more," the woman dispatcher said. When I persisted, she was polite but firm. "The cat will come down when it gets hungry enough."

"How do you know that?" I asked.

"Have you ever seen a cat skeleton in a tree?" she said.

Two hours later the cat was back, looking for breakfast.

TERRY CHRISTIANSEN

I always scoffed when my sister insisted that our three dogs are computer literate. Then one day when I was signing on to AOL, I noticed that when the "welcome" voice came on, the dogs immediately settled down. Later, when they heard the "good-bye" sign-off, all three dogs rushed to the door expecting to be walked.

MARGUERITE CANTINE

One of my mother's friends trains guide dogs and adopted a retired animal. While preparing tea and biscuits for a visitor, the lady briefly left the room; on her return she found the old dog sauntering up to the table and quietly stealing a mouthful of biscuits from the plate.

Issuing a loud, "Oi!" she received the most shocked look she'd ever seen on a dog's face. After all, it had been getting away with it for years.

KATIE BELL

SIGN LANGUAGE

"Homing pigeons free to good home. Must live far, far away."

SEEN IN A NEWSPAPER

Swan song

I was a fool to give Swan-upping a second thought. I won't say I should have ignored it. You can't ignore a thing that is called Swan-upping. The moment I heard of it, I should simply have said, "Swan-upping, eh?" or "Fancy that!" and gone about my business, instead of spending an afternoon in the Public Library reading about Swans.

Swan-upping sounds like a custom that should have been quietly dropped around the time, say, of Ethelred the Unready. But it has not been dropped – that's the whole point. Indeed, it flourishes, quite as it did on July 16th, 1308, when Edward II issued a commission of oyer and terminer about some Swans belonging to John de Fresingfeld, who kept his birds on the Waveney, at Mendham, Suffolk.

The Thames, of course, is *the* place for Swan-upping now, and July or August is the month, depending on the pleasure of the Vintners' Company, the Dyers'

Company, and the King of England, who divide the Swans on the river among themselves and annually up, or take up, the young ones and mark them on the bill with a penknife to show who owns which.

In the course of centuries England's Swan laws have attained such perfection that almost everybody has been seriously inconvenienced, from the King down. For instance, whenever Swan laws were broken, especially in regard to taxes (or Swannage), the King was supposed to seize the said

Swan or Swans appertaining thereunto, and sometimes he didn't want any more Swans. Nothing, by the way, can get on one's nerves like too many Swans.

Or sometimes the King wanted all the Swans he could possibly obtain, and the Queen hated the very sight of them. The King would prepare to seize some Swans. The Queen would be firm. I shouldn't wonder if there was Swan trouble between Edward II and Isabella the Fair. She had him murdered, you know.

Will Cuppy, *How to Attract the Wombat*

Then there's the law that any person found carrying a Swanhook, the same being neither a Swanherd in good standing nor accompanied by two certified Swanherds, or Swannerds (or Swanners, or Swanmasters), of known probity, should cough up thirteen shillings fourpence, three shillings fourpence going to the informer and the rest to the King. This looked like a fine bit of legislation until it developed that you can't collect from such people. They haven't got it. That's why they're out stealing Swans.

The strange thing is that anybody should try to carry a Swanhook around without attracting a lot of attention, let alone get by totally unobserved. A Swanhook is a rather cumbersome and conspicuous affair, generally attached to a long pole, by means of which it is possible to up, or capture, a Swan by the neck. It is not an object to be easily concealed about the clothing. Either you are carrying a Swanhook or you aren't.

We seldom hear of these miscreants nowadays. They seem to have lost interest. Doubtless they grew tired of telling inquirers, while making for the nearest Swannery, that they were only trying to get a cat out of a tree. The provision that they must be accompanied by two Swanherds probably discouraged them, too. It is a well-known fact that when you need a couple of Swanherds, you can't find even one.

Time was when simply mobs of festive Londoners would follow the Swan-upping barges along the Thames, either afoot or in gaily decorated boats. There would be collations and dancing on the grass while the uppers of the Dyers and the Vintners and the King, dressed respectively in blue, blue-and-white, and red jerseys, merrily upped the young Swans, or clear-bills, at Kingston, Stains, Maidenhead, and Henley. Of late the turnout has been sparser, and it has usually rained.

Nor are Swan-marks what they once were. The Vintners have got down to two nicks on the bill and the Dyers to one. The King's uppers don't even bother to nick the King's Swans any more. They just go along for the ride.

Things were very different among the old Dorset Stour crowd. The Abbot of Beaulieu, or Old Bewley, as everybody called him, marked his birds with only four short lines, but the Prior of Christchurch always insisted upon a small square in sinister chief, a black spot on the sinister edge of the middle of the bill, and a small circle in the middle of the lower half of the bill, with a line proceeding from it, sloping to dexter. A bit showy, perhaps.

Whatever I may think of Swan-upping as a sport, if such it be, I have no intention of trying to stop it. I know only too well what happened to the gentlemen who once replaced with silk cord and tassels the long leather thongs attached to the purses used at the ceremony of the Maundy money at Westminster Abbey. He was told to take the cords and tassels off and put the leather thongs back where they belonged. At the same time, I understand, a certain person gave him what could only be interpreted as a look. And quite right, too.

I saw two dogs walk over to a parking meter. One said to the other, **"How do you like that? Paying toilets."**

An adorable little girl walked into my pet shop and asked, "Excuse me, do you sell rabbits?"

"Yes," I answered, and leaning down to her eye level I asked, "Would you like a white rabbit or would you prefer to have a soft, fluffy black rabbit?"

She shrugged. "I don't think my python really cares."

C. PATTERSON

Each morning at 5:30, I take my Lhasa Apso, Maxwell, for a walk. He has the bad habit of picking up bits of paper or other rubbish along the way. When he does, I command him to "drop it" and he usually complies.

One morning, though, he absolutely refused to drop a piece of litter. So I told him to "sit" and then approached him to see what his treasure was. It was a £10 note.

ELSA BOGGS

When they found the man in a wood, he was emaciated and dressed in rags. However, because he was gnawing on an owl, charges had to be pressed. In court, the plaintiff explained to the judge that he understood he had committed a serious offence, but at the time he had been starving and had merely eaten the first creature he'd been able to catch. The judge decided to give the man a second chance and agreed to let him go free.

As he signed the paperwork, the judge looked up and asked, "Out of interest, what did the owl taste like?" The fellow pondered for a moment and replied, "Halfway between an osprey and a golden eagle."

MARTIN ROBERTSON

A French poodle and a collie were walking down the street. The poodle turned to the collie and complained, "My life is such a mess. My owner is mean, my girlfriend is having an affair with a German shepherd and I'm as nervous as a cat."

"Why don't you go see a psychiatrist?" asked the collie.

"I can't," replied the poodle. "I'm not allowed on the couch."

JOHN GAMBA

One morning when a locksmith arrived to change the locks in my house, I realised I had to go and run a few errands. I told the worker, a kindly older man, that I was heading out. When I got to the front door, I noticed my sad-faced dog staring at me from the living room. "I love you, sweet boy," I said. "Now you be good. OK?" From the other room I heard a voice answer, "OK."

ANGELA MILLER

"I'll negotiate, Stan, but I won't beg."

Our two dogs, a pointer and a mongrel, were missing. We looked everywhere, but finally I had to go to my work. Dressed in my dark-blue uniform and white shirt, I left in my car, an estate.

On my way, I spotted our dogs sitting by a bus stop where some 20 people stood. I stopped the car, got out and held the passenger door open. The dogs climbed into the front seat. I then closed the door, got in and drove off.

I'll never forget the faces of those people taking in the spectacle of two dogs, fetched by a uniformed chauffeur in a big car.

H. GEERTSMA

Two dog owners are arguing over whose dog is the cleverest. "My dog is so smart", says the first owner, "that every morning he waits for the paper boy to come round. He tips the boy and then brings the newspaper to me, along with my morning cup of coffee."

"I know," says the second owner.
"How do you know?"
"My dog told me."

After our dog died, my parents had her cremated, and they placed the ashes in a special box on

"It followed me home, can I keep it?!"

the mantelpiece. One day the boy next door came over to play and noticed the fancy container. "What's in the box?" he asked.

"That's our dog," my mum replied.

"Oh," the boy simply said. A minute later he remarked, "He's awfully quiet, isn't he?"

We went to visit our daughter and she prepared us a roast lunch. I noticed the chicken thawing in the kitchen sink with a dish drainer inverted over the bird. I asked what it was doing there.

"Mum, you always did it that way, didn't you?" said my daughter turning toher mother.

"Yes," my wife replied, "but you haven't got a cat."

A. STOKERS

My friend's husband, Ray, is a policeman and enjoys sharing the excuses people use when stopped for speeding. One day, however, the tables were turned. Ray maintains an aquarium of exotic fish, and a prized specimen had threatened to turn belly up. The off-duty officer called a pet shop, and they advised him to immediately purchase a special additive that would correct the water's pH.

Ray and his wife jumped into the car and rushed to the shop. A policeman signalled to them to pull over. "Go on," Ray's wife said. "Tell him you've got a sick fish!"

DEBRA MCVEY

After we moved into a new house my wife and I quickly learned our neighbour's name because we heard his wife using it. We often saw him walking his dog when we left for work and we always said, "Good morning, Bill." But he never replied.

Wondering if we had offended him, I asked another neighbour why he was so unfriendly. "That's because his name is Fred," they explained. "Bill is the dog."

DAVE WILLIAMS

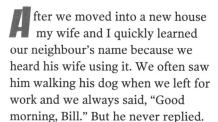

Enclosed with the worming tablets my friend received from a vet was a sheet of red heart stickers to place on a calendar as a reminder to give her pet the medication. She attached these stickers to her kitchen calendar, marking the first Saturday of every month. When her husband noticed the hearts, he grinned from ear to ear, turned to his wife and asked, "Do you have something special in mind for these days?"

MARY RUSSO

Snake 1:
Are we poisonous?

Snake 2:
I don't know.
Why?

Snake 1:
I just bit my lip.

FAITH LACKEY

When my younger sister and my mother bought three exotic birds, they named them This, That and The Other. After a few months, This died, and they buried the bird in the backyard. A few more months later, The Other passed away and they buried it next to This. Then the last bird died.

Mum called my sister and tearfully announced, "Well, I guess that's That."

GLORIA VITULANO

My niece bought her five-year-old daughter Kayleigh a hamster. One day he escaped from his cage. The family turned the house upside down and finally found him. A few weeks later, while Kayleigh was at school, the hamster disappeared again. After hours of searching, my niece was unable to locate the creature. So, in an attempt to make the loss less painful for her daughter, she removed the hamster's cage from her room.

When Kayleigh returned from school that afternoon, she climbed into her mother's lap. "We've got a serious problem," she sighed. "Not only has he disappeared again, but this time he's taken the cage with him."

PATSY STRINGER

"Maybe aerobics wasn't such a good idea."

I was in the pet section of a local shop when I overheard a woman singing the praises of a particular water bowl to her husband.

"Look, it even has a water filter!" she enthused, holding the doggie dish out for his inspection.

He had a different take on things: "Dear, the dog drinks out of the toilet."

JAMES JENKINS

To remind myself to give my pets some leftovers, I wrote a note reading "chicken" and put it in their empty food bowl. The next morning I noticed my daughter had added, "No! This is a bowl. Trust me – I'm at university."

LIZ BRAILSFORD

212

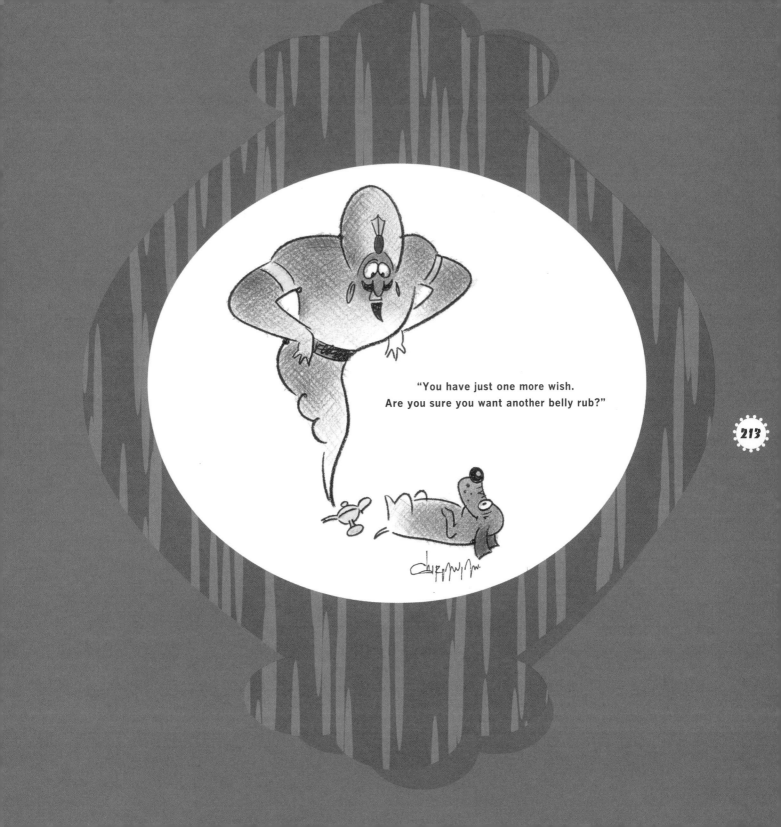

"You have just one more wish.
Are you sure you want another belly rub?"

213

My father and a friend were talking about the doors they had installed so their animals could let themselves in and out of the house.

My dad asked his friend, who had two massive Great Danes, **"Aren't you afraid that somebody might crawl through the dogs' door and steal something?"**

"If you saw an opening that big," said his friend, **"would you crawl through it?"**

H. JENKINS

 quirrels had infested three churches in town.

After much prayer, the vicar at the first church decided that the animals were predestined to be there by God and should be left in peace. Soon, the squirrels multiplied and overran the building.

The vicar at the second church felt he could not harm any of God's creatures, so he humanely trapped the squirrels and set them free on the edge of town. Three days later, they were back and breeding.

Only the third church succeeded in keeping the pests away. The vicar baptised the squirrels and welcomed them into the congregation. Now he only sees them at Christmas and Easter.

E.T. THOMPSON

I used to run a country pub which had a duck pond next to the car park. Early one morning I was alarmed to see two police cars driving at speed into the car park. Eight burly policemen emerged from their cars and strode purposefully towards the pond.

With horrid visions of floating bodies, I flew downstairs and out of the front door. "Good morning," said the sergeant with a beaming smile. "We've just come to admire your baby ducks."

PEGGY JACKSON

I bought my sons a pet rabbit after they promised they would take care of it. As expected, I ended up with the responsibility. Exasperated, one evening I said, "How many times do you think that rabbit would have died if I hadn't looked after it?"

"Once," my 12-year-old son replied.

L. PARSONS

"It's my way of showing support."

I was chatting about the scenery with my newborn daughter while out walking one day, when a man and his dog approached. I leaned over the pushchair and said, "See the doggy?"

Suddenly I felt very silly talking to my baby as if she understood. But just as the man passed, he reached down, patted his dog and said, "See the little baby?"

CATHERINE REARDON

One of my neighbours owns several cats. On a recent visit, she introduced them by name. "That's Astrophe, that's Erpillar, that's Aract, that's Alogue."

"Where on earth did you get such unusual names?" I asked.

"Oh, those are their last names," she explained. "Their first names are Cat."

MILTON ERSKINE

My wife gave me a dog whistle as a gift and I took our spaniel for a walk to try it out. I gave the whistle two sharp blasts and waited for our dog to reappear. Needless to say our spaniel did not return, but a Labrador did – followed by its panting owner.

RICHARD PRESCOTT

**"How many times have I told you –
No coffee after September!"**

A hypnotist was visiting the aquarium during feeding time. "You know," the hypnotist said to the man feeding the fierce shark, "I could hypnotise that shark."

"You're crazy! He'll rip you limb from limb," the feeder said, laughing. "But, hey, if you're so brave, be my guest."

The hypnotist jumped in, swam to the shark and stared it in the eye for a full minute. The animal paused, blinked, and then tore into him. The bleeding man slowly made his way out of the tank.

"I thought you could hypnotise him," sneered the feeder.

"I did," the hypnotist said, holding his arm. "Now he thinks he's an alligator."

JOHN CASON

My brother adopted a snake named Slinky, whose most disagreeable trait was eating live mice. Once I was pressed into going to the pet store to buy Slinky's dinner.

The worst part of this wasn't choosing the juiciest-looking creatures or turning down the assistant who wanted to sell me vitamins to ensure their longevity. The hardest part was carrying the poor things out in a box bearing the words "Thank you for giving me a home."

JOANNE MITCHELL

While I was working for a mining company we sent a small field party to the Yukon mountains in Canada. One day, one of the student trainees climbed over a ridge and was startled to find herself face to face with a young bear. To her relief there was one small tree nearby, to which she ran. On the way a brown blur passed her, and when she got to the base of the tree, she found the terrified bear safely perched at the top.

ROBERT BELL

"He likes you!"

Dave's parrot was always using bad language, so he asked the vet how he could stop it. "Every time the bird swears, put it in the freezer for 15 seconds," advised the vet.

The next time the parrot uttered an expletive, Dave did as the vet said. Then, feeling guilty, Dave opened the freezer.

Shivering, the parrot came out saying, "I'm sorry for all the bad language I've been using." Dave was astounded at the sudden change. Then the parrot said, "By the way, what did the chicken do?"

PAUL IRWIN

Our cat, Figaro, comes home between 10 or 11 at night to eat. If he's late, I turn on the outside light and call him until he appears.

One day my daughter was explaining to a friend where we live, and her friend said, "Is that anywhere near the house where the woman stands on her steps late at night and sings opera?"

MARGARET MATHES

Our friendly postman is in the habit of bringing biscuits in his bag for our peacock Charlie. One day the post was later than usual and Charlie, in his impatience, marched off up the road. He found the postman's bicycle outside the local railway station.

When the postman appeared he was met with the sight of Charlie rummaging through his postbag, plucking out the mail and scattering it everywhere in his eager search for biscuits.

CECIL GYSIN

One of the highlights of the biology course at my university was the monthly feeding of a caged rattlesnake kept in the laboratory. One time, the entire class gathered around the cage and, in complete silence, watched as the feeding took place.

"I'm jealous of the snake," the instructor said. "I never get the class's undivided attention like this."

A student answered matter-of-factly, "You would if you could swallow a mouse."

DIANE TALBOTT-MOSIER

TIMELESS HUMOUR

50s When my Great Dane puppy first came he howled the moment I was out of sight, so when a friend asked me to go to the cinema I explained I couldn't.

'He's more trouble in some ways than a baby – at least a baby could be taken along.'

'Wait,' said my friend. A few minutes later she appeared with an armful of baby clothes and we drove off. In the seclusion of the car-park we dressed the passive puppy – dress, coat, bonnet and pink socks. Wrapping him in a baby blanket I carried him into the cinema, where he snoozed contentedly through a double feature. Indeed, so perfect was his deportment that he won favourable comment from two ladies sitting behind us as 'Just the best baby.'

But on my way out I suddenly found myself the target of all eyes. People stared, nudged each other and burst into peals of laughter. I glanced down at my blanketed bundle and couldn't understand – until I caught a rear view in a mirror. From the folds of infant swaddling hung a puppy tail, wagging happily.

REINA HULIT

Recently I bought a large, three-tiered fountain cast in concrete. In order to "age" it, I took the advice of a gardening book and painted it with a yoghurt and oatmeal mixture to attract moss and lichen.

The following morning I discovered that it had all vanished and the concrete was as pristine as when I bought it. Mystified I repainted it with the mixture and watched from an upstairs window. I saw my three lurchers busily lick the mix from the lower tiers, while my two cats polished off the top where the dogs couldn't reach.

CHRISTINE WADE

The vet prescribed daily tablets for our geriatric cat, Tigger, and after several battles my husband devised a way to give her the medication. It involved wrapping Tigger in a towel, trapping her between his knees, forcing her mouth open and depositing the pill on the back of her tongue.

David was proud of his resourcefulness until one hectic session when he lost control of both cat and medicine. Tigger leaped out of his grasp, paused to inspect the tablet – which had rolled across the floor – and then ate it.

M. LEGERE

"Oh, yeah, like the stripes help."

As spring migration approached, two elderly vultures doubted they could make the trip north, so they decided to go by aeroplane. When they checked their baggage, the attendant noticed that they were carrying two dead armadillos.

"Do you wish to check the armadillos through as luggage?" she asked.

"No, thanks," replied the vultures. "They're carrion."

FRED BRICE

Our neighbour's Labrador is distinctly portly, thanks to his lifelong habit of begging scraps from the local butcher.

Alarmed by the dog's ever increasing girth, his owner finally hung a notice around his neck: "Please do NOT feed me."

It worked well for 24 hours. Then the dog ate the notice.

R. GODDARD

Last time my cat had a cough, I took her to see the vet. Not having a pet carrier in which to transport her, I put her in a cardboard box instead. When I arrived at the vet's surgery the receptionist eyed my box and said, "I'm sorry, but I don't think we can do much for you."

SIGN LANGUAGE

I was waiting in line to sort out a local council matter one afternoon and noticed a hand-lettered sign that read:
"Any child left unattended will be given a free kitten."

JEANNE MAULTSKY

It was only when I noticed what was written on the side of the box: "Deepfrozen Chicken."

CLARE ALTHAM

After agreeing to look after my parents' fish while they were away, I was delighted to spot a row of pink eggs nestled under a leaf at the back of the tank. Taking my role of tank supervisor seriously, I fashioned a protective nursery net around them.

When my mother returned, she thanked me for taking care of the fish – and also for finding my young cousin's doll's necklace that had been lost the previous month. She did wonder, however, why I had been feeding it fish food in her old tea-strainer.

LISA CULLIMORE

"Botox."

Law and disorder

The law is on your side, but who wants to put it to the test? Amusing criminal capers, comical policemen and the lawyers we love to hate.

220

Our friend, a lawyer, was defending a man accused of sending obscene literature through the post. Deciding to base his case on whether the material really was obscene, he asked court officials if he could see a copy. So they posted it to him.

ALAN BAINBRIDGE

Early in my career as a judge, I conducted hearings for those involuntarily committed to a psychiatric hospital. On my first day, I asked a man at the door of the hospital, "Can you tell me where the courtroom is?"

"Why?" he asked.

"I'm the judge."

Pointing to the building, he whispered, "Don't tell them that. They'll never let you out."

CHRISTOPHER DIETZ

My husband placed a perfectly good set of used tyres outside his repair garage with a sign that read "Free". After a few weeks with no takers, he changed the sign to "£10".

The next day, they were stolen.

J. CABIGTING

It was just another day at the driving test centre. I had taken a woman out on her test when a police car came up behind us – sirens wailing, lights flashing.

"Was I speeding?" she asked the police officer, after pulling over.

"No," he replied. "But you are driving a stolen vehicle."

Smiling awkwardly, the woman turned to me. "Does this mean I've failed my test?"

NADINE CARMOUC

While running a car repair business last winter with my two teenage sons, one of them cracked the windscreen of a Ford belonging to a very important customer.

I told my resourceful boys they must get hold of a new windscreen before going home. When I left work later, it was to find snow settling across the front seats of my own Ford.

DAVID LINTON

Any time the alarm goes off after-hours at the office where I work, the security company calls me at home and I have to go back and reset it. Late at night I got one of those calls. As I was getting ready to head out the door, my husband groggily said, "You're not going down there by yourself at this hour."

Just as I was thinking, how thoughtful of him, he added, "Better take the dog with you."

RUTH RODDICK

A case manager at the mental health facility where I work as a nurse needed a reference for a patient who was looking for a job. "I'll vouch for him," offered another client. "We were room-mates in prison."

JEANNE MULLER

I had a job wrapping hams at a meat-packing factory. At the end of one shift, I was leaving through the main gate right behind a woman who was oddly rotund. Or so I thought.

Just as she passed the security hut, a large ham dropped from beneath her skirt. Before the guard could react, the woman spun round, shouting, "All right! Who threw that at me?"

ROGER SCHOEN

221

SIGN LANGUAGE

On a billboard ad for a safe company:
"If your stuff is stolen, it's not our vault."

My father's pager beeped, summoning him to the hospital where he is an anaesthetist.

As he raced towards the hospital, a police car sped up behind him – lights flashing, siren blaring. He had no time to stop, so Dad hung his stethoscope out the window to signal that he was on an emergency.

Within seconds came the police officer's response: a pair of handcuffs flapping outside the police car window.

NICHOLAS BANKS

After practicing law for several months, I was talking with my brother, John, a doctor. "My work is so exciting," I said. "People come into my office, tell me their problems and pay me for my advice."

As older brothers will, John took the upper hand. "You know," he said, "in my work, people come into my office, tell me their problems, take off all their clothes and then pay me for my advice."

DAVID REUWER

Not long ago, I arrested a man for public drunkenness. When I brought him into the police station, the booking clerk asked the standard questions – name, address, phone number, etc. "Lastly," said the clerk, "who should we call in case of an emergency?"

Grinning and reeking of whisky, the drunk slurred, "999".

DEAN DANELSKI

I work for a security company that transports cash, and part of my job is to work with police if a crew is robbed. One afternoon my wife and I were packing to move, when I received a call to report to a crime scene.

"I have to go," I told my wife. "Two of our guards have been held up at gunpoint at a superstore."

As I dashed out the door, she called, "While you're there, pick up some big cardboard boxes."

BRIAN BURTON

"In future, a reg number will suffice, OK."

TIMELESS HUMOUR

50s Recently, I was hauled before a judge for driving an unlicensed vehicle. The judge listened attentively while I gave him a long, plausible explanation.

Then he said with great courtesy, "My dear sir, we are not blaming you – we're just fining you."

D. CROWHURST

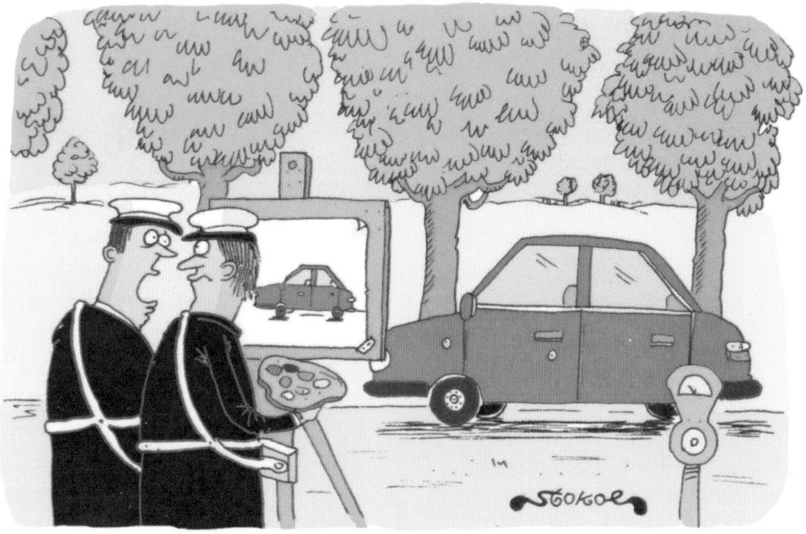

When the driver in front of my police car began weaving in and out of his lane, I put the siren on and pulled him over. As I approached his window, I was hit with the stench of alcohol.

"Sir," I said, "can you tell me when you started drinking and how much you've had?"

"Well, officer, I can't tell you how much I've had," he slurred. "But I started drinking in 1967."

ROBERT MILLER

"The prisons are overcrowded, Mr. Woodlee, so I'm sentencing you to five years of jury duty."

223

My son, a policeman, stopped a woman for going 15 miles over the speed limit. After he handed her a ticket, she asked him, "Don't you give out warnings?"

"Yes, madam," he replied. "They're all up and down the road. They say, 'Speed Limit 30'."

PATRICIA GREENLEE

I had just pulled over someone for driving under the influence when another car pulled up behind us. I stopped what I was doing and ventured back to see if the driver needed assistance.

"No, I don't need any help," he said, reeking of booze. Then, pointing to the flashing lights on the roof of my car, he continued, "I just stopped for the red light."

D. RUGEE

Guards escorted a handcuffed prisoner into the courtroom where I stood as the court deputy. "Is this a tough judge?" the prisoner asked.

"Yes," the bailiff said. "A tough but fair judge."

"Yeah? How tough?"

"The toughest judge since Pontius Pilate," the bailiff replied.

"I don't know him," said the prisoner. "I'm not from around here."

JOSEPH WRIGHT

An old man living alone on a farm wrote to his only son, Walter, in prison.

"Dear Walter:
I'm feeling bad because it looks like I won't be able to plant my potato garden this year. I'm just getting too old to be digging up a garden plot.
I wish you were here – I know you would take care of it for me.
Love, Dad."

About a week later, the farmer received this letter.

"Dear Dad:
Don't dig up the garden! That's where I buried the bodies.
Love, Walter."

The next morning, a group of policemen stormed the property and dug up the entire garden. They didn't find any bodies, though, so they apologised to the old man and left.

Soon the farmer received another letter. It read:

"Dear Dad:
You can go ahead and plant the potatoes now. It's the best I could do under the circumstances.
Love, Walter."

NICHOLA BANKS

When I worked in a bank, one morning one of the managers entered the safe to prepare that day's cash for the cashiers. When a client called asking for him, the clerk who answered the phone let the caller know that the manager was busy.

"He can't come to the phone now," she said. "He's tied up in the vault."

N. HENSLEY and J.SIMMONDS

In the news the other day – first a lorry carrying brand new file folders was hijacked, then a van loaded with Post-it notes was stolen.

Detectives believe the robberies were the work of organised crime.

RON DENTINGER

As a judge, I was sentencing criminal defendants when I saw a vaguely familiar face. I reviewed his record and found that the man was a career criminal, except for a five-year period in which there were no convictions.

"Milton," I asked, puzzled, "how is it you were able to stay out of trouble for those five years?"

"I was in prison," he answered. "You should know that – you were the one who sent me there."

"That's not possible," I said. "I wasn't even a judge then."

"No, you weren't the judge," the defendant countered, smiling mischievously. "You were my lawyer."

PHILIP RILEY

I drive a police patrol-car, and one night after stopping a driver for speeding, I returned to my vehicle to make out a ticket for him. When I'd finished and was leaving my car, without thinking I pushed the lock down and closed the door. As it shut, I realised that there on the motorway, with lights flashing, I had locked myself out.

The most embarrassing moment was yet to come. I had to walk up to the stationary car, hand the driver a ticket – and ask him for a lift to the police station.

E.M.

QUOTABLE QUOTES

The only way to get rid of temptation is to yield to it.
OSCAR WILDE

Few things are harder to put up with than the annoyance of a good example.
MARK TWAIN

Thieves respect property. They merely wish the property to become their property that they may more perfectly respect it.
G. K. CHESTERTON

Lawyers are like beavers: They get in the middle of the stream and dam it up.
DONALD RUMSFELD
in The Wall Street Journal

Trust in God – but tie your camel tight.
PERSIAN PROVERB

A little inaccuracy sometimes saves tons of explanation.
SAKI

A little rebellion now and then is a good thing.
THOMAS JEFFERSON

If you obey all the rules, you miss all the fun.
KATHARINE HEPBURN,
The Making of the African Queen (Knopf)

If a man can't forge his own will, whose will can he forge?
W.S. GILBERT

Once when I was lost I asked a policeman to help me find my parents. I said to him, "Do you think we'll ever find them?"
He answered, "I don't know, kid. There are so many places they can hide."
RODNEY DANGERFIELD

225

My husband reversed his new car into the wall that runs alongside our drive. He contacted our insurers and the the dented bumper was replaced straight away.

Less than a week later he did the same thing. "I'm so embarrassed," he moaned as he phoned the insurance company for the second time.

"Why not tell them it was me this time?" I suggested.

He looked at me sheepishly and confessed, "I said that last time."

CAROL MIDWOOD

Three lawyers – an American, a Russian and a Czech – went bear hunting in Canada. After three weeks they hadn't returned, so the authorities got up a search party and went looking for them.

At the lawyers' campsite they found signs of a violent struggle. And then, to their horror, they spotted two well-fed bears not far from the camp. Fearing the worst, the rangers shot them both. After cutting open the female and finding the American and Russian inside, they concluded that, in true lawyer fashion, the Czech was in the male.

LUKE BREWER

It was time to tell my ten-year-old son the facts of life, so I took books out of the library and prepared myself for any questions he might ask. At the end of our lengthy chat, he looked confused. "If you have any questions," I said, "please ask them. There are no silly questions."

"Well, suppose I was married," he said with some embarrassment, "my wife was pregnant and I had to rush her to the hospital. OK?"

I nodded supportively.

"Can I go through red lights?" he asked.

C. LESSARD

One snowy evening my brother, a police officer, stopped a car at a roadside check for drunk drivers. "Good evening, madam," he greeted the lady. "How are you this evening?"

"Fine, thank you," she replied.

My brother continued, "Anything to drink this evening?"

Surprised, the lady answered, "No, thank you."

DONNA FILSHIE

My cousin was standing behind the bakery's till when a gunman burst in and demanded all the cash. As she nervously handed over the money, she noticed the rolls of coins in the back of the till. "Do you want the rolls too?" she asked.

"No," said the robber, waving his gun. "Just the money."

PHIL LEMAN

Dear Revenue & Customs: I'm sending you this money because I cheated on my income tax and my conscience has been bothering me. If it doesn't stop, I'll send you the rest.

ROY PATE

My grandmother is fascinated by my husband's career as an undercover drugs-squad officer. One evening, she telephoned me after he'd driven her home from our house. "I think Rick took me on a drug deal," she said.

I assured her that he would do no such thing. She insisted he had. In detail she described a small black box that he had dropped off without comment in front of a building.

When Rick got home, I asked him what had happened. "I didn't take Grandma on a drug deal," he said. "But I did stop at the video shop to drop off the film we watched last night."

MARY SANDFORD

Recently, I spent the afternoon shopping with my friend. As she searched for somewhere to park, she suddenly pulled up on a yellow line, reached into the glove compartment and pulled out a card on which, "Sorry, ran out of petrol" was already written. "It always works," she smiled smugly, as she secured it under the windscreen wiper. After a while we returned to the car only to find a parking ticket and another note with read, "Sorry, ran out of patience. This is the second time this week."

DAWN TATE

While working as a television-news cameraman, I arrived at an accident scene, and a cameraman from another channel pulled up behind me. As I parked the work vehicle I was driving, I heard a policeman on his radio using the radio phonetic alphabet to alert other officers.

"Be aware that the Mike Echo Delta India Alpha has arrived," he said.

I approached the officer, looked him in the eye and said, "You might be surprised to know that some of us in the Mike Echo Delta India Alpha can Sierra Papa Echo Lima Lima."

A. GIRARD

227

SIGN LANGUAGE

A sign on the side of the road with a message from the police:

"If you drink and drive, we'll provide the chasers."

J. BERNTSEN

"As a matter of fact, yes, this would hold up in court. Any other questions?"

I answered the phone one day in the lawyer's office where I worked. The caller gave his name, saying our office had just served him with divorce papers.

I was unable to place him immediately because this was a new case. Eager to talk, he blurted out, "I'm the despondent!"

CAROLINE NIED

Just ahead of me in a busy street, a car drew up on double yellow lines – to the annoyance of a passing lady traffic warden. "Sorry, you can't park here'" she told the driver.

"I'm only going to be a few minutes," he retorted angrily.

"You can't park here," she repeated, raising her voice. "Move on."

As she drew level with me, I remarked: "You do get some awkward people, don't you?"

"Yes," she replied, "and that one should know better. He's my husband."

J.R.W.

The lawyer I work for specialises in divorce cases. He is a refined man who maintains a wry sense of humour about what can be rather depressing work.

One day, I took a call from a potential new client who informed me that he was telephoning from prison where he was serving a life sentence for murdering his wife. I put the man on hold as I relayed this to my boss.

"What does he need me for?" he quipped.

"He appears to have solved all his marital problems by himself."

R. CHAN

Travelling home on a very crowded train, I was surprised to see a girl suddenly thrust her arm up into the air grasping the hand of the man behind her.

It all became clear when she shouted: "Does anyone own this? I just found it on my bottom."

CAROLINE HALLAS

As part of a Comparative Religions course, I had to listen to a lecture on psychic phenomena. The speaker told the group about a woman who contacted police working on a missing persons case. She gave them eerily detailed instructions on where to find the body. In fact, the detectives discovered the corpse exactly as she had described. Next, the lecturer asked what we would call this type of person.

While the rest of us pondered the question, a police officer taking the course raised his hand and replied, "A suspect."

L. PEEBLES

A friend and I used to run a small temporary-staffing service. Our agency did mandatory background checks on all job candidates, even though our application form asked them if they'd ever been convicted of a crime.

One day after a round of interviews, my colleague was entering information from a young man's application into the computer. She called me over to show me that he had noted a previous conviction for manslaughter. Below that, on the line listing his skills, he had written, "Good with people."

JANA RAHRIG

229

FELMORE
MINIMUM SECURITY FACILITY

The civil trial dragged on and on and everyone in the courtroom – including my former boss, the judge – found themselves fighting a losing battle against boredom.

The first one to fall asleep was the clerk. After his snoring began to interrupt the testimonies, one of the barristers addressed the bench.

"Um, Your Honour," he asked, "should I wake him up?"

"Leave him alone," the judge replied. "He's the only one here enjoying himself."

JACKIE REEVES

My father began teaching business classes at the local prison through a community college. On his first night of class, he started a chapter on banking. During the course of his lecture, the subject of cash machines came up, and he mentioned that, on average, most machines contain only about £1500 at a given time.

Just then a man at the back raised his hand. "I'm not trying to be disrespectful," he told my father, "but the machine I robbed had about £5000 in it."

JENNIFER JOHNSON

At the court where I work, I once received a phone call from a woman who asked to have her jury duty postponed. "I want to do my civic duty," she said, "but I really think you should inform the judge that you also sent my mother a jury summons. If we're both selected to serve on a case, it's going to be a hung jury for sure!"

Her request was approved.

V. ALTHOUSE

As a trainee local-newspaper reporter, I was sent to cover a trial at an unfamiliar court. Though slightly late, I strode confidently into the courtroom, sat down at the press bench and started taking notes on

what the defendant in the witness box was saying. I could tell my entrance had made a big impression as everyone, including the magistrates, was staring at me.

Just then an usher approached and asked, "Are you a member of the press?"

"Yes," I replied. "Why?"

"Because the press bench is over there. You're sitting in the dock."

ANDY GREENWOOD

I was riding my bike through a small town when the traffic in front of me slowed to a crawl. Peering ahead, I saw a police officer standing beside his patrol car holding what appeared to be a speed gun. But as I got closer, I realised that it was actually a hairdryer.

"What are you doing?" I asked.

"Our gun's being repaired," said the police officer. Surveying the slow parade of cars, he added, "But they don't know that."

LOREN MILBURY

A defence barrister was cross-examining the police officer who had responded to an accident in which the defendant had rear-ended another car. The policeman testified that he had smelled alcohol on the accused's breath.

The lawyer got the officer to agree that the collision had ruptured the radiator of his client's car, spilling antifreeze onto the ground. "So," the legal eagle continued, "might it not be true that you smelled antifreeze, not alcohol?"

"Yes," replied the officer, "if that's what he was drinking."

WILLIAM PRINCE

I requested identification from a department-store customer who had just written a personal cheque for her purchase. After fumbling through her purse, she presented me with what she said was the only thing that bore both her name and address.

It was a notice of insufficient funds from her bank.

STEVE GOODWIN

M y husband's job of fire safety inspector took him to the roof of a tall office building. There was a high wind and he had gone only a few steps when the heavy metal door slammed and locked. He was marooned.

Nearby there was a higher building, but every window was closed and there was no use yelling. Spotting a girl looking out, he tried some spirited pantomime, but she seemed merely bored. Despair gave him an idea. Slowly he started taking off his clothes, and was rewarded by startled attention. When he got to his trousers he saw the girl reach for a telephone. The building manager and the police closed in on him before he complete his striptease.

REBECCA MORRIS

I am a lawyer in a small town and will admit to having a few extra pounds on me. Not long ago, I was questioning a witness in an armed robbery case. I asked, "Would you describe the person you saw?" The witness replied, "He was kind of short and stout."

"You mean short and stout like me?" I asked.

"Oh, no," he said. "He wasn't that fat."

WILLIAM GOODWIN

A n artist friend of mine used to work for the police, drawing the faces of crime suspects based on descriptions given by the public.

For the most part, she said, people were pretty good at describing the criminals, but sometimes she had to admit defeat.

For instance, on one occasion, a lady told her "Well, he looks a bit like Uncle Robert, but not as tall, and something about him reminds me of Mr Jones up the road."

DEBORAH MERCER

"For robberies and murder, it still has the old siren, but for stuff like cats in trees, it plays 'Que Sera, Sera'."

Access denied

It's odd how keys tend to play a high profile role in domestic dramas. A friend of mine, the distracted mother of a grumpy infant, grizzling toddler and yelling baby, was telling me how she arrived home from a stressful shopping trip and after an increasingly frantic search of bag, pockets, doormat, etc., remembered last seeing her key lying on the kitchen dresser. Her husband's key was, like her husband, en route for New York. Faced with a house like Fort Knox and with children now screaming for food, drink and urgent attention, she had a blaze of inspiration – the police – surely they would have a master key! She rushed to the police house, where the policeman was just getting up for the afternoon shift. Between yawns and scratches he explained that the police no longer have skeleton keys, and suggested she go back and search for an open window. Accepting the offer to leave her kids with his wife (thank God this happened in the country –

can you imagine that suggestion coming out of Bow Street?) she rushed home and found – joy of joys – a slit-like crack in the upstairs bathroom window.

Her elderly neighbour brought a ladder and gallantly insisted on climbing up to the window. At which point the policeman (a six-foot seven-inch giant) arrived in a Panda car to check on the situation. Seeing gallant elderly neighbour up ladder he heaved a sigh of relief: "Can't stand heights meself," and beat a hasty retreat. Meanwhile the gallant elderly neighbour discovered that the bathroom window opened upwards like the flap on a letter box; he climbed down ladder, fetched tool-box, climbed up ladder, unscrewed latch, descended ladder in search of stick to wedge flap open, climbed up ladder, and posted elderly self through window, scattering a sill full of toiletries, medicines, pills, etc. (Mother-of-three, heart in mouth, head in hands, made mental note to purchase bathroom cabinet

on next shopping trip.) Saintly neighbour then descended through house, opened front door and was mobbed by effusive mother, incoherent with relief and gratitude. Fending off wild woman, he reascended ladder, removed prop, rescrewed latch, closed window, descended ladder for last time, and carried it home.

Mother-of-three hurriedly replaced everything on bathroom window sill, noting with despair the state of the bedrooms, landing, stairs as revealed to neighbour's unfamiliar eyes. Suddenly mindful of fractious infants and by now demented policeman's wife, she rushed downstairs and out of front door, slamming it behind her. Too late she remembered key still sitting on kitchen dresser.

A silent scream, followed by mad head banging. She briefly considered hurling herself into nearby river, or better still through lounge window. Stoically, though, she dismissed these as easy ways out, and with heavy heart and carefully rehearsed

Maureen Lipman, *Something to Fall Back On*

speech, returned grimly to gallant elderly neighbour ...

One of the happiest married couples I know are our friends Bryan and Edith, who first started courting at the age of fourteen and have been together ever since – about thirty-seven years. Edith tells of how she parked her bike outside Bryan's house, dressed in her school uniform and beret, and while waiting for him heard his mother say, "Bryan, there's that brazen hussy outside!" When we lived in the flat above them we used to race down for the rows, because it was – is – so wonderful to see them both revert to adolescence. They disagree on just about every issue, and do so at the tops of their voices, yet it's forgotten within minutes.

One of the main bones of contention between them is Bryan's supposed super-efficiency.

Once, after a spate of burglaries at their flat, he replaced the small window through which the thieves had gained access, and had an alarm fitted. About a week later he arrived home from work without

his key. As Edith wasn't due back for some time, he decided to scrape away the putty on his new window and gain access the same way as the burglars had. Finding a sharp object in his pocket, he scraped and pushed and pushed and scraped until finally the new putty began to give. He pressed and scraped a bit more, until at length the window fell in, setting off the ear-splitting sound of the alarm. Only then did he glance down at the sharp object with which he'd been scraping at the putty.

It was, of course, his key.

233

Having been a store detective for five years, I should be surprised at nothing. Occasionally, however, I have to fight a powerful urge to scream, "You've got to be joking!"

One such occasion was the seemingly routine matter of a nice, motherly old woman who had helped herself to an assortment of beauty products. In my office I asked her to empty the contents of her large handbag onto the desk. As she did, there, mixed with the stolen toiletries, were three small potted cacti.

Why, I asked her, would she steal a cactus?

"Well," she replied, "I haven't had much luck with African violets."

JILL HILDEBRAND

The policeman arrived at the scene of an accident to find that a car had struck a telegraph pole. Searching for witnesses, he discovered a pale, nervous young man in work clothes who claimed he was an eyewitness.

"Exactly where were you at the time of the accident?" inquired the officer.

"Mister," exclaimed the telephone lineman, "I was at the top of the pole!"

LARRY BLACK

I was reviewing my client's case with him in prison when it was announced that visitors had 15 minutes to leave or be locked in for the three-hour prisoner head count. I bade my client farewell and left. But somehow, I managed to get lost on my way out.

Desperate for directions to the exit, I noticed some men wearing jumpsuits. Mistaking them for workmen, I called out to one of them, a no-necked, barrel-chested man. "Sir," I said, "I need to get out of here."

He shrugged. "Darling, so do I."

SUZAN PORTO

Our chief financial officer was giving a tour of corporate headquarters to a special group of senior executives from whose bank we had recently received a loan. As our CFO came to the jewel of the tour, the computer centre that had been financed with the bank's help, he proudly pointed to a small metal box on the wall next to the entrance.

"This box," he boasted, "is part of our new security system. The only way to gain admittance to the computer room is by inserting a properly encoded card in the slot."

He pressed a button next to the box, and a buzzer sounded. His face went pale when a voice from the other side of the door shouted, "Come in. It's open!"

BILL MIDWIG

"Only ONE phone call?! Now you tell me!"

A friend was assigned a new post teaching English to inmates in prison. Feeling a little nervous on his first day, he began by asking the class a basic question: "Now, who can tell me what a sentence is?"

PETER MCDONAGH

When my husband, Jack, was a police officer, he once approached a home guarded by two ferocious dogs. They lunged at the front door with such force that it opened, and they rushed out into the front garden. Thinking quickly, Jack stepped into the house, closing the door tightly behind him.

"It's all right, madam," he reassured the homeowner. "I'm a police officer."

"Not a very brave one," she observed.

L. HENDERSON

After years of hard work establishing my law practice, I had many satisfied clients and the respect of my peers. When my father passed away, I took over my mother's affairs, handling her investments and paying her bills.

One day, she let me know how much she appreciated my help. "It's so nice, your taking care of everything for me," she said. "Otherwise, I'd have to hire a real solicitor."

ARNOLD BERWICK

Attempting to park our car recently, my wife dented the bumper of an occupied car parked at the kerb. She completed an accident report form for our insurance company, and asked me to check it before posting it. I found everything else in order until I came to the question: "What could the driver of the other vehicle have done to avoid the accident?"

Her reply: "He could have parked his car somewhere else."

G.H.J.

A neighbour of mine, in her 70s, invited a girlhood chum to come for a visit. On the way home from the airport, engaged in animated conversation, my neighbour drove through a red light. A young police officer stopped her and proceeded to give her a terrific tongue-lashing.

When he finally paused for breath, she reached out and gently patted his arm. "Young man," she said, "I never would have done it if I'd known it was going to upset you so."

MADELINE RATHJEN

235

TIMELESS HUMOUR

50s As I entered the police station the other evening to pay a parking fine, I noticed that an old lady just ahead of me was trembling all over. I paid the money and was about to leave when I saw the lady sitting on a bench in the corner absorbed in a book. "What's the trouble?" I asked. "Is there anything I can do?"

"No, thank you," she replied sedately. "You see, I was sitting at home all alone reading this murder story and I got so scared that I came down here to finish it under police protection."

GEORGE ROE

As a policeman, I occasionally work off-duty as a security officer in shops. I was handling crowd control for a going-out-of-business sale, and people were massed around the two cash registers. Determined to establish order, I climbed onto the checkout counter and announced, "Please, I want to organise you into two lines, one for each register. Remember, you all can't be first – someone has to be second."

A woman at the back raised her hand and called out, "I volunteer to be second!"

NICK WALTMAN

In honour of my brother's retirement from the police force, my sister-in-law decided to throw a surprise party for him. Plans made in secrecy over a two-month period included catering and entertainment decisions as well as travel and accommodation for over 100 friends and relatives from all over the country.

At the party, my brother stood up to address his guests. As he looked around the room at everyone who had secretly gathered on his behalf, he shook his head and said, "After 25 years in the police force, I finally know why I was never made a detective."

LAWRENCE WRIGHT

As a lawyer, I am perhaps more used to being criticised than praised. At the end of a difficult case I once received a letter of thanks from a client that concluded,

"I shall always think of you as a friend and not as a good lawyer."

PETER WILKINSON

As a potential juror in an assault-case, I was sitting in a courtroom, answering questions from both sides. The Crown Prosecutor asked such questions as: Had I ever been mugged? Did I know the victim or the defendant?

The defence lawyer took a different approach, however. "I see you are a teacher," he said. "What do you teach?"

"English and drama," I responded.

"Then I guess I'd better watch my grammar," the defence lawyer quipped.

"No," I shot back. "You'd better watch your acting."

When the laughter in the courtroom died down, I was excused from the case.

MACEY LEVIN

friend of mine, a policeman, responded to an accident call one day. When he arrived, he noticed an ambulance technician trying to apply a spine board to a man standing near one of the cars involved in the accident. The patient appeared to be resisting.

"Really," he objected, "I ... "

The ambulance technician interjected, explaining that because of regulations, he had to take necessary precautions.

"No, I'm okay, really, I am."

Again the ambulance technician cut him off, explaining the rules he had to follow.

By then, my friend had reached them and, recognizing the patient, asked, "Are you sure you're okay? The accident looks pretty nasty."

"I reported the accident – I wasn't in it," he was finally able to explain.

DAVID BLOOM

policeman heard this plea on his radio: "Does anyone know where I am? I'm all screwed up." It was a policeman who had lost his way.

Another voice rang out, bold and authoritative: "Would the officer making that last transmission please identify himself?"

After a short silence, a third unidentified voice said, "He's not that screwed up."

MICHAEL VIOLET

237

TIMELESS HUMOUR

60s A young man I know, who recently became clerk to a prominent judge, was asked to prepare a suggested opinion in an important case. After working on the assignment for some time, he proudly handed in a 23-page document.

When he got it back, he found a terse comment in the judge's handwriting on page 7: "Stop romancing – just propose."

S. JANOFF

---

was a brand-new lawyer, in practice on my own, and I had a likewise inexperienced secretary straight out of school. The importance of proofreading the results of my dictation was highlighted one day when a reminder to a client's tenant to pay her rent or suffer eviction was transcribed as follows: "You are hereby notified that if payment is not received within five business days, I will have no choice but to commence execution proceedings."

MARY RASAMNY

s a nightclub owner, I hired a pianist and a drummer to entertain my customers. After several performances, I discovered the drummer had walked away with some of my valuables. I notified the police, who arrested him. Desperate for another drummer, I called a friend who knew some musicians.

"What happened to the drummer you had?" he asked me.

"I had him arrested," I replied.

We said good-bye and hung up. A few minutes later my friend called back and asked, "How badly did he play?"

MIKE CAVALLO

A traffic policeman friend of ours had stopped at our café for coffee and was getting ready to leave. "Go out and get 'em!" I said. "I suppose everyone gets a ticket today?"

"I don't really give out many tickets," he said seriously.

"Oh, come on," I teased, "you'd give your own mother a ticket."

"No, my mother never drove a car," said Bill, still serious. Then a grin spread over his face. "I did catch her on a pedestrian crossing when the light was red once," he said, "and I gave her a warning. But that's all."

D. JONES

A group of prospective jurors was asked by the judge whether any of them felt they had ever been treated unfairly by a police officer. "I once got fined for running a red light," offered one woman, "even though it had been on amber when I got to the light."

"Did you pay the fine?" the judge questioned.

"Yes."

"If you thought you were innocent," the judge went on, "why didn't you contest it?"

"There have been so many times I didn't get a ticket for running a red light that I decided this evened things out a little," she replied.

CHARLES KRAY

A woman was driving down the street and got stopped by a police officer. **"May I see your driver's licence?"** he said.

She looked at him with disgust. **"What's the matter with you people? I wish you'd make up your minds. You took my licence from me yesterday."**

L. BENTON

Investigating a case as a CID officer, I visited an old lady. As I showed her my warrant card, she grabbed it and scrutinised my photograph. After a minute or so, she handed the card back. "No," she said. "I've never seen him before."

BRYAN HAMMOND

When I worked as a prison teacher one of my charges kept missing classes. First of all it was because he had a tooth extracted, then his tonsils were removed. Finally, he chopped off the end of his finger in a workshop.

All of this led one guard to comment, "You know, I think we'd better keep an eye on this chap. He seems to be trying to escape one bit at a time."

LUCY GRACE

While I was serving as a juror, I happened to share the lift one morning with a visiting judge. He asked me where the jurors parked, and I informed him that we had our own area a little way away.

Then it occurred to me that he might be having a problem finding a place for his car, so I continued, "but, Your Honour, they have a special place reserved for judges down below."

"Yes," he said dryly, "I'm sure they do."

HELEN BAYS

A female lawyer in a law office found a typewriter on her desk with this note: "We are short of secretarial help and need your assistance."

Recognizing that this was yet another prank by her male colleagues, she quickly typed a response that forever squelched the jokes: "I wold lov to hep out eny wey I kan."

BRENDA OLIVER

Part of my job at the local court is to send letters to people accused of crimes, informing them of when their trial will be. One such notice was returned, clearly by a criminal mastermind, with this jotted on the envelope:

"I DO NOT LIVE HERE."

C. GALINDO

While taking a routine vandalism report at a junior school, I was interrupted by a little girl about six years old. Looking up and down at my uniform, she asked, "Are you a policeman?"

"Yes," I answered, and continued writing the report.

"My mother said if I ever needed help I should ask the police. Is that right?"

"Yes, that's right," I told her.

"Well, then," she said as she extended her foot toward me, "would you please do up my shoe?"

CAROL WIRGES

While decorating a customer's home, my husband answered the door to a traffic policeman.

The officer asked if the van parked outside the property belonged to my husband and he confirmed it did.

"Would you mind moving it," requested the policeman, "as we've set up a speed trap and everyone is slowing down because of your vehicle."

JUNE STILL

When a thief snatched a necklace a friend of mine was wearing, she grabbed at his collar, trying unsuccessfully to stop his getaway. Asked for the thief's description later, she said, "Don't bother looking for him. He only got a costume-jewellery necklace of mine. But when I grabbed him by the collar, I got his chain, and it's real gold!"

ROCHELLE ADELMAN

I once called upon an elderly lawyer, who greeted me warmly and invited me to be seated. As I was about to take the chair in front of his desk, he motioned me into a different one. Before I left, however, he invited me to try the first chair. I did so, and after a short time noticed an uncomfortable desire to rise.

"That chair I reserve for law-book sellers, bill collectors and pesky clients," my host explained. "The front legs are sawn off two inches shorter than the back ones."

ROBERT DEMER

"I'm advising my client not to answer any more questions, or to even make eye contact."

Some prisoners are chatting in the exercise yard. "I heard the prison governor's daughter married a bloke down in cell block D," says one. "The governor's very upset about it too."

"Why?" asks another. "Because she married a con?"

"No. Because they eloped."

ADAM SMARGON

Phil was driving down a country lane late one night when he felt a large thud. He got out of the car and looked around, but the road was empty. Since there was nothing else to be done, Phil drove home. In the morning a policeman was waiting for him on his doorstep.

"You're under arrest for hitting a pig and leaving the scene," the officer told him with a frown. "Please come with me."

Phil couldn't believe his ears. "But how could you possibly know that's what happened?" he asked.

"It wasn't hard," the detective replied. "The pig squealed."

SANDRA BINGHAM

Someone I know was towing his boat home from a fishing trip when his car broke down. He didn't have his mobile phone with him, but he thought he might be able to raise someone on his marine radio to call for roadside assistance. He climbed into the boat, clicked on the radio and said, "Mayday, mayday!"

A voice came on and said, "State your location."

My acquaintance gave the number of the road and explained he was about two miles south of the coast.

After a pause, the voice asked, "How fast were you going when you reached the shore?"

MARY MARINEAU

As I entered the supermarket, I noticed there were only two shopping trolleys available and they were jammed together so tightly they looked like one. A woman came in behind me and, as I held the handle of one trolley, she went to the end of the other and pulled. The trolley remained stuck. Then she held on fast while I tried to yank them apart. No luck. As a last resort we both pulled tug-of-war style.

A woman who had just been through the checkout queue came up to us. "You don't need to fight over it," she said. "One of you can have my trolley."

EMMY DAVIS

"I've got a funny feeling about this, Dave. Are you sure you ran it by legal?"

Some years ago, my dad, a lawyer, took me to a fancy restaurant. When the bill arrived, there was a £1.50 charge for bread and butter. Dad paid the bill, including the charge for bread and butter. However, the next day, he sent a letter to the restaurant stating that the charge was uncalled for. Enclosed in the same envelope was a bill for £500 in legal services.

Someone from the restaurant called immediately and asked, "What is this £500 bill for? We didn't order any legal services."

Dad replied, "I didn't order any bread and butter."

The £1.50 was returned.

CARL FIELD

My husband, a lawyer, is frequently consulted by clients who, after learning what the cost of legal services will be, decide to do without his aid. Recently the elderly minister of a small, struggling church came in with a legal problem.

After patiently listening to an explanation of my husband's fees, he left the office with a prudent: "Thank you, sir, but I believe I'll just pray this one through."

JAN LYONS

A man is pulled over by a police officer for a broken headlight. The policeman looks in the car and sees a collection of knives on the back seat. "Sir," he says. "Why do you have all those knives?"

"They're for my juggling act," the man replies.

"Prove it," says the policeman.

The man gets out of the car and begins juggling the knives just as two men drive by.

"Wow," says one guy. "I'm glad I stopped drinking. These new sobriety tests are hard."

BASIL HENDRICKSON

One weekend, a doctor, a priest and a lawyer were out in a fishing boat. Their motor had conked out and one of the oars had drifted off. Just as the doctor was about to dive in to retrieve the oar, the boat was surrounded by sharks.

"I can't go now," the doctor said. "If someone gets bitten, you'll need my services."

"I can't go either," said the priest. "If the doctor fails, I'll need to give last rites."

"Fine," said the lawyer. "I'll get it."

He dove in, the sharks moved, he retrieved the oar and climbed back into the boat. The doctor and priest looked flabbergasted. The lawyer just smiled and said, "Professional courtesy."

M. LEE

Our dinner party was heading for complete disaster.

One man, an insurance salesman, was monopolizing the conversation with a lengthy account of recent litigation involving himself. Since two other guests were solicitors, I became increasingly uneasy. "In the end," the salesman said, "you know who got all the money?" I cringed. "The lawyers!" he shouted.

There was an embarrassed silence at the table. My heart pounded until the wife of one solicitor exclaimed, "Oh I love a story with a happy ending."

JANE GHEGAN

While discussing the plight of driving test examiners, a former examiner told a story about a woman who was parallel parking. "Could you get a little closer?" the examiner asked.

And she slid over.

NEIL MORGAN

TIMELESS HUMOUR

70s As a new driver, I was very nervous about my first solo venture into town traffic. Not sure of my way, and intimidated by the congested streets, I soon found myself going the wrong way along a one-way street.

As luck would have it, the only place to turn around was in front of the police-station, and as I drove up I spied a young officer watching my manoeuvres. Completely flustered, I pulled the car round and waited to see what would happen.

Sure enough, the officer headed my way. Reaching the car, he enquired with a grin, "Giving yourself up?"

JOANNE MYLES

As a freelance secretary, I type story manuscripts. When an author pays me, I print the name of the story across the top of his cheque. Once when I took a cheque to the bank, the cashier suddenly froze. Only after I had explained my procedure to a bank officer did the reason for the cashier's reaction become clear.

The story was called "Your Money or Your Life," and that, of course, was what I had written in bold letters across the top of the cheque.

E. DESIDERIO

On a particularly busy day at my local supermarket I noticed a woman with a trolley-load of goods join the queue for the express checkout. Then a man with less than the maximum ten items came and stood behind her.

Seeing the trolley, he tapped her on the shoulder and told her this was the express checkout. She ignored him.

The man pointed to the notice which said "Ten items or less" and the woman snapped at him, "I can read."

He replied: "Ah yes, but can you count?"

JANICE MCGUIRE

My son, a lawyer, was approached by his friend, a priest, who wanted a will drawn up.

When the work was completed and ready to be sent out, my son could not resist inserting this note: **"Thy will be done."**

MARJORIE SUMMERS

I hear many excuses by those caught speeding. Once, the driver ran back to my police car to tell me someone in the car was sick and he was taking her to the hospital. I let the man go, but was suspicious when he declined my offer of a police escort. I decided to follow him.

By the time we reached the emergency entrance of the local hospital, I was feeling a little foolish about not trusting the man. When I noticed he was having difficulty getting an elderly woman out of his car, I walked over to offer my assistance. It was then that I overheard the struggling woman say, "Leave me alone. You told him someone was sick, so you be the sick one."

I wrote the ticket.

D. GUILLORY

My law partner was presenting a no-fault divorce case at court. The couple involved had no children, but they did have a dog, of whom both were very fond.

My partner stated that both parties agreed to share whatever medical expenses might be necessary for the care of the animal. They also agreed that the wife would have custody, but that the husband would be allowed visitation rights.

The judge, looking somewhat startled, peered down at the husband and asked, "Is this true?"

The husband replied, "Yes, Your Honour."

"Well," intoned the judge, with a trace of a smile on his face, "you should know that there is nothing this court can do for you if the dog refuses to see you."

STEPHEN MECKLER

SIGN LANGUAGE

Sign in a police station:
"In God we trust – others we polygraph."

TIMELESS HUMOUR

70s My grandfather, who was an ardent lay preacher, was concerned that he was speaking only to the converted. Then one day the Deacon rushed up to him after a service, and announced: "Somebody has taken my new raincoat from the cloakroom."

Grandfather raised his eyes heavenwards, and exclaimed with delight: "The Lord be praised, we're getting the sinners in at last."

MARY CARTER

Driving along a mountain road one night, my dad complained about the car behind us.

"That driver must be drunk," he said. "Every time I move over to let him overtake, he slows down. When I get back on the road, he gets closer and stays right behind me."

About 30 minutes later, the vehicle switched on a flashing blue light and my dad pulled over. Striding up to our window, the police officer said, "I'd like you to take a breathalyser test. You've been swerving on and off the road for over half an hour."

PRISCILLA YEN

Pavements were treacherous after a heavy snowstorm blanketed my university campus. Watching people slip and slide, I gingerly made my way to lectures.

Suddenly I found myself on a clean, snow-free section of pavement. This is weird, I thought – until I noticed that it was directly in front of the law building.

REBECCA HARRIS

My father was the presiding judge in a case involving a man charged with tax evasion. As the defendant stood before him alone, Dad asked if he had counsel.

Looking toward the ceiling, the man replied, "Jesus Christ is my counsellor and defender."

My father nodded slowly while framing his next question, which was, "Do you have local counsel?"

TOM CECIL

243

"Red means stop – not attack."

We were pulled over for speeding on a deserted road out in the countryside. The road was empty, and the policeman was almost apologetic about writing the ticket. He even complimented us for wearing our seat belts.

At that point, my wife leaned over and said, "Well, Officer, when you drive the speeds we do, you've got to wear them."

C. HUNT

Growing increasingly impatient as I drove round trying to find a well-known computer shop, I stopped to ask two young policemen.

"Excuse me," I said. "Could you tell me where PC World is?"

I cheered up no end when one replied, "Sorry. Never heard of him."

MARGARET FINCH

"I don't need to check anything with 'the boys in forensics', I know it was you."

My mum has a tendency to drive a little quickly, so I wasn't surprised when a policemen pulled us over as we made our way along a main road.

Hoping to get off with a warning, Mum tried to appear shocked when he walked up to the car.

"I have never been stopped like this before," she said to the officer.

"What do they usually do, madam?" he asked. "Shoot the tyres out?"

JOAN TORELLO

Amen to that

From the pulpit to the Pearly Gates, and everything in between,
this is higher humour at its best.

246

During his children's sermon, our assistant vicar asked the kids, **"What is grey, has a bushy tail, and gathers nuts in the autumn?"**

One five-year-old raised his hand. **"I know the answer should be Jesus,"** he began, **"but it sounds like a squirrel to me."**

REV. RICHARD O'HARA

As part of his talk at a banquet, our minister told some jokes and a few funny stories. Since he planned to use the same anecdotes at a meeting the next day, he asked reporters covering the event not to include them in their articles.

Reading the paper the following morning, he noticed that one well-meaning reporter had ended his story on the banquet with the observation "The minister told a number of stories that cannot be published."

DAN BETTS

Our synagogue was throwing a coming-out party of sorts for our new officiant, which was to be billed as "Coffee With the Cantor". The guest of honour, an Argentinian, suggested that rather than coffee we serve mate, a variation of a South American tea.

That idea was quickly vetoed, however, when we realised that we would be inviting the congregation to "Mate With the Cantor".

PHILLIP HAIN

We were celebrating the 100th anniversary of our church, and several former priests and the bishop were in attendance. At one point, our priest got the children to gather at the altar for a talk about the importance of the day. He began by asking them, "Does anyone know what the bishop does?"

There was silence. But finally, one little boy answered gravely, "He's the one you can move diagonally."

LILLIE LAMPE

At an ecumenical round-table discussion, various religious leaders tried to answer the question "When does life start?"

"At conception," said the Catholic priest.

"No, no," said the Presbyterian minister. "It begins at birth."

"It's in between," said the Baptist. "Life begins at 12 weeks when the foetus develops a functional heartbeat."

"I disagree with all of you," said the rabbi. "Life begins when your last child leaves home and takes the dog with him."

L. LEATHERMAN

My young son ran out of school shouting, "Mum! Mum! Are you a prostitute?"

"No!" I replied, aghast.

He looked at me quizzically.

"Well, what religion are you, then?"

DAWN LEWIS

247

While waiting in the checkout queue at a Christian bookstore, a man in front of me asked the assistant about a display of hats with the letters WWJD on them. The assistant explained that WWJD stood for "What would Jesus do?" and that the idea was to get people to consider this question when making decisions.

The man pondered a moment, then replied, "I don't think he'd pay that much for that hat."

T. ASH

Prior to our wedding, David and I met with our minister to discuss the marriage ceremony and various traditions, such as lighting the unity candle from two individual candles. Couples usually blow out the two candles as a sign of becoming one. Our minister said that many people were now leaving their individual candles lit to signify independence and personal freedom.

He asked if we wanted to extinguish our candles or leave them burning.

After thinking about it, David replied, "How about if we leave mine lit and blow out hers?"

C. TAUCHER

Shortly after my husband passed away, one of my daughter's Jewish friends approached her with a question. "Kate," he said, "I've never attended a Catholic wake before. What is the significance of the widow not wearing shoes?"

Kate replied, "My mother's feet hurt."

MARIE MAY

Operating high-pressure boilers can be stressful – like the time my two colleagues and I discovered a potentially dangerous leak in a boiler. Scorching steam was billowing out, filling up the room and decreasing visibility.

"I hope this doesn't get any bigger," said one colleague. "I don't want this steam to be the last thing I see in this world."

"That wouldn't be so bad," my other colleague replied. "As long as it's not the first thing you see in the next."

ROGER WILDEMAN

A distinguished minister and two elders from his congregation attended an out-of-town meeting that did not finish until rather late. They decided to have something to eat before going home, but unfortunately, the only spot open was a run-down café with a questionable reputation.

After being served, one of the elders asked the minister to say grace. "I'd rather not," the clergyman said. "I don't want him to know I'm here."

P. MARTIN

One Sunday our priest announced he was passing out miniature crosses made of palm leaves. "Put this cross in the room where your family argues most," he advised. "When you look at it, the cross will remind you that God is watching."

As I was leaving church, the woman in front of me walked up to the priest, shook his hand, and said, "I'll take five."

AARON RUPP

Our vicar's sermon was about how the institution of marriage is under assault in popular culture. He cited the TV programme *Desperate Housewives*.

"How many are going to watch the final episode?" he challenged.

When no one raised a hand, he smiled. "Nobody's willing to admit to being a fan?"

My mum whispered to me, "Actually, the series has ended."

DIANA JUE

During a school trip to north Wales, which I had volunteered to help with, we went hill walking.

Unfortunately, the weather was not brilliant, and as we were nearing the summit of a hill the cloud began to descend.

When we reached the top, I felt a tugging on my sleeve. It was a small girl. With a slight trace of concern in her voice, she whispered, "Miss, are we in heaven?"

SUSAN CONWAY

During a Sunday service, the pastor asked the congregation for their intentions. We heard the usual requests to pray for sick people and the acknowledgments for those who helped when a parishioner died. The sombre mood was broken when the last intention was heard.

A woman stood up and said, "My granddaughter turned 17 this week and received her driver's licence. Let us pray for us all."

KEN MALLORY

A young parish minister about to deliver his first sermon asked a retired cleric for advice on how to capture the congregation's attention. "Start with an opening line that's certain to grab them," the older man said. "For example: 'Some of the best years of my life were spent in the arms of a woman who was not my wife.'" He smiled at the younger man's shocked expression before adding, "She was my mother."

The next Sunday the young clergyman nervously clutched the pulpit rail in front of the congregation. Finally he said, "Some of the best years of my life were spent in the arms of a woman."

He was pleased at the instant reaction – then became panic-stricken. "But for the life of me, I can't remember who she was!"

GIL HARRIS

"Good to see you in church, Frank – but it doesn't change anything, I'm afraid ... you're still going to hell."

249

Sharma, my cousin, was telling me about an evening service at the church we've both attended for years. She and her husband usually sat in the back, but this time they moved up front to be sure to hear the Scripture reading. They sat beside a longtime church member who cheerfully said, "Good to have you with us! Where are you from?"

Taken by surprise, Sharma mumbled, "The back."

LAUREN GRISHAM

As our vicar went along the line of worshippers, giving them Holy Communion, he saw what he thought was a communion wafer lying on the floor. Because, as blessed bread, it had to be consumed, he popped it into his mouth.

"Mummy, Mummy," the small boy next to me cried out. "The vicar's eaten my Save the Children badge."

PAM DAVIES

The teacher in our Bible class asked a woman to read from the Book of Numbers about the Israelites wandering in the desert.

"The Lord heard you when you wailed, 'If only we had meat to eat!'" she began. "Now the Lord will give you meat. You will not eat it for just one day, or two days, or five, or ten or twenty days, but for a month: until you loathe it."

The woman paused, looked up and said, "Hey, isn't that the Atkins diet?"

DAVID MARTINO

While serving as church usher, I was carrying out our tradition of escorting parishioners to their seats before the service began. After I returned to the entrance of the sanctuary to escort the next party, I greeted two strangers and asked where they would like to sit.

Looking confused, the young man smiled and said, "Non-smoking, please."

JOHN PREWITT

Having stopped to take in a spectacular sunset, my husband, sons and I were on our way back to the car when four Buddhist monks dressed in orange

"Could it be under another name?"

robes walked past. When our sons asked about them, I explained, "Their life is a quest for enlightenment."

"I wonder what kind of car they drive," my husband said, and jokingly suggested, "a Ford Focus?"

The monks got into a Pathfinder.

DAWN PELLETIER

Both full-time students, my son and his wife don't have time or money for anything other than studying. I was with them in church one day when the vicar gave a sermon on marriage.

"The three most common problems that can lead to divorce," he warned, "involve money, children and sex."

My son whispered to his wife, "Then we should be OK. We don't have any of those."

SUSAN BRUNTON

Every Catholic church in town but one had its Mass schedule posted at the front of the building. The exception announced the time weekly bingo started. I phoned the priest to complain.

"My son," he replied, "our parishioners know when we hold Mass, but we have to be sure the Protestants know when we hold bingo."

JAMES DAILY

SIGN LANGUAGE

Seen when passing a church:

"Get in touch with God by knee mail."

DOROTHY CZARNECKI

During birth-preparation class we were learning relaxation techniques, and the instructor asked us to come up with ideas to lower stress levels. Silence pervaded the room, but one dad, a slight fellow with round glasses and a religious T-shirt, finally offered: "Prayer?"

"Good," the instructor replied. "Anything else?"

"How about sex?" suggested another father-to-be.

Once again, silence followed. Then the devout dad-to-be muttered under his breath, "What do you think I've been praying for?"

TRACY AND SCOTT YANCEY

There is a folk belief that if you bury a statue of St. Joseph on a piece of property, it will be sold more quickly. When I was getting ready to move, I took the Saint Joseph from my Nativity scene and buried it near my front door. A few days later a woman made an offer. Since she had to sell her property I suggested she enlist the help of the saint as well.

After a month of burying the statue in various places on her lawn, she had no buyers and, in disgust, put the statue out with her rubbish. A week later she opened her local paper and read: "Town Sells Landfill to Private Developer."

FRANCES LACASSE

I am a nun and was the only one in the main office of a small church when a deliveryman came to the door with several boxes. I assured him that it was the correct address, but he seemed hesitant to leave them with me.

It wasn't until I went to move the boxes that I understood his confusion. Stamped in bold letters across the sides were the contents: "Madonna Calendars".

JANET CARR

Toward the close of a meal held during an Episcopal Church convention some years ago, the bishop of the diocese stood up and quite disrupted the entire affair by announcing, "We will reserve the entertainment of the evening until the waitresses have taken everything off."

W. LEAR

A group of guys I know took a trip to France and decided to attend Mass in a small town, even though none of them understood French. They managed to stand, kneel, and sit when the rest of the congregation did, so it wouldn't be obvious they were tourists. At one point, the priest spoke and the man sitting next to them stood up, so they got up too. The entire congregation broke into hearty laughter.

After the service they approached the priest, who spoke English, and asked him what had been so funny. The priest said he had announced a birth in the parish and asked the father to stand up.

JEFF POWELL

252

One Sunday morning my sister Liz was surprised to receive a phone call from her priest. He reported that he'd just been in a minor car accident and asked if she could inform the congregation he'd be unable to conduct services that day.

Liz was flattered that out of the entire congregation, she was the one he had called – until the priest went on to say that since Liz was always the last to arrive at church, he knew she would be the only person he could still reach at home.

WILLIAM HIMROD

A doctor died and went to heaven, where he found a long line at St. Peter's gate. As was his custom, the doctor rushed to the front, but St. Peter told him to wait in line like everyone else. Muttering and looking at his watch, the doctor stood at the end of the line.

Moments later a white-haired man wearing a white coat and carrying a stethoscope and medical bag rushed up to the front of the line, waved to St. Peter, and was immediately admitted through the Pearly Gates.

"Hey!" the doctor shouted. "How come you let him through?"

"Oh," said St. Peter, "that's God. Sometimes he likes to play doctor."

PATRICIA THOMAS

I admit I'm not a regular church goer, so I was a bit uncomfortable when my wife talked me into being a greeter one Sunday. But after a few minutes passing out bulletins, I started to warm to the job. Things were going pretty well until a distinguished-looking gentleman approached. "Good morning," I offered. "It's a pleasure to have you with us today."

"Thank you very much, and may I say the same to you," said the man, shaking my hand, "as your minister."

RICHARD HIMES

At church, the lay reader who had been leading us so beautifully through the service was suddenly unsure whether we should sit or kneel. "Let us knit," she said.

J. STUART-WHITE

The ten-year-old boy was failing maths. His parents tried everything to get him to do well in school, but nothing worked. Finally they enrolled him in a Catholic school. From his first day, the boy spent every night poring over books. When his first report card came, he had received an A in maths.

"Son," his father asked, "what made the difference in maths class? The nuns? The textbooks?"

"Dad, I had never taken maths seriously before," the boy admitted. "But when I walked in and saw that guy nailed to the plus sign, I knew this place meant business!"

SCOTT BIHL

Coal black nights make parachute jumps very difficult and dangerous. As a result, we attach small lights called chemlites to our jumpsuits to make ourselves visible to the rest of our team.

Late one night, lost after a practice jump, members of my unit knocked on the door of an isolated cottage. When a woman answered, she was greeted by the sight of five men festooned in glowing chemlites.

"Excuse me," I said. "Can you tell me where we are?"

The startled woman replied, "Earth."

BILL BLACK

For the past year or so, my husband has helped count the collection money after church. One Sunday a visitor placed a £500 cheque in the plate. After the service my husband congratulated the priest on the large donation. "I'm sure it was because of your wonderful sermon," he gushed.

"Oh, boy," replied the priest. "If you can't be more honest than that, how can I trust you to count our money?"

SANDRA CROPSEY

My brother-in-law has a great e-mail address. It starts PS81_10b@, to represent the second half of the Bible verse Psalms 81:10, which states, "Open wide your mouth and I will fill it."

By the way, he's a dentist.

JEANNE WARSING

Taking advantage of a balmy day, my brother and three other priests swapped their clerical garb for polos shirts and khakis and time on the golf course. After several horrible shots, their caddy asked, "Are you guys priests?"

"Actually, yes," one cleric replied. "Why?"

"Because," said the caddy, "I've never seen such bad golf and such clean language."

PAULA O'GORMAN

While in seminary, I taught the Old Testament to prisoners. One evening as I waited for a guard to appear and check me in, I noticed the fellow ahead of me fidgeting and constantly checking his watch. Take a chill pill, I thought.

Finally the guard came. The man scribbled his name in the visitors' book and rushed inside. "What does that guy teach?" I asked the guard.

"Serenity Through Meditation."

DAN FITZGERALD

SIGN LANGUAGE

Slogan for a now out-of-business restaurant:

"Karma Café. We don't have a menu. We give you just what you deserve."

JAN VEDER

Doug was leaving church after Christmas services when Father McCarthy took him aside. "Douglas, my son," he said, "it's time you joined the Army of the Lord. We need to see you every Sunday."

"I'm already in the Army of the Lord, Father," Doug replied.

"Then why do we only see you at Christmas and Easter?"

Doug looked to the right and to the left, and then leaned over to whisper in Father McCarthy's ear. "I'm in the Secret Service."

LOREEN BRODERICK

NEW! BROADBAND CRUCIFIX – FASTER ACCESS TO GOD!

IAN BAKER

255

The young couple met with their vicar to set a date for their wedding. When he asked whether they preferred a contemporary or a traditional service, they opted for the former.

On the big day, a big storm forced the groom to take an alternate route to the church. The streets were flooded, so he rolled up his trouser legs to keep them dry. When he finally reached the church, his best man rushed him into the sanctuary and up to the altar, just as the ceremony was starting. "Pull down your trousers," whispered the vicar.

"Uh, Reverend, I've changed my mind," the groom responded. "I think I want the traditional service."

The Presbyterians were convening in Scotland. After a couple of days of sitting on hard pews, a group decided to stretch their legs in the countryside. Soon they approached a rickety old bridge over a river. They were so busy talking they missed the Keep Off the Bridge sign.

A villager saw them step onto the dangerous span and yelled for them to stop. "That's all right," one of the ministers responded. "We're here from the Presbyterian convention."

"I dinna care aboot that," came the reply. "But if ye go much farther, ye'll all be Baptists!"

CLYDE MURDOCK

A friend of mine, a professional organist, was asked to play for a wedding. Unfamiliar with the church's organ, she went to the sanctuary to practice. Curious about a small keyboard that slid out from under the two regular keyboards, she tapped out a couple of bars of a children's song but heard nothing. Then she played a few more notes, but still no organ music.

Just then a man came running into the church, shouting, "Who's playing 'Three Blind Mice' on the church-steeple bells?"

She had been operating the carillon.

JUDY BURRESS

Not long after I resigned as vicar of a small community church, the phone rang. "Is the reverend there?" a man asked.

I explained that I was a minister, though not the current vicar.

"You'll do," he said. The man wanted to know which Scripture verses applied to funeral services.

I gave him several references, and he jotted them down.

"What about the 'ashes to ashes, dust to dust' part?" he asked.

I read it to him slowly. Then, intending to offer him some sympathy, I inquired, "And who is the deceased?"

"My daughter's rabbit," he replied.

FRED FIRSTBROOK

The ordination of women as Episcopal ministers occasionally presents awkward situations as to what to call us. "Father" sounds inappropriate to some; "Mother" is traditionally used for unordained women overseeing religious communities.

Last year, one of my colleagues, dressed in her clerical garb, was in an airport. A man summoned the courage to ask her, "Pardon me, but what do you call a female father?"

My colleague smiled mischievously and replied, "Ambisextrous."

MARY APPLETON

In the newsroom of the newspaper where I'm employed, my colleagues and I were busily working during an afternoon thunderstorm. Suddenly an unusually loud clap of thunder rattled the windows, and every light in the place went out – except one.

Bathed in the glow of the remaining light sat our religion writer, a minister, at his desk. Apparently not surprised, he stood and bowed, receiving our applause with aplomb.

JEAN GIGANTE

I was working as a phone-order sales assistant for a textbook publisher. One very busy day, many customers had been put on hold. When I took my next call, I heard a soft yet annoyed voice on the line muttering, "Darn, darn, damn, darn, darn it!"

I chuckled and said, "What may I help you with today?"

There was a brief silence, followed by, "I'm so sorry. I wish to place an order."

"Don't be sorry," I replied. "That's hardly the worst thing I've heard today. Now, first I need your name."

"Oh, dear," she said, "how embarrassing. My name is Sister Patience."

R. WINGROVE

Work was being done on the roof of my church's tower and I climbed up into the bell chamber to see how it was going.

As I talked to the foreman, one of his men was outside on the roof trying to open a trapdoor that probably hadn't been touched for centuries.

As he struggled and struggled, the air turned increasingly blue.

Concerned for my sensibilities, the foreman shouted, "Bill, cut out the swearing. I've got the bl**dy vicar here!"

REVEREND JOHN BOURNE

257

Notice outside a church:
"God loves all sorts."

Graffiti underneath:
"Except the coconut ones."

ELAINE TRENT

When a bishop came to visit a nearby church, the congregation was keen to impress, particularly with the "responses" during the service.

Unfortunately, he experienced some problems with his microphone and just as he was about to say, "The Lord be with you," it broke down completely. "There's something wrong with this," he announced.

"And also with you," came the quick response.

ROSEMARIE DARBY

Saying her evening prayers, my daughter began: "Dear Peter, please look after Mummy and Daddy ... "

Thinking Sunday School had confused her with tales of the disciples, I tried to correct her.

"But that's his first name," my daughter insisted. "We always say it at the end of prayers: 'Thanks Peter God'."

CHRISTOPHER CAMPBEL

My husband is a preacher. At a revival meeting, the visiting choir sang at the beginning and then turned the service over to him. Wanting to compliment them, my husband said, "The singing was so good, we could all leave right now without any preaching."

A parishioner called out, "Amen, brother!"

PAM LOCKE

The preacher, arriving in a small town to be guest speaker at a local church, wanted to post a letter to his family back home. He stopped a young boy on a bike and asked him where the post office was. The boy gave him directions, and the preacher thanked him.

"If you come to church this evening," the preacher said, "I'll tell you how to get to heaven."

"I don't think I'll be there," the boy said. "You don't even know your way to the post office."

ARTHUR GAMMON

"Somehow, I thought it would be different up here."

One Easter Sunday, my husband was trying unsuccessfully to get our young sons to eat lunch. It was no wonder they weren't hungry as they had been scoffing enormous chocolate eggs just an hour before.

My mother-in-law, who had been to church that morning, commented without thinking, "It's Easter Sunday. What do you expect? A miracle?"

JENNIFER SMITH

Going over our church finances, I found a receipt for paint from a DIY store.

It said that the paint had been purchased for us by someone called Christian. I wasn't aware of anyone buying any such product, so I called the shop to point out its mistake.

"I'm sorry," I told the manager, "but there are no Christians here at First Baptist Church."

R. MAYHEW

Bob is taking a walk when his foot gets caught in some railway tracks. He tries to pull it out, but it gets wedged in tighter. Then he spots a train bearing down on him. Panicking, he starts to pray, "Please, Lord. Get my foot out and I'll stop drinking." But it's still stuck. As he struggles to free himself, he prays again, "Please! Help me and I'll stop drinking and swearing." Still nothing.

"I'm begging you, Lord," Bob pleads. "Let me live and I'll stop drinking, swearing and I'll give all my money to the poor." Suddenly, his foot slips free and he lunges to safety as the train thunders past. "Whew," he says. "Thanks anyway, God, but I took care of it myself."

CHRIS PARKE

Roy Delgado

259

SIGN LANGUAGE

A bulletin in a local church listed hymns for the service. The last one was:

"Jesus, Remember Me (if time permits)."

RUTH HEINECKE

Our vicar was teaching Proverbs 16:24: "Pleasant words are as an honeycomb, sweet to the soul, and health to the bones."

The minister then added, "You can catch more flies with honey than with vinegar."

My wife leaned over, put her head on my shoulder, and whispered in my ear, "I just love to watch your muscles ripple when you take out the rubbish."

TOM KOLOSICK

A motorist was driving in the country when he came upon a priest and a rabbi standing on the shoulder of the road, fishing. Next to them was a sign that read "Turn Around. The End Is Near."

The motorist didn't like to be preached to, so he rolled down the window and yelled, "Mind your own business, you religious nuts!"

A few seconds later the two fishermen heard tyres screech, then a splash.

The rabbi turned to the priest and said, "I told you we should've just written, 'Bridge Out'."

C. RIGGS

The newly appointed priest was being briefed by the housekeeper on problems in the rectory that required immediate attention. "Your roof needs repair, Father," she said. "Your water pressure is bad and your boiler is not working."

"Now, Mrs. Kelly," the priest allowed, "you've been the housekeeper here five years, and I've only been here a few days. Why not say our roof and our boiler?"

Several weeks later, when the priest was meeting with the bishop and several other priests, Mrs. Kelly burst into the office, terribly upset. "Father, Father," she blurted, "there's a mouse in our room and it's under our bed!"

DORIS CYPHER

A preacher was asking for contributions to the church's programme to buy food for the needy. The town gambler, who also owned the saloon and several other shady operations, offered the preacher a donation.

"You can't take that," a scandalised deacon told the preacher. "That's the devil's money."

"Well, brother," said the preacher, cheerfully accepting the gift, "in that case, the devil has had his hands on it long enough. Now let's see what the Lord will do with it."

JAMES DENT

It was a typical back-seat scene between my two boys: Keaton was flicking Kade in the ear. "Stop!" said Kade, punching his brother lightly on the arm.

Immediately Keaton began to scream and cry as if his arm had been severed. I looked at him in the rearview mirror and said, "Did he really hurt you that badly?"

"Yes! He hit me very hard!"

"Keaton," I said, "Jesus knows when you're lying."

My son paused. "Well, yeah," he said. "But does he tell you?"

M. COATES

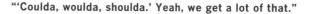

"'Coulda, woulda, shoulda.' Yeah, we get a lot of that."

QUOTABLE
QUOTES

It is absurd to divide people into good and bad. People are either charming or tedious.

OSCAR WILDE

Learn to enjoy your own company. You are the one person you can count on living with for the rest of your life.

ANN RICHARDS in O: The Oprah Magazine

The children of Israel wandered the desert for 40 years. Even in Biblical times, men wouldn't ask for directions.

RUMESA KHALID

My dad believes in reincarnation, so in his will he left everything to himself.

JACKIE GRAZIANO

The true measure of a man is how he treats someone who can do him absolutely no good.

ANN LANDERS

I used to be Snow White, but I drifted.

MAE WEST

An eye for an eye only leads to more blindness.

MARGARET ATWOOD

For two people in marriage to live together day after day is unquestionably the one miracle the Vatican has overlooked.

BILL COSBY Love and Marriage (Doubleday)

261

Bill goes to church one Sunday and hears a sermon about the Ten Commandments. He has an epiphany and goes to confession.

"Forgive me, Father, for I have sinned," he begins.

"Go ahead," the priest says.

"Well, I lost my hat and I came to church to steal one. But then I heard your sermon and I changed my mind."

"I'm glad," the priest replies. "'Thou shalt not steal' is a powerful commandment."

"True," Bill says. "But it was when you said, 'Thou shalt not commit adultery' that I remembered where my hat was."

The teenager asked his father for a car. "Not until you start studying your Talmud and get your hair cut," his father said.

A month later the boy approached his father again. "Well," the father said, "I know you've been reading the Talmud quite diligently, but your hair's still long."

"You know, Dad," the boy replied, "I've been thinking about that. All the prophets had long hair."

"That's true," the boy's father said. "And everywhere they went, they walked."

Kevin was not an ideal child. He managed to get into mischief frequently, and was always trailed by his younger brother, Ken. Finally, at her wits' end, his long-suffering mother took him to see their parish priest. The father decided to focus Kevin's mind on higher levels.

"Kevin," he asked with great seriousness, "where is God?"

Kevin gave no reply.

"Kevin, where is God?"

Again there was silence.

For a third time the priest asked the question, and this time Kevin bolted out of the office and ran all the way home. He burst into his brother's room.

NO!

It was the answer to his prayers. Not the one he was hoping for, but an answer nonetheless.

"Ken," he panted breathlessly, "Father can't find God and he thinks we had something to do with it!"

JAN SCHREDL

Desperate for a child, a couple asked their priest to pray for them. "I'm going on sabbatical to Rome," he replied. "I'll light a candle in St. Peter's for you."

When the priest returned three years later, he found the wife pregnant, tending two sets of twins. Elated, the priest asked to speak to her husband and congratulate him.

"He's gone to Rome," came the harried reply, "to blow out that candle."

K. YODER

Our well-built, six-foot tall curate read out his own marriage banns and finished by saying,

"If anyone knows just cause or impediment why we should not be joined in holy matrimony, please meet me outside the south door at the end of this service."

NEIL DAWTRY

After my five-year-old, Ryan, had told me what I assumed to be his first little fib, I decided it was time to tell him about the boy who cried wolf. He liked the story and had me tell it to him several times. Hoping the moral would sink in, I asked if he had learned anything. "Yes," Ryan answered. "You can only tell a lie twice."

KELLY SARE

At the gates of heaven, a woman asked St. Peter, "How do I get into heaven?"

"You have to spell a word," said St. Peter.

"Which word?" she asked.

"Love," he replied. She spelled it correctly and was welcomed into heaven.

A year later, she was watching the gates for St. Peter when her husband arrived. "How've you been?" she asked.

"Oh, I've been doing pretty well since you died," he answered. "I married the young nurse who took care of you while you were ill. I won the lottery, so I sold the house we'd lived in and bought a mansion. We travelled the world and were in Cancún when I fell and hit my head, and here I am. How do I get in?"

"You have to spell a word," she told him.

"Which word?" he asked.

"Czechoslovakia."

KERRY BARNUM

Two priests died at the same time and met St. Peter at the Pearly Gates. "Our computer's down," said St. Peter. "You'll have to go back for a week, but you can't go back as priests. What'll it be?"

The first priest said, "I've always wanted to be an eagle, soaring high above the mountains."

"So be it," said St. Peter, and off flew the first priest.

The second priest thought for a moment and asked, "Will any of this week count?"

"No," said St. Peter.

"Well," the priest said, "I've always wanted to be a stud."

"So be it," said St. Peter. A week later, the computer was fixed, and the Lord told St. Peter to recall the two priests. "Will you have any trouble locating them?" he asked.

"The first one should be easy," said St. Peter. "He's somewhere over the Alps, flying with the eagles. But the second one could prove more difficult."

"Why?" asked the Lord.

"He's on a snow tyre somewhere in Canada," said St. Peter.

RUMESA KHALID

On business in Edinburgh, my husband popped into a church hall which was offering morning coffee to passers-by.

He asked a young man pouring drinks if the church served agnostics.

The helper ruminated on this for a while before answering, "No, only what's on the counter."

RAY MARR

263

TIMELESS HUMOUR

70s While I was saying a few farewell calls before moving to a new parish, one elderly parishioner paid me the compliment of suggesting that my successor would not be as good as I had been. "Nonsense," I replied, flattered. "No, really," insisted the old lady. "I've lived here under five different vicars, and each new one has been worse than the last."

REV. ERIC DAVIS

A big, burly man paid a visit to a vicar's home.

"Sir," he said, "I wish to draw your attention to the terrible plight of a poor family. The father is unemployed and the mother can't work because of the nine children she must bring up. They are hungry and will be forced on to the street unless someone pays their rent."

"How terrible!" exclaimed the vicar. Touched by the concern of a man with such a gruff appearance, he asked, "May I ask who you are?"

"Yes," sobbed the visitor. "I'm their landlord."

On my first day in a Sky sales department, I had to make a call to a potential customer with my managers listening in.

A very elderly lady answered and, because I was so nervous, I found myself saying, "Hello, this is Gabriella calling from the sky" rather than "This is Gabriella from Sky".

"Oooh, I'm terribly sorry for not making a donation at church last week," the old dear replied, sounding concerned. "Please don't take it out on Albert."

I became so flustered that I put down the phone. Perhaps I should have explained first that I was from a TV company and not, as she clearly thought, an angel.

GABRIELLA EDE

A man is about to be savaged by an enormous bear. Terrified, he cries out, "God help me."

A bright light appears in the sky and a voice booms, "Why should I help you when you've led a wicked life and never even believed in me?"

"I know, I'm sorry," says the man. "But I promise that I'll become a Christian if you save me."

"No," says God. "It's too late for you to change now."

"Well, could you at least make the bear a Christian?" begs the man.

"Fair enough," God replies.

The bright light disappears and the man notices the bear has fallen to its knees. Then it puts its hands together and says, "For what we are about to receive ... "

BRENDA SMITH

264

We accompanied our son and his fiancée when they met with her priest to sign some pre-wedding ceremony papers.

While filling out the form, our son read aloud a few questions. When he got to the last one, which read **"Are you entering this marriage at your own will?"** he looked over at his fiancée.

"Put down 'yes'," she said.

LILYAN VAN ALMELO

An old friend and I were on holiday in Israel and decided to take a trip on the Sea of Galilee. The boat operator told us how much he charged. My friend was astounded at the high price and told the operator so.

"But these are the waters on which Christ himself walked," the man protested.

"If that's how much it is to take the boat, no wonder," my friend replied.

DANIEL LANNON

One Sunday, shortly after receiving my provisional driving-licence, I drove my parents to church. After a long, rough ride, we reached our destination. I stopped at the entrance to drop my mother off, and when she got out of the car, she said "Thank you."

"Any time!" I replied.

As my mother slammed the door shut, I heard her call out, "I wasn't speaking to you. I was talking to God."

AMY LOWE

At church recently, I stopped to study an announcement promoting the youth choir's charity sale. Being an English teacher, I couldn't resist the temptation to

Moses Separating His Laundry

correct the last line, which read "Donations Excepted". I crossed out the misused word and pencilled in "Donations Accepted".

After the service, I glanced at the announcement again, this time noting yet another pencilled-in correction. It now read "Donations Expected".

LORI DIGBY

During the last few days before our university finals, everyone in my comparative-religion class was frantic with revision.

The lecturer had just reviewed an Eastern concept he identified as

Taoist, when a frazzled and confused student protested to him, "You said that was a Buddhist belief!"

The lecturer looked up and informed him, "I'm afraid not. That was Zen. This is Tao".

TIM WATERS

Jesus, Moses, and an old bearded guy were playing golf. On the first tee, Moses shanked his ball into a lake. He parted the water and hit his ball onto the green.

Jesus teed off, hitting his ball into another water hazard. But he walked on water and stroked his ball just short of the cup.

Then the old man with the beard stepped up for his tee shot. He hit the ball with tremendous force, but hooked it badly. The ball bounced off the clubhouse roof, hit the cart path, and rolled down a hill into a pond, coming to rest on a lily pad. A frog hopped over and picked up the ball, then an eagle swooped down, snatched the frog, and flew over the green. The frog dropped the ball, and it rolled into the cup for a hole in one.

Moses turned to Jesus and said, "I hate playing golf with your dad."

RICHARD WRIGHT

265

A crafty cleric

As he sat himself down in the railway carriage, confronting the bishop and Mrs. Proudie, as they started on their first journey to Barchester, [the Rev. Obadiah Slope] began to form in his own mind a plan of his future life. He knew well his patron's strong points, but he knew the weak ones as well. He understood correctly enough to what attempts the new bishop's high spirit would soar, and he rightly guessed that public life would better suit the great man's taste than the small details of diocesan duty.

He, therefore, he, Mr. Slope, would in effect be Bishop of Barchester. Such was his resolve, and, to give Mr. Slope his due, he had both courage and spirit to bear him out in his resolution. He knew that he should have a hard battle to fight, for the power and patronage of the see would be equally coveted by another great mind – Mrs. Proudie would also choose to be Bishop of Barchester. Mr. Slope, however, flattered himself that he

could outmanoeuvre the lady. She must live much in London, while he would always be on the spot. She would necessarily remain ignorant of much, while he would know everything belonging to the diocese. At first, doubtless, he

must flatter and cajole, perhaps yield, in some things; but he did not doubt of ultimate triumph. If all other means failed, he could join the bishop against his wife, inspire courage into the unhappy man, lay an axe to the root of the

Anthony Trollope, *Barchester Towers*

woman's power, and emancipate the husband.

Such were his thoughts as he sat looking at the sleeping pair in the railway carriage, and Mr. Slope is not the man to trouble himself with such thoughts for nothing. He is possessed of more than average abilities, and is of good courage. Though he can stoop to fawn, and stoop low indeed, if need be, he has still within him the power to assume the tyrant; and with the power he has certainly the wish. His acquirements are not of the highest order, but such as they are they are completely under control, and he knows the use of them. He is gifted with a certain kind of pulpit eloquence, not likely indeed to be persuasive with men, but powerful with the softer sex. In his sermons he deals greatly in denunciations, excites the minds of his weaker hearers with a not unpleasant terror, and leaves an impression on their minds that all mankind are in a perilous state, and all womankind too, except those who attend regularly to the evening lectures in Baker Street. His looks and tones are extremely severe, so much so

that one cannot but fancy that he regards the greater part of the world as being infinitely too bad for his care. As he walks through the streets, his very face denotes his horror of the world's wickedness; and there is always an anathema lurking in the corner of his eye ...

Mr. Slope is tall, and not ill-made. His feet and hands are large, as has ever been the case with all his family, but he has a broad chest and wide shoulders to carry off these excrescences, and on the whole his figure is good. His countenance, however, is not specially prepossessing. His hair is lank, and of a dull pale reddish hue. It is always formed into three straight lumpy masses, each brushed with admirable precision, and cemented with much grease; two of them adhere closely to the sides of his face, and the other lies at right angles above them. He wears no whiskers, and is always punctiliously shaven. His face is nearly of the same colour as his hair, though perhaps a little redder: it is not unlike beef – beef, however, one would say, of a bad quality. His forehead is capacious and high, but

square and heavy, and unpleasantly shining. His mouth is large, though his lips are thin and bloodless; and his big, prominent, pale brown eyes inspire anything but confidence. His nose, however, is his redeeming feature: it is pronounced, straight and well formed; though I myself should have liked it better did it not possess a somewhat spongy, porous appearance, as though it had been cleverly formed out of a red-coloured cork.

I never could endure to shake hands with Mr. Slope. A cold, clammy perspiration always exudes from him; the small drops are ever to be seen standing on his brow, and his friendly grasp is unpleasant.

Of Mr. Slope's conduct much cannot be said, as his grand career is yet to commence; but ... [he has] a pawing, greasy way with him, which does not endear him to those who do not value him for their souls' sake, and he is not a man to make himself at once popular in a large circle such as is now likely to surround him at Barchester.

267

Jake, Johnny and Billy died and went to heaven. "Welcome," Saint Peter said. "You'll be very happy here if you just obey our rule: never step on a duck. If you step on a duck, it quacks, then all the other ducks start quacking and it makes a terrible racket."

That sounded simple enough until they passed through the Pearly Gates and saw thousands of ducks everywhere. Jake stepped on one straight away. The ducks quacked, making an unholy racket, and Saint Peter came up to Jake bringing with him a ferocious-looking woman. "I warned you you'd be punished," he said. Then he chained the woman to Jake for eternity.

Several hours later, Johnny stepped on a duck. The duck quacked, they all quacked and Saint Peter stepped up to Johnny with an angry-looking shrewish woman. "As your punishment," Saint Peter told Johnny, "you'll be chained to this woman for all eternity."

Billy was extremely careful not to step on a duck. Several months went by. Then Saint Peter appeared with a gorgeous woman and chained her to Billy.

"Wow!" exclaimed Billy. "I wonder what I did to deserve this?"

"I don't know about you," said the beautiful woman, "but I stepped on a duck."

PENNY WILLIAM

"I think we may have flown too far south."

My friend and I delivered a large refrigerator to the local priest's home. With difficulty we had managed to get the fridge into the porch, but struggled for over 20 minutes to make the 90-degree turn through the narrow door. The priest, seeing our difficulty, asked what we usually did when confronted with such a situation.

Rubbing some badly skinned knuckles, I replied, "Well, Father, at this point we usually start cursing."

"Well, gentlemen," Father replied, "allow me time to move out of earshot so you can continue your work."

JOHN GILLIS

On holiday in Hawaii, two priests decide to wear casual clothes so they won't be identified as clergy. They buy Hawaiian shirts and sandals and hit the beach.

They notice a gorgeous blonde in a very small bikini. "Good afternoon, Fathers," she says as she strolls by. The men are stunned. How can she tell that they are clergy? Later they go out and buy even wilder attire: surfer shorts, tie-dyed T-shirts and shades. Next day, they go back to the beach.

The fabulous blonde, now wearing a string bikini, passes by again. "Good morning, Fathers," she says politely.

"Just a minute," says one of the priests. "We're priests and proud of it, but how in the world did you know?"

"Don't you recognize me? I'm Sister Catherine from the convent."

MICHAEL RANA

"The fool's paradise is the next gate down."

The funeral directors of the mortuary where I am a receptionist were asked by a grieving family if they could place a golf club in the casket alongside their uncle, who had been an avid golfer. "Of course," was the answer.

On the day of the funeral, as the pallbearers descended the steps toward the hearse, a loud rattling and rolling came from the coffin. "Sounds like a pinball machine," murmured one startled director.

Later a family member of the deceased came to the chapel office to apologise. At the last minute, they had decided to place in the casket, along with the club, a half-dozen golf balls.

SHIRLEY THOMPSON

Finally! After 25 years on a desert island, Joe was being rescued. As he climbed onto the boat, the curious crew noticed three small grass huts. "What are those?" they asked.

"The first one is my home," Joe said. "The second is my church."

"What about the third hut?" the rescuers wanted to know.

"Oh," says Joe, "that's the church I used to belong to."

THOMAS ALLEN

Once when I was a pastor, I visited a lady with a bad back. She was lying down on the lounge floor – the most comfortable position she could find. I asked if she would like me to lay my hands on her back and pray, to which she said "yes".

I quickly felt a significant surge of warmth from her back, and I excitedly explained that this could be God performing the healing process.

"I'm sorry to disappoint you," she sighed, "but that is my hot water bottle."

DAVID HILL

It was my friend's first night working at the nursing home run by an order of Catholic nuns. She was assigned Mr. Jones, a patient known for being difficult. No amount of persuasion could convince him that it was time to go to bed.

In desperation, my friend sought the night sister's help. "Now, now, Mr. Jones," the sister began as she bustled into the room. "It's time for us to go to bed."

Without hesitating, Mr. Jones answered, "Sure as we do, we'll get caught."

RUTH WILLEMS

I can't believe I locked my keys inside, again!

St. Peter

Reynolds

A solicitor I know once drafted wills for an elderly husband and wife who had been somewhat apprehensive about discussing death. When they arrived to sign the documents, he ushered the couple into his office.

"Now," he said to them, "which one of you wants to go first?"

ROBERT CUNNINGHAM

After the evening service at my local church began, there was a torrential downpour. When the rain ceased I heard the persistent trickle of water as it flowed off the roof.

This was so distracting that at the end of the service I told the minister: "I've spent the evening listening to an annoying drip!"

I only realised what I had said when I saw the shock on his face.

ISHBEL MACKAY

One Sunday my teenage son was in church. When the collection plate was passed around, he pulled a coin from his pocket and dropped it in. Just at that moment the person behind him tapped him on the shoulder and handed him a £20 note.

Secretly admiring the man's generosity, my son placed the £20 in the plate and passed it on. Then he felt another tap from behind and heard a whisper: "Son, that was your £20. It fell out of your pocket."

MARY LOWE

Do you know how to make holy water?

You take some regular water and you boil the hell out of it.

JACKIE MARTLING

"Please serve me the fibrous chicken, give me a headset that cuts in and out, and ask the passenger in front of me to recline fully, that I may achieve the purified state of total suffering."

My husband, who believes in avoiding doctors and hospitals at all costs, had to have emergency surgery for an inflamed appendix. In pain, but still protesting the whole idea of an operation, he muttered, "When God gave man an appendix, there must have been a reason for putting it there."

"Oh, there was," said the surgeon. "God gave you that appendix so I could put my children through university."

JUDITH STOLTZ

"If I sold my house and my car, donated my possessions to charity, and gave all my money to the church, would I get into heaven?" a teacher asked the children in her Sunday school class.

"No!" the children all answered.

"If I cleaned the church every day, mowed the lawn, and kept everything neat and tidy, would I get into heaven?"

Again the answer was, "No!"

"Well," she continued, "then how can I get to heaven?"

A five-year-old boy shouted out, "You have to be dead!"

R. WARNER

"Frankly, I'm quite disappointed with the technology."

The vicar of my church hates to plead for money. But when the coffers were running low, he had no choice. "There's good news and there's bad news," he told the congregation. "The good news is that we have more than enough money for all the current and future needs of the parish. The bad news is, it's still in your pockets."

ILES SCHMITT

Our priest suddenly became ill and asked his twin brother, also a priest, to fill in for him and conduct a funeral Mass scheduled for that day. His brother, of course, agreed. It was not until the brother was accompanying the casket down the aisle, however, that he realised that he had neglected to ask the sex of the deceased. This was information that he would need for his remarks during the service.

As he approached the first pew where the deceased's relatives were seated, he nodded toward the casket and whispered to one woman, "Brother or sister?"

"Cousin," she replied.

GEORGE MILHAM

One night when my son was five years old, I told him the Bible story about Noah and the Ark. I gave him the full treatment, complete with animal sounds and howling winds and detailed descriptions of the beasts arriving two by two. I could tell he was captivated as he stared at me in wonder, and as I finished the story, I asked him if he had any questions.

His stare never wavered as he replied, "Where were you hiding?"

B. WILLIAMS

TIMELESS HUMOUR

50s My first church was a small country one. Full of enthusiasm and eager to build up the congregation, I decided that my sermons would set a standard of excellence heretofore unknown in the community. With high hopes I went to work.

The sermon was a masterpiece. The comments of the congregation at the conclusion of the service merely reaffirmed what I already knew – I was terrific! The last parishioner to leave was a lady of great age.

"Did anyone ever tell you how wonderful you are?" she asked softly. My answer of "no" lacked all vestige of conviction.

"Well, then," she said, "wherever did you get the idea?"

N. LINDNER, CHAPLAIN

A man walks into a church one day and kneels down to pray. "Lord," he says, "I've made mistakes, but I'm determined to change. If you let me win the lottery, I promise to be a good servant and never bother you again."

Nothing happens. So the next week the man tries again. "Please, God, let me win the lottery, and I'll come to church every week."

Again nothing happens. So the man decides to try one last time. "Lord," he implores, "why haven't I won the lottery? Have you abandoned me?"

Suddenly a deep voice booms down from above. "My son, I have not abandoned you, but at least meet me halfway – buy a ticket!"

SIMON MCDERMOTT

On a school trip to a cathedral, we were guided around the site in our tutor groups, which are referred to by the initials of the class teacher. My class, 12JC, spent ages studying the main altar area.

We got some odd looks from other visitors when our guide, in full cathedral dress, stood at the altar declaring, "Hurry up, JC. We haven't got all day"

DANIEL HANCOCK

A human-resources director found herself at the Pearly Gates. "We've never had a human-resources director here before," said St. Peter. "So we're going to let you spend one day in heaven and one in hell, and you can choose where to spend eternity."

"I'll go to hell first and get it over with," said the HR director.

To her surprise she spent a wonderful day with her former fellow executives, playing golf on a beautiful course. The game was followed by a sumptuous meal at the clubhouse. When she returned to heaven, she spent her day there sitting in a cloud, playing a harp.

"Have you decided where you'd like to spend eternity?" St. Peter asked.

"Yes," she said, "heaven was great, but too boring. I choose hell."

"Okay," said St. Peter, "off you go."

This time when she arrived in hell, she found everything barren and desolate. Confused, she confronted Satan. "Where's the golf course?" she asked. "And where are my friends?"

Satan smiled. "Yesterday we were recruiting you; today you're staff!"

STEVEN SCHWARTZ

273

An elderly couple, admitted by St. Peter through the Pearly Gates, found conditions there just heavenly.

Said the man to his wife, "I could have been here two years ago if you hadn't fed me all that oat bran."

PAUL IZDEPSKI

My sister's dog had been deaf and blind for years. When she started to suffer painful tumors, it was time to put her down. As I explained this to my seven-year-old son, he asked if Jazzy would go to heaven.

I said I thought she would, and that in dog heaven, she would be healthy again and able to do her favourite thing: chase squirrels.

Jacob thought about that for a minute, then said, "So dog heaven must be the same as squirrel hell."

JUDY SUTTERFIELD

My boyfriend was working in the souvenir shop at Canterbury Cathedral. One afternoon he was talking with an attendant who worked in the cathedral when they were approached by two tourists. "Are you a monk?" one of the women asked.

"No," the attendant explained, "I wear this robe as part of my job, but I'm not a member of any religious order."

"Then where are the monks?" asked the woman.

The man replied, "Oh, there haven't been any monks here since 1415."

Hearing this, the woman looked at her watch and announced to her friend, "Betty, we missed the monks."

SHAWNDA URIE

The Pope gets to heaven.

"Frankly," St. Peter says, "you're lucky to be here."

"Why?" the Pope asks.

"What did I do wrong on earth?"

"God's really angry with the stance you took on women being ordained into the priesthood," St. Peter tells him.

"He's mad about that?" the Pope asks.

"She's furious!" St. Peter says.

SHARON HENDRICKSON

On a Papal visit abroad, the Pope is riding in a limousine when he has an idea. "Driver? Do you think I could take the wheel for a while?" the Pope asks.

"Certainly," says the driver. How can I say no to the Pope? he thinks.

So the Pope starts driving – like a maniac. He ignores the speed limit, dodges in and out of traffic and cuts other cars up.

Before long, a traffic policeman pulls him over. But when the Pope rolls down the window, the officer stops dead in his tracks and goes back to his car.

"We've got somebody really important here," he radios in.

"Who is it?" the dispatcher asks. "A politician?"

"No. More important."

"The Queen? Who?"

"I couldn't tell, but the Pope is the driver."

A Sunday school teacher was discussing the Ten Commandments with her five- and six-year-old charges. After explaining the commandment to "Honour thy father and thy mother," she asked, "Is there a commandment that teaches us how to treat our brothers and sisters?"

Without missing a beat, one little boy answered, "Thou shall not kill."

JESSICA LASALLE

Word play

It's your mother tongue, so how can the words come out all wrong?
Revel in these ridiculous mistakes and hysterical utterances.

When our air conditioner broke down, we called for an engineer to come and have a look at it. The engineer, a man called Love, turned out to be an old classmate of my husband's. He said to ask for him the next time we had any problems.

The following year, when we needed work done again, we requested Mr Love. I took the day off from my job to be there.

After he'd finished repairing our air conditioner, he left his work order behind. On it was written my name and the scheduling instructions: "Wants Love in afternoon".

DONNA MELLER

A pregnant woman lapses into a deep coma. She awakens and frantically calls for the doctor. "You had twins. A boy and a girl. They're fine," he says. "Your brother named them."

Oh no, the new mother thinks. He's an idiot. Expecting the worst, she asks, "What's the girl's name?"

"Denise," the doctor says. Not bad, she thinks. Maybe I was wrong about him.

"And the boy?"

"DeNephew."

Pity the poor insomniac dyslexic agnostic. He stays up all night wondering if there really is a dog.

Our regimental sergeant major was well known for his abuse of the English language, and we all joked about it. At parade one morning, he announced in a stentorian voice, "Certain people have been making allegations about me. If I catch these alligators, they will be in for a hard time."

C. MALEY

Stuck in traffic, I couldn't help noticing the personalised number plate on the car in front of me. It read: BAA BAA.

I wondered why anyone would choose this – until I looked at the vehicle to which the plate was attached: a black Jeep.

ROBERT LALONDE

Can you be a closet claustrophobic?

GINA FADELY

I can't swim, but often wish that I could. So when I went to the optician's for some contact lenses I was very pleased with what he told me: "You can do anything wearing these lenses. You'll even be able to swim with them in."

JENNY HARRIS

Job applicants at the company where my friend Diane works are asked to fill in a questionnaire. Among the things candidates list is their school and when they attended.

One man dutifully wrote the name of his place of learning, followed by the dates he was there: "Monday, Tuesday, Wednesday, Thursday and Friday."

JENNIFER CARUANA

277

SIGN LANGUAGE

Today was the day. I was going to get a tattoo. I walked into a local shop to check out their designs. But I had second thoughts when I noticed the two "artists" working there had the last names of **Pane and Burns.**

LINDSAY HALVERSON

Sitting in a posh restaurant, a man spots a gorgeous redhead at the next table. He spends ages checking her out, but doesn't have the nerve to speak to her.

Suddenly, she sneezes and her glass eye comes hurtling out of its socket towards him. He reaches out, grabs it in the air and gives it back to her.

"Oh, I am so sorry," the woman says as she pops the eye back in. "Let me buy you dinner to make it up to you."

They enjoy a fantastic meal together then go to the theatre, followed by drinks. They talk, they laugh, she shares her deepest thoughts and he shares his.

After paying for everything, she invites him back to her place. Next morning, she cooks them both a gourmet breakfast.

The man is amazed. "You are the perfect woman," he says. "Are you this nice to every man you meet?"

"No," she replies. "You just happened to catch my eye."

REGINA LALLY

There were only two people in the line ahead of me at the electronics store, but the wait was dragging on forever. Finally the

"Do you have the root of all evil?"

customer behind me muttered, "Mr. Hare must be on holiday."

Only then did I notice the name tag on the man at the register. It read: "Mr. Turtle, sales associate."

B. WRIGHT

Did you hear about the man who, in an attempt to get in touch with his feminine side, went to the library and took out a book called "How to Hug"?

He got home and found it was volume seven of the encyclopaedia.

At the end of a long, hard day, I found myself standing in a line at a fast-food restaurant with my husband, Stan, and our three-year-old daughter. The service was painfully slow, and my husband's temper began to mount.

"Look, darling, it's been a long day," I said, trying to console him. "You're tired, I'm tired, she's tired."

Before I could say another word, Stan interrupted me, smiling. "You conjugate well," he said.

S. DEPASSE

A large publishing house sent me a mailing containing the phrase, "Wether or not you would like to subscribe ... "

I wrote back pointing out that "whether" denoted a choice of alternatives, but a "wether" was a castrated ram.

I may well do business with the firm as a swift reply came back saying, "With reference to your letter: thank ewe for pointing this out."

M. S.

For anyone who gets confused about proper grammar and style in writing, we offer, from the Internet, the following tip sheet, "How to Write Good":

- It is wrong to ever split an infinitive.
- Contractions aren't necessary.
- The passive voice is to be avoided.
- Prepositions are not the words to end sentences with.
- Be more or less specific.
- Who needs rhetorical questions?
- Exaggeration is a billion times worse than understatement.

Sitting at a red light, I was puzzling over the meaning of the vanity plate on the car in front of me. It read "Innie".

Then I got it. The make of the car was Audi.

KATHY JOHNSON

My husband is a pilot and our five-year-old son has an insatiable interest in flying. One day he went to the library to join other children who were being shown where the books were and how to find them.

"Does anybody know what 'information' means?" the librarian asked the children.

My son proudly answered, "Aeroplanes flying side by side."

J. ELIAS

Standing in a department store, my sister overheard a woman in the next aisle saying loudly: "You're not normal. You've never been normal!" Curious, my sister peered around the edge of the display shelving. There stood two women choosing shampoo.

FELICITY REES

Students in a science class at school were studying astronomy. "What do we call a group of stars that makes an imaginary picture in the sky?" the teacher asked.

"A consternation," one student replied.

RALPH HEDGES

A policeman pulled his vehicle up alongside a speeding car and was shocked to see that the little old lady behind the wheel was knitting. The officer switched on his lights and sounded his siren, but the driver was oblivious. So the policeman got out his loudspeaker and shouted to the woman, "Pull over."

"No," the old lady shouted back. "Cardigan."

The teacher asked the class to write a short composition dealing with four major subjects: religion, nobility, sex and mystery.

In a flash, Anna's hand shoots up. Amazed at the rapid response, the teacher asks her to read her piece out loud.

"'Oh my God!' exclaimed the countess, 'I'm pregnant, and I don't know by whom.'"

GRACIELA SUAREZ

"The labs are back."

News that her third child was going to be a girl thrilled my cousin, who already had two boys. "My husband wants to call her Sunny," she told me, "and I want to give her Anna as her middle name in memory of my mum."

I thought they might want to reconsider their decision, since their birth announcement would herald the arrival of Sunny Anna Rainey.

CAROLYN WALLIS

During a trip to Dublin, my friend and I visited a typical Irish pub. I thought I'd try a pint of Guinness while my friend wanted something refreshing and decided on a bitter lemon.

I ordered the drinks and the barman pulled the pint of Guinness and served it with a large piece of lemon on the side of the glass.

"What's this?" I asked.

"What you ordered," said the barman. "A Guinness and bit o' lemon."

C. ALLEN

Police are investigating the murder of Juan Gonzalez. "It looks like he was killed with a golf gun," one detective observes.

"A golf gun?" asks his partner. "What in the world is a golf gun?"

"I don't know. But it sure made a hole in Juan."

Two weevils grew up in the countryside. One moved to the big city and became a famous actor. The other stayed back home in the fields and never amounted to anything.

He became known as the lesser of two weevils.

DUSTIN GODSEY

"You have to admire the way she juggles family and career."

Our manager at the restaurant where I worked was a much-loved, jovial man. But there was one subject you didn't dare discuss in front of him – his height. Or, rather, the lack of it.

One day, he stormed through the door and announced angrily, "Someone just picked my pocket!"

My fellow waitresses and I were speechless, except for the one who blurted out, "How could anyone stoop so low?"

B. MOEGGENBORG

"We request low bail as my client is not a flight risk."

A happy accident

A poll has discovered that the favourite word of the British is "serendipity". A surprising choice, perhaps, but then with so many words to choose from it's hard to think of a word that wouldn't have been surprising.

I suppose I'd have guessed that the top choice would have been a pushy new shaven-headed word, freshly coined to infuriate and intimidate traditionalists, a word such as "sorted" or "innit" or "saddo". But the tweedy are in no position to feel smug: "serendipity" is in fact a pretty modern word, new-fangled enough to be flash, even a little vulgar, like the windchimes its sound resembles.

Serendipity's birth can be dated to exactly 1754, when Horace Walpole coined it – or at least purloined it – from the title of a Persian fairy tale, "The Three Princes of Serendip". How it would have upset Dr Johnson, whose *Dictionary* was to appear for the first time the following year, to think that Serendip, the Persian name for Ceylon, or, if you'd prefer, the Iranian name for Sri Lanka, would one day be voted the favourite word of the British people.

Like so many, Johnson was upset by new words, particularly those in which he sniffed the whiff of America. He hated, for instance, the freshly coined word "mob" which was then a recent and yobbish abbreviation of "mobile", itself an abbreviation of the Latin "mobile vulgus", meaning common people. He also damned newly fashionable words like "jeopardy", "glee" and "smoulder" as hideous Americanisms, though he was etymologically wrong (they were in fact all old English words that had gone out of currency in Britain but, like many others – "gotten" among them – had been preserved intact in America).

There is nothing new about the mistrust of the new. Samuel Taylor Coleridge so hated one new word that he condemned it as "vile and barbarous". The word was "talented", now the mainstay of school reports written by even the crustiest of schoolteachers.

Anyone with children will know the speed with which new words – and new meanings for old words – pop up. In the past few weeks, I have heard "shod" meaning absolutely terrible (e.g. "Your BB gun doesn't work. It's really shod") and "mint" meaning very good (e.g. "My BB gun is the best. It's mint").

In a world owned and operated by the over-15s, the under-15s have the understandable urge to coin new words of their own. Inevitably, their attraction to a new word diminishes the moment the word is colonised by oldies. A week or two ago, I used the word "sad" in its new, or new-ish, meaning of "socially inadequate". My nine-year-old son winced at someone of my age employing such a young word. "You saying 'sad' is what's *really* sad," he said.

Of course, not every fresh-faced word that pokes its head around the door of English letters is then permitted a permanent seat. It's a

Craig Brown, *This is Craig Brown*

long time, for instance, since I've heard anyone use the word "crucial" meaning "splendid", yet in the early 1980s it was as prevalent as the current "wicked!", which means the same thing. (In fact, "wicked" itself is not quite so up to date as its users might hope: Scott Fitzgerald was using it in this ironic, jazzy manner as early as 1920, when he had one of his characters say at a dance, "Phoebe and I are going to shake a wicked calf".)

Trademark words such as "Gonk" "Filofax" "shell-suit" and "Tamagotchi" are destined to perish alongside the trend that gave them birth, though occasionally one of these words is able to fly free of its product's corpse. I suspect that this might be true of "anorak". Back in the 1920s, it was a word taken from the Eskimo for a waterproof jacket with a hood. By the mid-80s, it had taken on a second meaning: it was now also a gawky social misfit with an obsessive interest in something uncool such as trainspotting or collecting stamps. This second meaning then grew so pervasive that manufacturers of anoraks were forced to rename them. In a few years' time, the original meaning of

anorak may well have been jettisoned altogether.

The speed with which language changes can come as a shock even to those who live through it. In the late 1940s, when the Beatles were roughly the same age as my son, the *Daily Mail* published with a shudder a list of new-fangled American expressions it believed to be "positively incomprehensible" to the average Englishman. These included the words "commuter", "seafood", "mean" (in the sense of nasty), "living room", "dumb" (in the sense of stupid) and "rare" (in the sense of underdone). Fifty years later, can there be anyone in Britain who doesn't know what they mean? In fact, nowadays most of them

seem dull, almost stale, and one of them – dumb – has been overtaken many times, most recently, I think, by "durbrain". (Or should that be "duh-brain"? It is hard to know, as it is too recent for any refence work.)

My own favourite word is still ex-directory. It is "pimpsqueak" meaning simple. "That's pimpsqueak!" my children say when they know the answer to a question. I imagine its etymology can be traced from "simple" to "pimps" via "pipsqueak", to "pimpsqueak". Could it be the nation's favourite word in the year 2100? In many ways, it would seem a less radical choice than the Iranian word for Sri Lanka.

283

My friend John came into our French class one Monday with a pillow that he placed on his seat. He had been skiing and mildly fractured his tailbone. Our teacher promptly asked him to explain, *en français,* why he was sitting on a pillow.

To our amusement, John answered, "Sorbonne."

GEORGE SHUPING

Today in the markets, helium was up; feathers were down. Paper was stationary. Lifts rose, while escalators continued their slow decline. Mining equipment hit rock bottom. The market for raisins dried up. Coca-Cola fizzled. Balloon prices were inflated. And toilet paper reached a new bottom.

ERIC CAMPBELL

Stuck in rush-hour traffic, I couldn't help but stare when a burly biker wearing black leather jacket and chaps pulled up next to me on a shocking pink Harley Davidson. My first thoughts were, "Is that really a pink Harley? I wonder if he's … "

Just then the traffic cleared and he pulled in front of me. On the back of his helmet were stencilled the words "Yes it is. No I'm not."

AMY CARPENTER

While recording the vital statistics of a soon-to-be mother, I asked how much she weighed. "I really don't know," she said.

"More or less," I prompted.

"More, I suppose."

AGNES HALVERSON

A keen amateur clarinettist for many years, I didn't start to learn my instrument until I was in my thirties. During the early stages, I produced many strange and unmusical sounds. One day I complained to my cousin, "After all this blowing, I can't even play a recognizable tune."

"I think you've done very well," she replied encouragingly. "After all you started from screech."

EILEEN WALLACE

When my mother asked me what I wanted for my birthday, I replied that I would like something for the bath.

In due course, a heavy, beautifully wrapped parcel arrived and, my mind dwelling on the luxurious perfumed extravagance it must contain, I eagerly tore the paper off. Inside were four drums of scouring powder.

MRS M. MAGUIRE

As a fund-raiser, the chemistry club designed and sold T-shirts. Written across the front were our top "Stupid Chemistry Sayings":
- Have yourself a Merry Little Bismuth
- What do you do with dead people? Barium
- You stupid boron!
- We hope your year is very phosphorous.

SHANE HART

If you arrest a mime, do you still have to tell him he has the right to remain silent?

While waiting in a queue to pick up some items I had bought earlier, I heard one of the salesmen shout out, "E I E I O." "Here," the woman standing next to me answered.

Curious, I asked if she was married to a farmer, or maybe taught at a primary school.

"Neither," she replied. "My name is McDonald."

JIM PIERCE

A favourite beach restaurant of ours has a simple way of advertising its hours. During the day, the window panes sport large letters spelling "Open."

After hours, the "N" is moved forward to spell "Nope".

PHIL TRIPP

I was buying a lacy black nightie, and thought I'd better check that it would not run in the wash.

"Is it fast?" I asked.

The salesgirl studied the nightie for a moment, then replied: "Not really, madam. Sophisticated, perhaps – but not fast."

MRS A. STUART

While driving through the countryside a friend found that his tyre was punctured and his spare was under-inflated. As he was looking for an air point at a nearby garage an old man emerged from behind a shed.

"Excuse me," asked my friend, "do you have an airline here?"

"No we don't, son," replied the old man, "but the bus stops twice a week."

ROBERT BARBOUR

Expecting delivery of a piano, my son left me a key for the removal men and stuck a note on the sitting-room wall saying, "Piano here please."

He returned to find the instrument in place and a message added to his note: "Sorry, can't get piano to stick to wall – have left it on the floor."

ELIZABETH CANDLISH

I went to the butcher's the other day and I bet him fifty pounds that he couldn't reach the meat on the top shelf.

He said, "No, the steaks are too high."

ED THOMPSON

285

I believe in an open mind, but not so open that your brains fall out.

ARTHUR HAYS SULZBERGER

Polite conversation is rarely either.

FRAN LEBOWITZ,
Social Studies (Random House)

What's another word for thesaurus?

STEVEN WRIGHT

The first thing I do in the morning is brush my teeth and sharpen my tongue.

DOROTHY PARKER

Experience is the name every one gives to their mistakes.

OSCAR WILDE

My early choice in life was either to be a piano player in a whorehouse or a politician. And to tell the truth, there's hardly any difference.

HARRY S. TRUMAN

The problem with people who have no vices is that they're pretty sure to have some annoying virtues.

ELIZABETH TAYLOR

Time's fun when you're having flies.

KERMIT THE FROG

I looked up the word *politics* in the dictionary. It's actually a combination of two words: *poli*, which means many, and *tics*, which means bloodsuckers.

JAY LENO on "The Tonight Show"

Our son recently married a Russian woman. During the reception, various guests proposed toasts with someone translating between Russian and English. My sister-in-law said, "Good health, good fortune. Go and multiply." I couldn't help noticing that some of the guests looked confused. We found out later that this had been translated as, "Good health, good fortune. Go and do maths."

DAVID MACLEOD

The gladiator was having a rough day in the arena – his opponent had sliced off both of his arms. Nevertheless, he kept on fighting, kicking and biting as furiously as he could. But when his opponent lopped off both feet, our gladiator had no choice but to give up. After all, he was now both unarmed and defeated.

TEDDEM YEE

My friend Nancy was Catholic, but her fiancé Chris was not. They were planning to marry in a Catholic church, and at one prenuptial meeting there, the priest turned to Chris and told him that since he was not Catholic, they would have the ceremony without Eucharist.

Later that day, Chris was noticeably upset, so Nancy asked him what the matter was. "I just don't understand," he told her moodily. "How can we possibly have the ceremony without me?"

KURT SHELLENBACK

Did you hear about the satellite dishes who married?

The ceremony was awful, but the reception was great.

SANDRA CORONA

"I think I'll just stay in tonight, maybe open a can of worms."

We opened a bridal-gown business and checked out the competition in a nearby town, which had two bridal shops. We visited one, but couldn't find the other, so we asked two women the way. One started giving directions, but was interrupted by her friend who thought the shop had closed down. This prompted a heated debate. "Oh, well," I said in the end. "I suppose this town is a bit small for two bridal shops, anyway."

"Yes," agreed the first woman. "There aren't enough horses to keep one shop going, never mind two."

RICHARD ROCHE

287

Harry drove over to the next county to buy a new bull for the farm. It cost more than expected, and he was left with only one pound. This was a problem, since he needed to let his wife, Sue, know that he'd bought the bull so she could come and get it with the truck – and telegrams cost a pound per word. Harry thought hard for a minute. Finally he said, "All right. Here's my pound. Go ahead and just make it this one word: Comfortable."

"How's that going to get your point across?" the clerk asked, scratching his head.

"Don't worry," Harry said. "Sue's not the greatest reader. She'll say it really slowly."

RICHARD SCHEUB

After a long career of being blasted into a net, the human cannonball was tired. He told the circus owner he was going to retire. "But you can't!" protested the boss. "Where am I going to find another man of your calibre?"

Looking in my local library for two books by communications expert Deborah Tannen turned into an Abbott and Costello routine.

"What's the first book?" the librarian asked.

"That's Not What I Meant," I said.

"Well, what did you mean?"

"That's the title of the book I want," I explained.

"OK," she said, looking at me sceptically. "And the other book?"

"You Just Don't Understand."

"Excuse me?"

I got both books. Eventually.

N. WILLIAMS

I was surprised when a customer came into the carpet shop where I work and handed me a neatly drawn diagram of his living-room, complete with clearly written measurements. "In feet," he explained. Closer inspection revealed a second set of figures beside the first, and I asked him what these meant.

"They're my wife's," he replied brightly. "She's got smaller feet than me."

P. BUTTON

Working in a personnel department has its lighter moments – one of which is spotting inadvertent spelling mistakes made on application forms. One young judo fanatic with six children listed his only hobby as "marital arts".

SUE LEWIS

Aoccdrnig to rscheearch at an Elingsh uinervtisy, it deosn't mttaer in waht oredr the ltteers in a wrod are, the olny iprmoetnt tihng is taht teh frist and lsat ltteer is at the rghit pclae. The rset can be a toatl mses and you can sitll raed it wouthit aporbelm.

Tihs is bcuseae we do not raed ervey lteter by istlef but the wrod as a wlohe.

JOHNATHAN POWELL

Tiffany adopts two dogs, and she names them Rolex and Timex. "Where'd you come up with those names?" asks her friend Mandy. "Oh, that was easy," Tiffany replies. "They're watchdogs!"

GUSTAVO YEPES

"I'm sorry."

When our daughter arrived to take my wife shopping an odd-job man was working in the garden. After a few hours, he left and I put on an old cap and jacket to do some tidying up. When my daughter returned she remarked: "That man's still out there working."

"That's not a man," said my wife looking out of the window. "It's your father."

LOUIS DAY

My wife walked into a coffee shop on Halloween to find the woman behind the counter with a bunch of sponges pinned to her uniform.

"I'm assuming this is a costume," said my wife. "But what are you supposed to be?"

The waitress responded proudly, "I'm self-absorbed."

SCOTT PIPER

Rick, a banker, is showing off his fancy new boat to his friend Jim. But the boat sinks, and Rick can't swim. So Jim starts pulling him to shore.

Finally, with only 50 feet to land, Jim says, "So do you think you could float alone?"

Rick gasps back, "This is a heck of a time to be asking for money!"

Did you hear about the self-help group for compulsive talkers? It's called On & On Anon.

SALLY DAVIS

Planning to purchase some new animals, a zookeeper started to compose a letter: "To whom it may concern, I need two mongeese." That doesn't look right, thought the zookeeper. So he started again: "To whom it may concern, I need two mongooses." That doesn't look right either, he thought.

Finally he had an idea: "To whom it may concern, I need a mongoose. And while you're at it, make it two."

An American friend was telling me about her boyfriend's habit of misusing words. On one occasion, he had referred to the crispy chunks of bread in his soup as "futons". I told her that in the UK we called that a malapropism.

"Really?" she said. "In America we call them croutons."

MARILYN THORNTON

"Honey, I'm taking the dog out to do his business."

Eye halve a spelling chequer
It came with my pea sea
It plainly marques four my
  revue
Miss steaks eye kin knot sea
Eye strike a key and type
  a word
And weight four it two say
Weather eye am wrong
  oar write
It shows me strait a weigh
As soon as a mist ache is maid
It nose bee fore two long
And eye can put the error rite
Its rarely ever wrong
Eye have run this poem threw it
I am shore your pleased two no
Its letter perfect in it's weigh
My chequer tolled me sew.

Our personnel department sent the following message to people who play sport at lunchtime: "Due to the recent heavy snow fall we regret to inform you that the all-weather pitch is unavailable."

THERESA JONES

Our school chaplain was thrilled by a request to stand in for a well-known minister. During the service he noticed a piece of cardboard covering a hole in a lovely stained-glass window.

Telling the congregation of his joy at being asked to preach in that church, the chaplain said that he was like the cardboard standing in for the stained glass.

Later, as he shook hands with the departing throng, an elderly woman said to him, "Oh, you weren't a piece of cardboard – you were a pane."

P.P.O.

A policeman looked up to see a woman racing down the centre of the road at 100mph. He pulled her over and said, "Madam, would you mind telling me why you're going so fast down the middle of the road?"

"Oh, it's okay, Officer," she replied. "I have a special licence that allows me to drive like that."

"Oh, really? Can I see it?" The policeman looked at the licence and then concluded, "Madam, there's nothing special about this. It's just a normal licence."

"Look at the very bottom, though," the woman insisted. "See? It says 'Tear along the dotted line.'"

R. MEYERSON

If a pig loses its voice, is it disgruntled?

Sometimes the words just get in the way...

I work for a mail order company where a customer once rang to complain that we had sent her a blue jumper instead of a white one.

"I ordered it in cornflower," said the customer.

"That's right," I replied. "Cornflowers are blue."

"Well mine isn't," insisted the customer. "I've just looked in the kitchen cupboard and my cornflour is white."

S. HARNEY

My son was filling in college application forms. One asked him for extra-curricular activities. He answered: "Wrestling".

The next question requested positions held. He entered: "Pinned, mostly".

MARK SMITH

At the school summer fair, I joked with my wife that I would take part in the games if there was a veteran's section.

Moments later a voice came over the public address system declaring that there would shortly be a race for 45-year-olds.

I was walking to the start line when the announcer said: "So will all four- and five-year-olds make their way to the track, please."

CLIVE WEBSTER

Buying new clothes is anathema to my husband, but when we were invited to a wedding I insisted that he purchase a new suit.

When we entered a men's outfitters, he grumpily asked the sales assistant which was the cheapest suit in the shop.

Noticing my horrified expression, the assistant fetched a full-length mirror and stood it in front of my husband.

RACHEL ALDRED

As a community psychiatric nurse, I was asked to assess an elderly lady who was showing signs of confusion.

Although she wasn't sure what month or year it was, I was delighted when she identified the country, county and town in which she lived.

Nodding encouragingly as she correctly told me her address, I finally asked her what floor we were on. Pausing momentarily, she sat forward in her chair, prodded her fingers into the carpet and responded, "I reckon it's concrete, duck."

BERNADETTE WARD

Entering a luxury car showroom, a man is grabbed by a salesman and guided round the latest, gleaming convertible sports car.

The prospective customer announces that he is interested in purchasing the vehicle and enquires after the price.

The salesman types some figures into his calculator and says, "That particular model will cost you two pink fluffy notes with rhinos on and seven yellow clown coins, sir."

"I'm not paying that," protests the customer, "it's silly money."

When my mother and I stopped to visit the woman who was baking my wedding cake, she had trouble placing us – was our cake vanilla or chocolate? Then she looked at my mum and it dawned on her. "Now I remember. You're the fruitcake!"

MICHAL LOEPRICH

Recently, one of the blokes at the warehouse called my husband, the general manager, to tell him that he wouldn't be in that day.

"I'm having my autopsy," he said. "But, with any luck, I'll be in tomorrow."

T. RITTER

292

SIGN LANGUAGE

Sign over a display of pine panels at a timber yard:
"Knotty, but nice."

While measuring my 14-year-old brother for his first suit, the tailor asked him, "Which side do you dress on?"

My brother looked rather troubled.

"Erm, the one furthest away from the window," he replied.

KATH CLEMENTS

Callie, my friend's daughter, had signed up for Spanish lessons taught by a native speaker.

"I'm not familiar with that name," he said. "Does it start with a K?"

She replied, "C."

Ever since, he has spelled her name "Kallie."

WILLIAM HERRINGTON

If there's an award for Worst Waiter of the Year, I've got a candidate. He was working at my aunt's favourite restaurant when we took her there for her birthday.

He messed up every order. She asked for pork – he brought beef. We requested beans – we got sweetcorn. At the end of the meal, he asked, "Does anyone want dessert?"

My aunt said, "What do I have to order to get a piece of cheesecake?"

JEFF PINSON

A real-life native American Indian was a special guest at my sister's primary school. He talked to the children about his tribe and its traditions, then shared with them this fun fact: "There are no swear words in the Cherokee language."

One boy raised his hand. "But what if you're hammering a nail and accidentally bash your thumb?"

"That," the Indian answered, "is when we use your language."

ANGELA CHIANG

While at dinner in a pub, I called the waitress over and asked for the condiments. Swiftly disappearing into the kitchen she re-emerged a few minutes later and informed me, "There's a machine behind the door in the gents."

ANN KELLY

A friend of ours once answered the front door to a stranger who declared, "Census takers."

"You've come to the wrong place," Barry quipped. "We've taken leave of ours."

BRENDA JENNINGS

Harvey becomes claustrophobic every time he reaches the great outdoors.

While I was relaxing in the lounge of my friend's Florida home, another guest, also a Brit, strode in looking peeved. He'd lost his credit card and had to ring the card company to report it.

Going through some details with the customer services rep, we heard him say, "What do you mean, 'What state am I in?' I'm bloody worried someone will use it! You could say I'm distraught!"

The rep said something back, then he replied sheepishly, "Oh ... Florida."

STUART UNSWORTH

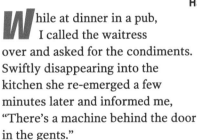

LAUGHINGSTOCK

Things you need to know if your son wants to leave school and become a rock star:

- What do you call a guitar player who breaks up with his girlfriend? Homeless.
- What's the difference between a rock musician and a 16-inch pizza? The pizza can feed a family of four.
- What's the definition of an optimist? A rock musician with a mortgage.
- How do you define perfect pitch? It's when you throw your son's guitar into the dustcart and it lands right on top of his amplifier.

I was waiting to board a plane when a flight attendant stopped a woman in front of me to question her about the number of carry-on bags she had. The woman vehemently defended herself, claiming the extra bag was really her handbag. It was the size of a large briefcase, but she insisted that it shouldn't count as a carry-on item. The flight attendant finally let the woman pass.

As the next man stepped up, the flight attendant's gaze settled on his bags. Immediately, he held up his briefcase and exclaimed, "This is my wallet."

KIMBERLEY LEVACY

While redecorating my bathroom, I phoned a shop to see if it stocked a particular model of toilet. "We haven't got one here," said the assistant.

"Oh, no!" I said, crestfallen. His number had been the fourth one I'd called.

"Don't worry," he added helpfully. "I'll contact our other outlets to see if there's anybody out there sitting on one."

DOUG BINGHAM

In a remote part of Colombia, police discovered a field full of marijuana and decided to burn the lot. The fire was blazing when an officer noticed that a flock of terns was flying around the area. Concerned about the effects the smoke would have on them, he called the animal-welfare department.

Sadly, his worst fears were confirmed. No tern was left unstoned.

JOHN ARENDS

If athletes get athlete's foot, do astronauts get mistletoe?

Fear factor. Are you scared of heights? Cramped spaces? If so, you've got plenty of company. Some people, though, have to wrestle with phobias that may surprise you.

- Automatonophobia = fear of ventriloquist dummies
- Ecclesiophobia = fear of church
- Aulophobia = fear of flutes
- Selenophobia = fear of the moon
- Venustraphobia = fear of beautiful women
- Logizomechanophobia = fear of computers.

Reporter: "Brzinlatowskiczinina is the name of the man who was struck by lightning earlier today."

City editor: "What was his name before he was struck?"

Did you hear about the Buddhist who refused his dentist's Novocain? He wanted to transcend dental medication.

Sitting in the first row of economy class during a lengthy flight, my wife and I were able to hear a flight attendant as he pushed a wine trolley down the aisle in the first-class section. "Would you care for chardonnay or burgundy?" he asked the high-paying passengers.

A few minutes later the attendant opened the curtain between the two sections, offered wine to one final first-class patron, then wheeled the same trolley forward to our aisle. "Excuse me," he said, looking down at us, "would you care for a glass of wine? We have white and red."

WILLIAM COPELAN

Did you hear about the university professor who was involved in a terrible car crash? He was marking papers on a curve.

JACK KISER

I was playing a game of Trivial Pursuit with some friends and family. My team was asked, "In Roman religion, who was the chief goddess and wife of Jupiter?"

Everyone else looked blank. "Juno?" I ventured.

My gran shrugged her shoulders and shook her head. "No," she said. "I haven't got a clue."

JO AUSTIN

Our surname is Stead, pronounced to rhyme with "bed". But, much to my family's annoyance, people often call us Steed.

One day an acquaintance from the local council came to see me. My mother opened the front door. "Is Mr Steed in?" the woman asked.

"He's Stead," my mother snapped.

"Oh, my God," the woman gasped. "I was talking to the poor man only yesterday."

J. STEAD

Does Santa call his elves "subordinate clauses"?

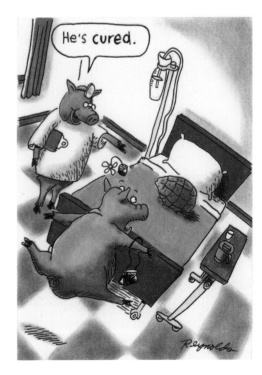

A man called the phone company to complain about his listing in the directory. "I told you that my last name is Sweady," he said, "but you have it listed as Cyirwu."

"I'm sorry, sir," the phone-company representative said. "I'll fix it so it'll be correct the next time we publish the directory. Now how do you spell your name?"

"Just like I told you before," the customer said. "It's S as in sea, W as in why, E as in eye, A as in are, D as in double-u and Y as in you."

BILL GAULEY

P sychiatry students were in their Emotional Extremes class. "Let's set some parameters," the professor said. "What's the opposite of joy?" he asked one student.

"Sadness," he answered.

"The opposite of depression?" he asked another student.

"Elation," he replied.

"The opposite of woe?" the professor asked a young woman.

She replied, "Sir, I believe that would be giddyup."

"D octor, you've got to help me. Every time I drive down a country lane, I find myself singing 'Green Green Grass of Home.' Every time I see a cat I sing 'What's New Pussycat?' And last night I sang 'Delilah' in my sleep. I tell you, my wife was not at all amused."

"I wouldn't worry. It seems you have the early symptoms of Tom Jones syndrome."

"I have never heard of that. Is it common?"

"It's not unusual."

Y ears after I had last been there, I visited a small Scottish town where I had taught at the secondary school.

As I looked around, a young woman rushed up to me. "I know you!" she said excitedly. My chest swelled with pride at the impact I had clearly had on a former pupil.

"You teached me English!" she continued.

MAY MACKAY

O ur suppliers in China sent me a fax which was completely incomprehensible. I replied to them: "Thank you for your fax, but I am none the wiser."

The following day I received another which read: "Dear None the Wiser, please pass this to your colleague Mr Landau."

DANNY LANDAU

Bob never got tired of fishing for compliments.

A linguistics professor is teaching her students about grammar in foreign languages. "In English," she says, "A double negative forms a positive. In other languages, such as Russian, a double negative is still a negative. However, there is no language where a double positive is a negative."

Just then a voice from the back of the class pipes up, "Yeah, right."

MAIREAD DOHERTY

Last laughs

Classic jokes and those fantastic and funny snippets of humour that we just couldn't resist.

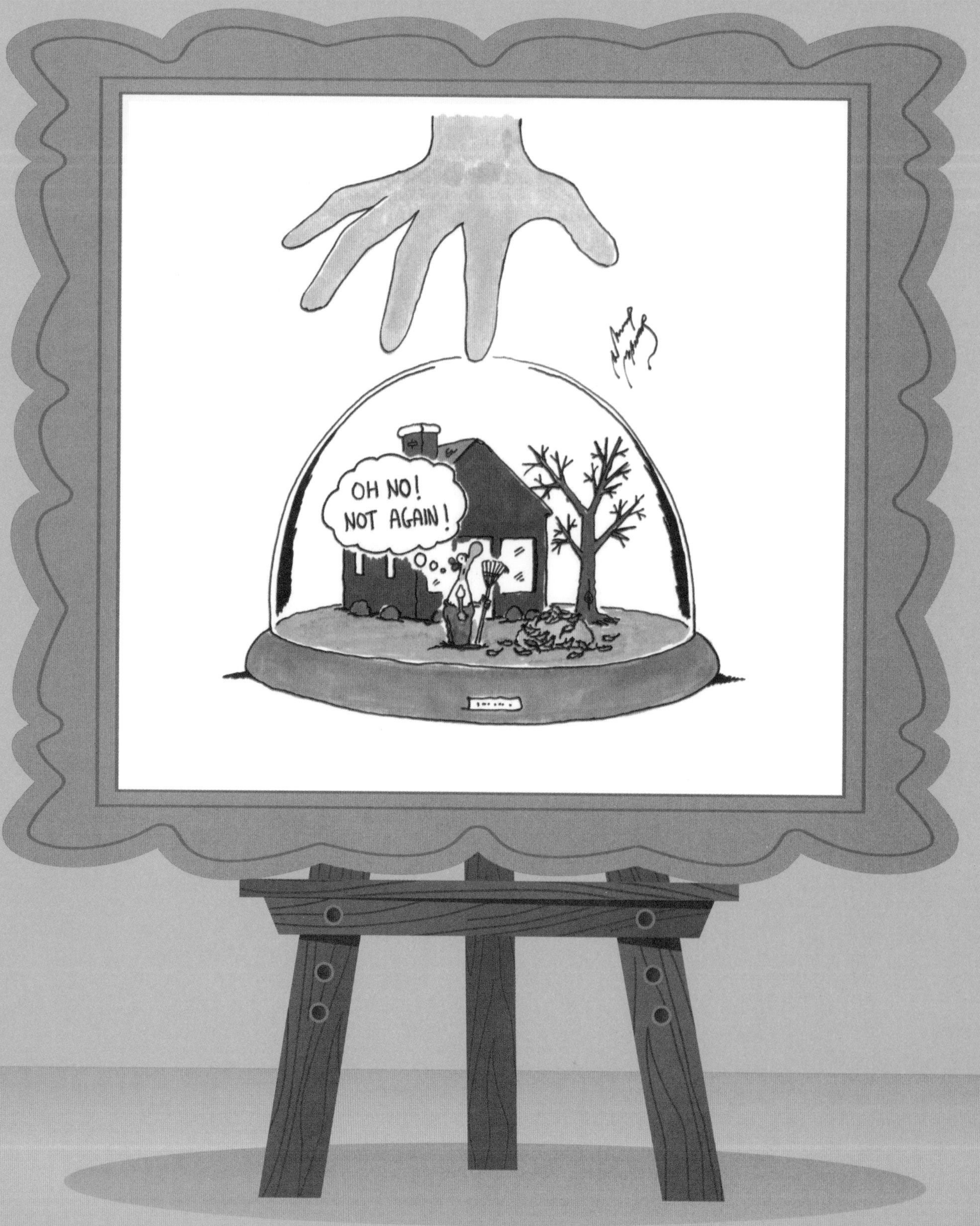
OH NO!
NOT AGAIN!

An older father noticed his son's Viagra tablets in the medicine cabinet. "Could I try one?" he asked. "Sure," his son said, "but make the most of it. Each of those pills costs ten pounds."

His dad was shocked by the price. "Don't worry," he promised, "I'll pay you back."

The next morning the son found an envelope under his breakfast plate. Inside was £110.

"Dad," he said, "that pill only cost ten pounds."

"I know," his father said, smiling. "The ten is from me. The hundred is from your mother."

D. KELLY

Police officers arrest a con artist for selling bottles filled with a liquid that he claims slows the aging process.

One officer tells his partner, "Frank, check his record. My instinct tells me that our boy has played this game before."

Frank reports back. "You're right, he's got form. He was nicked for the same thing in 1955, 1898, 1721 ... "

RON DENTINGER

Harold and David are out hunting when David suddenly collapses and stops breathing. Desperately,

Harold searches for a pulse but can't find one. He whips out his mobile phone, dials 999 and blurts, "My friend has just dropped dead! What should I do?"

A soothing voice at the other end says, "OK, OK. Just relax. First, let's make sure he's really dead."

After a brief silence the operator hears a shot ring out. Then Harold comes back to the phone. "OK," he says nervously, "what should I do next?"

When the policeman saw the man speed past, he pulled him over and asked for his licence and registration. "I lost my licence after my fifth drink-driving offence," the guy replied calmly. "I'll give you the registration, but don't freak out when I open the glove compartment because I've got a couple of guns in there. And if you should search the car, don't be surprised if you find some drugs and illegal immigrants in the boot."

Alarmed, the policeman went back to his car and called for back-up. Moments later a police van swept down on the car. The driver was handcuffed as the team searched the vehicle.

"There's no drugs or guns in this car, mate'" the team leader said to the driver.

"Of course there aren't," the driver replied. "And I suppose that policeman told you that I was speeding, too."

D. ELMORE

Holidaying in Arizona, a group of British tourists spot a cowboy lying by the side of the road with his ear to the ground. "What's going on?" they ask.

"Two horses – one grey, one chestnut – are pulling a wagon carrying two men," the cowboy says. "One man's shirt is red, the other's black. They're heading east."

"Wow!" says one of the tourists. "You can tell all that just by listening to the ground?"

"No." replies the cowboy. "They just ran over me."

JOHN GAMBA

299

TIMELESS HUMOUR

50s "For 20 years," mused the man at the bar, "my wife and I were ecstatically happy."

"Then what happened?" asked the barman.

"We met."

ROBERT SELLECK

In A&E, a young woman explains to the doctor that her body hurts wherever she touches it. "Impossible," he says. "Show me."

The girl pushes her chest with her finger and screams, then pushes her elbow and screams even more. Pushing her knee, her shoulder and thigh is just as bad. Everywhere she touches causes her great agony.

"Hmm," says the doctor. "I think I know what this condition is."

"Is it fatal?" asks the young woman nervously.

"No. You've got a broken finger."

RICHARD LENTON

"If I've only got two weeks to live, I'll take the last week in July and first week in August."

one of his partners asked, "How did you do that?"

The golfer shrugged. "You have to know the bus schedule."

A woman goes to the chemist's and asks for arsenic. "What do you want that for?" the pharmacist asks.

"I want to kill my husband," she replies. "He's having an affair with another woman."

"I can't sell you arsenic to kill your husband," says the pharmacist, "even if he is cheating."

The woman pulls out a picture of her husband with the pharmacist's wife. The pharmacist turns pale and replies, "Oh, I didn't realise you had a prescription."

M. SCHAUER

The police officer pulled over a guy driving a convertible because he had a penguin riding in the passenger seat. "Excuse me sir, is that an actual penguin?"

"Yeah. I just picked him up."

"Well, why don't you take him to the zoo?"

The guy agreed, but the very next day the policeman saw him drive by again with the penguin sitting beside him. "I thought I told you to take that thing to the zoo," said the officer.

"I did," the guy replied. "And we had such a good time, tonight we're going to a football match."

The 16th tee featured a fairway that ran along a road fenced off on the left. The first golfer in a foursome teed off and hooked the ball. It soared over the fence and bounced onto the street, where it hit the tyre of a moving bus and ricocheted back onto the fairway.

As they all stood in amazement,

I got thrown out of a mime show the other day for having a spasm. They thought I was heckling.

JEFF SHAW

A Doctor who went on a ski trip and got lost on the slopes? He stamped out "HELP" in the snow, but nobody could read his writing.

H.Z.

A pale-looking man staggers into a pub and sits down at the bar. The barman looks at him nervously and says, "What can I get you?" The man says, "Set me up with ten double shots of your best whisky."

The barman does this and the man slugs them down one after another, until he's knocked back the lot in under a minute. Concerned, the barman asks why he's hitting the bottle so hard.

"You'd drink this fast if you'd got what I've got," the man says, staring sadly into his empty glass.

Wondering what this terrible affliction could be, the barman asks, "What have you got?"

The man replies, "About eighty-six pence."

ERIC PICKERING

O n holiday, a guy gets lost and walks into a local village pub to ask the quickest way back to town.

"Are you walking or driving?" asks the barman.

"Driving," answers the man.

"Well," says the barman, "that's the quickest way."

CHRIS GIBBONS

A n electrician goes for a job on a building site.

"I need to ask you a few questions to see if you're what we're after," the foreman tells him. "Firstly, can you roll your hard hat down your arm and make it pop up on to your head?"

"Yes," the electrician replies, puzzled.

"OK," says the foreman, ticking his clipboard. "Secondly, can you bounce your spanner on the ground, spin round and catch it in your tool belt?"

"Yes. Yes, I can" says the electrician, getting excited.

"Righty-ho," says the foreman, making another tick. "Lastly, can you quick-draw your wire stripper, twirl it and slip it into your pouch like it's a holster?"

"Yep. I've been doing that for years!"

"Right," says the foreman and looks at his clipboard. "Well, I'm afraid I can't use you. I've got 15 people doing all that already."

A n engineering student was strolling across campus when a fellow engineer rode up on a shiny new motorcycle. "Where did you get that great bike?" asked the first student.

"I was walking along minding my own business," his friend replied, "when a gorgeous woman rode up on this motorbike. She jumped off, threw it to the ground, ripped off all her clothes and said, 'Take what you want.'"

The first engineer nodded his approval. "Good choice," he said. "The clothes probably wouldn't have fitted."

E. PERRATORE

301

CALDWELL

One day a genie appeared to a man and offered to grant him one wish. The man said, "I wish you'd build a bridge from here to a beautiful island so I could drive over there anytime."

The genie frowned. "I don't know. It sounds like quite an undertaking," he said. "Just think of the logistics. The supports required to reach the bottom of the ocean, the concrete, the steel! Why don't you pick something else?"

The man thought for a while and then said, "Okay, I wish for a complete understanding of women – what they're thinking, why they cry. I wish I knew how to make a woman truly happy."

The genie was silent for a minute, then said, "So how many lanes did you want on that bridge?"

LISA FREDERICK

TIMELESS HUMOUR

60s Breathless scientist, to returning spaceman: "Is there any life on Mars?"

Spaceman: "Well, there's a little on Saturday night, but it's awfully dead the rest of the week."

A priest, a nun, a rabbi, a lawyer and a doctor walk into a bar. The bartender takes one look at them and says, "What is this? A joke?"

SEAN MORRISON

Henry's wife was going into labour, so he dialled 999 in a panic. When the operator came on the line, he cried, "My wife is having a baby. Her contractions are only two minutes apart. What am I supposed to do?"

The operator said, "Calm down, sir. Is this her first child?"

"No," shouted Henry. "This is her husband!"

Up in heaven, the vicar was shown his eternal reward. To his disappointment, he was only given a small shed. Down the street he saw a taxi driver being shown a lovely estate with gardens and pools.

"I don't understand it," the vicar moaned. "I dedicated my whole life to serving God and this is all I get, yet a cabbie is awarded a mansion?"

"It's quite simple," Saint Peter explained. "Our system is based on performance. When you preached, people slept; when he drove, people prayed."

JOEL BERGMAN

A pair of cows were talking in the field. One says, "Have you heard about the mad cow disease that's going around?"

"Yes," the other cow says. "It makes me glad I'm a penguin."

Scrawled on the wall in the Ladies' Room: "My husband follows me everywhere."

Scribbled underneath: "No I don't."

BYRON CALLOWAY

Carol offers her friend Michelle a lift home from work. During the drive, Michelle notices a brown paper bag on the front seat between them. Curious, she asks her colleague what is inside.

"It's a bottle of wine," says Carol. "I got it for my husband."

Michelle nods. "That's a good swap."

ALAN OWENS

Bless you!

Reynolds

A local charity had never received a donation from the town's most successful lawyer so the director asked for a contribution.

"Our records show you earn £500,000 a year, yet you haven't given a penny to charity," the director began. "Wouldn't you like to help the community?"

The lawyer replied, "Did your research show that my mother is ill, with medical bills several times her annual income?"

"Um, no," mumbled the director.

"Or that my brother is blind and unemployed?" The stricken director began to stammer out an apology.

"Or that my sister's husband died in an accident," said the lawyer, his voice rising in indignation, "leaving her penniless with three kids?"

The humiliated charity director said helplessly, "I had no idea."

"So," said the lawyer, "if I don't give any money to them, why would I give any to you?"

The dying penny pincher told his doctor, lawyer and vicar, "I have £90,000 under my mattress. At my funeral I want each of you to toss an envelope with £30,000 into the grave." And after telling them this, he died.

At the funeral, each threw his envelope in the grave. Later, the vicar said, "I must confess. I needed £10,000 for my new church, so I only threw in £20,000."

The doctor admitted, "I needed £20,000 for new equipment at the hospital, so I only had £10,000 in the envelope."

"Gentlemen, I'm shocked that you would blatantly ignore this man's final wish," said the lawyer. "I threw in my personal cheque for the full amount."

Jim's doctor tells him he has only one day to live. When Jim goes home to share the bad news with his wife, she asks what he wants to do with the little bit of time he has left.

"All I want," Jim tells his beloved wife, "is to spend my last few hours reliving our honeymoon." Which is exactly what they did.

But after four hours of blissful romance, she announces that she's tired and wants to go to sleep.

"Oh, come on," Jim whispers in her ear.

"Look," his wife snaps, "I've got to get up in the morning. You haven't!"

In the hospitality suite at a bar association convention, a young lawyer meets the Devil. The Devil says, "Listen, if you give me your soul and the souls of everyone in your family, I'll make you a full partner in your firm."

After mulling this over, the lawyer says, "What's the catch?"

A destitute musician stood on a street corner playing his guitar. After an hour or so, he was confronted by a policeman who demanded to see his busking licence. The musician confessed that he didn't have one.

"Right," said the policeman. "Then you'll have to accompany me."

"OK," shrugged the busker, "what do you want to sing?"

DEBRA RAMSEY

The Japanese eat little fat and suffer fewer heart attacks than Brits or Americans. The French eat a lot of fat and suffer fewer heart attacks than Brits or Americans. Italians wash down their pasta with red wine and suffer fewer heart attacks than Brits or Americans.

Conclusion: Eat and drink what you like. Speaking English is what kills you.

IRWIN KNOPF

Proudly showing off his new apartment to a friend late one night, the drunk led the way to his bedroom, where there was a big brass gong. "What's that big brass gong for?" asked the friend.

"It's not a gong. It's a talking clock," the drunk replied.

"A talking clock? How's it work?"

"Watch," said the drunk. He picked up a hammer, gave the gong an ear-shattering pound and stepped back.

Someone on the other side of the wall screamed: "Hey, you jerk. It's three in the morning!"

E.T. THOMPSON

These two green beans are crossing the motorway when one of them is hit by an enormous lorry. His friend scrapes him up and rushes him to the hospital. After hours of surgery, the doctor says,

"I have good news and bad news."

The healthy green bean says, "Okay, give me the good news first."

"Well, he's going to live."

"So, what's the bad news?"

"The bad news is he'll be a vegetable for the rest of his life."

A junior manager, a senior manager and their boss were on their way to a lunch meeting. In the cab, they found a lamp. The boss rubbed it and a genie appeared. "I'll grant you one wish each," the genie said.

Grabbing the lamp from his boss, the eager senior manager shouted, "I want to be on a fast boat in the Bahamas with no worries." And, poof, he was gone.

The junior manager couldn't keep quiet. He shouted, "I want to be in Monte Carlo with beautiful girls, food and cocktails." And, poof, he was gone.

Finally, it was the boss's turn. "I want those idiots back in the office after lunch."

ASHFAQ AHMED

Two tourists met for a drink. "Does your hotel overlook the sea?" asked the first.

"Yes," replied the second. "It also overlooks good food, comfortable beds, soap and towels."

ROY BERRY

"I don't have a good feeling about this."

One night a thug and his girlfriend were strolling down the street, holding hands and gazing in shop windows. Passing a jeweller's, the girlfriend spotted a shiny ring. "Oh!" she exclaimed. "I'd love to have that."

The lout looked round and, without a word, threw a brick through the window, reached in and grabbed the ring. "There you go, darling," he said.

The girl was impressed. They walked on until she spotted a leather jacket in another window. "Wow," she said. "That's beautiful."

"Hold on," said the bruiser. He threw another brick through the window and handed her the coat.

A few blocks later she spotted an attractive pair of boots. "Oh," she began, but the thug interrupted.

"Come on, darling," he said, "you think I'm made of bricks?"

STEPHEN McCULLOUGH

Jason showed his friend the beautiful diamond ring he had bought his girlfriend for her birthday. "I thought she wanted a four-wheel-drive vehicle," ventured his friend.

"She did," Jason said. "But where am I going to find a fake Jeep?"

ZHANG WENPENG

/ SMELTZER

The blind man walks into a bar and says, "Want to hear a blonde joke?"

The barman tells him, "Well, I'm blonde and I won't appreciate it. The man sitting next to you is 18 stone and is also blonde. The man behind you is 20 stone and he's a blonde too. Do you still want to tell it?"

"No way," says the blind man. "Not if I have to explain it three times!"

PAT PATEL

A farmer on a tractor approached a driver whose car had become stuck in a muddy hole.

He offered to haul the vehicle out of the quagmire for a fee of £10. After brief consideration, the driver fished into his pocket and handed over the money.

As he attached the tow rope, the farmer mentioned that this was the tenth car he had rescued that day.

"Really?" asked the astonished motorist. "When do you find time to work on your land? At night?"

"No," said the farmer, shaking his head. "Night is when I fill the muddy hole with water."

"Pour me a double whisky, I've just had a blazing row with the little woman," Mike tells Charlie the pub landlord.

"Oh, yeah?" says Charlie. "Who won?"

"Put it like this, when it was all over, she came crawling to me on her hands and knees."

"Really?" says Charlie. "What did she say?"

"'Come out from under the bed, you little coward.'"

R. LALLY

Reporter interviewing a 104-year-old woman: **"What is the best thing about being 104?"** She replies, **"No peer pressure."**

SYLVIA SHINER

A biologist assigned to work in deepest Africa hired a guide to take him upriver to the remote site where he would do his study. As they were making their way into the jungle, the scientist heard the sound of drums. "What is that drumming?" he asked his guide nervously.

The guide, who spoke little English, replied, "Drums okay, but very bad when they stop." The drumming continued for two weeks while the biologist conducted his fieldwork. Finally, on the last day, the drums suddenly stopped, and the forest fell eerily silent.

Alarmed, the scientist called out to his guide, "The drums have stopped! What happens now?"

The guide crouched down, covered his head with his hands and, with despair in his voice, answered, "Bass solo."

Phoning a patient, the doctor says, "I have some bad news and some worse news. The bad news is that you have only 24 hours left to live."

"That is bad news," the patient replies. "What could be worse?"

The doctor answers, "I've been trying to reach you since yesterday."

Bob sees a sign in front of a house: "Talking Dog for Sale." Intrigued, he rings the bell and the owner shows him the dog. "What's your story?" Bob asks.

The dog says, "I discovered I had this gift when I was just a pup. The CIA signed me up, and soon I was jetting around the world, sitting at the feet of spies and world leaders, gathering important information and sending it back home. When I tired of that lifestyle, I joined the FBI, where I helped catch drug lords and gunrunners. I was wounded in the line of duty, received some medals, and now a movie is being made of my life."

"How much do you want for the dog?" Bob asks the owner.

"Ten dollars," says the owner.

Bob is incredulous. "Why on earth would you sell that remarkable dog for so little?"

"Because he's a liar. He didn't do any of that stuff."

STEVE DERIVAN

307

So... which one is yours?

Everything is changing. People are taking their comedians seriously and the politicians as a joke.

WILL ROGERS

Inviting people to laugh with you while you are laughing at yourself is a good thing to do. You may be the fool, but you're the fool in charge.

CARL REINER, My Anecdotal Life (St. Martin's)

I have my standards. They may be low, but I have them.

BETTE MIDLER

Deep down, I'm pretty superficial.

AVA GARDNER

308

I can live for two months on a good compliment.

MARK TWAIN

If a thing is worth doing, it is worth doing badly.

G.K. CHESTERTON

You know there is a problem with the education system when you realize that out of the three R's, only one begins with an R.

DENNIS MILLER, "Dennis Miller Live," HBO

No matter what happens, somebody will find a way to take it too seriously.

DAVE BARRY, Dave Barry Turns 50 (Crown)

How come if you mix flour and water together you get glue? And when you add eggs and sugar you get cake? Where does the glue go?

RITA RUDNER

A scoutmaster asks his troop to list three important things to bring in case they get lost in the desert. Food, matches, a bandana are all mentioned. Then Timmy suggests a compass, a canteen of water, and a deck of cards.

"I get the first two items," says the leader. "But what good are the cards?"

"Well, as soon as you start playing patience, it's guaranteed someone will come up to you and say, 'Put the red nine on top of the black ten.'"

This duck walks into a shop one day and asks the sales assistant, "Do you have any grapes?"

Thes sales assistant replies, "Sorry, no."

The next day the duck walks into the same shop and again asks, "Do you have any grapes?"

The sales assistant says, "No."

The next day the duck walks into the shop and asks, "Do you have any grapes?"

This time the sales assistant says: "No. And if you ask me again, I'll staple your feet to the floor."

The next day the duck walks into the shop and asks, "Do you have any staples?"

The sales assistant says, "No."

So the duck says, "Do you have any grapes?"

GREG WILKEY

"Knock, knock."
"Who's there?"
"Control freak."

"Now you say, 'Control freak who?'"

Why Elephants Never Forget...

Last night I played a blank tape at full blast. The mime artiste next door went nuts.

STEVEN WRIGHT

Mary told the funeral director to spare no expense on her father's funeral. So when a bill for £5000 arrived soon after the service, Mary happily paid it. The next month, she received a bill for £200. Thinking it must have been left off the original tally, Mary paid this too.

A month later, Mary received another bill for £200. And the next month, yet another. So she called the funeral director.

"You said you wanted the best funeral we could arrange," the director told her. "So I rented him a dinner jacket."

RICHARD REYNOSA

309

On the way home from work, Tom is stopped on the street by an attractive woman in a suggestive outfit.

"For £100, I'll do anything you ask in three words or less," she whispers.

"Okay," agrees Tom, handing over the cash. "Paint my house."

BILL UPDIKE

Overheard: "If Batman is supposed to be so smart, how come he wears his underwear outside his clothes?"

ASHLEY COOPER

"How much is 10 plus 13?"

Slowly the blonde replied, "16."

"Sorry," he said, shaking his head.

Once again the crowd roared, "Give her another chance."

"This is your last try," warned the speaker. "How much is two plus two?"

Carefully she ventured, "Four?"

And the crowd yelled, "Give her another chance!"

JAMES DORSEY

Overheard: "I hate talking cars. A voice out of nowhere says things like, 'Your door is ajar.' Why don't they say something really useful, like 'There's a speed camera hidden behind that bush'?"

A businesswoman is sitting at a bar. A man approaches her. "Hi, gorgeous," he says. "Want a little company?"

"Why?" asks the woman. "Do you have one to sell?"

CAROLYN STRADLEY

The husband came home unexpectedly and found his wife in the arms of another man.

"What do you think you're doing?" he shouted.

"See?" the woman said to her companion. "I told you he was stupid."

The man auditioning for the circus was confident, even though he'd been told the impresario had seen it all. "I have the most unusual act," the performer said before he began. "Just watch. I'm sure you'll be amazed."

He proceeded to climb a tall tower, then jump off, his arms flapping wildly. Nearing the ground, the artiste's fall suddenly slowed and he soared upwards. He swooped past the impresario twice and then fluttered gently to the ground, where he beamed triumphantly.

The impresario sat for a moment staring at the man. Finally he said, "So is that all you've got? Bird impressions?"

Two lawyers go into a restaurant, order drinks and pull their lunches from their briefcases.

"Sorry," the waiter says, "but you can't eat your own food in here."

The lawyers look at each other, shrug their shoulders and swap sandwiches.

LYDIA PRINCE

So this neutron walks into a bar and orders a beer. "How much will that be?" the neutron asks.

"For you," replies the bartender, "no charge."

L. LEATHERMAN

At a convention of blondes, a speaker insisted that the "dumb blonde" myth is all wrong. To prove it he asked one pretty young volunteer, "How much is 101 plus 20?"

The blonde answered, "120."

"No," he said, "that's not right."

The audience called out, "Give her another chance."

So the speaker asked the blonde,

Phil visits his doctor after weeks of not feeling well. "I have bad news," says the doctor. "You don't have long to live."

"How long have I got?" asks a distraught Phil.

"Ten," the doctor says sadly.

"Ten? Ten what? Months? Days?"

Suddenly the doctor interrupts, "Nine ... "

A man goes to his GP and says, "Doctor, I think I'm a moth."

"You don't need a doctor, you need a psychologist," the GP replies.

"I know," says the man. "But I was passing and your light was on ... "

E. BAGGOTT

Otto the vampire bat came flapping in from the night – his face covered in fresh blood – and settled on the roof of the cave to get some sleep. Soon, all the other bats smelled the blood and hassled Otto to tell them where he got it. He hissed at them to go away and let him get some rest. But they persisted, getting increasingly excited at the prospect of a feast.

"OK, follow me," he said and flew out of the cave with hundreds of his fellow residents behind him. Down through a valley they went, across a river and into a forest. Finally, he slowed down and the other bats milled around him, tongues hanging out expectantly.

"Do you see that large tree over there?" he said.

"Yes, yes!" the bats all screamed, whipping themselves into a frenzy.

"Good for you," said Otto, " 'cos I blooming didn't."

R. L.

TIMELESS HUMOUR

70s A mother was writing an excuse to the kindergarten teacher for her five-year-old daughter, who had been out of school with a cold.

"Okay," said the little girl. "But don't write that I threw up. I want to save that for show and tell."

"The first thing you have to understand is that when they throw your ball, they're not trying to get rid of you."

"I think we can separate you."

A scrawny little fellow turned up at a lumber company looking for work. "Just give me a chance to show you what I can do," he said to the head lumberjack.

"All right," said the boss. "Take your axe and cut down that oak tree."

Five minutes later the skinny man was back. "I've cut it down," he said, "and split it up into lumber."

The boss couldn't believe his eyes. "Where did you learn to cut down trees so fast?"

"The Sahara," the man answered.

"The Sahara desert?"

"Desert? Oh, yes, if that's what they call it now."

KUMIKO YOSHIDA

Do you know what you get when you play a country-and-western song backward? You get your job back, you get your house back, your wife back, your truck back ...

Sitting on the veranda at a nudist colony, two history professors are watching the sun go down. "Have you read Marx?" one asks the other.

"Yes," his colleague replies. "I think it's these wicker chairs."

DOROTHY GRAY

Mother Teresa arrives in Heaven. "Be thou hungry?" God asks.

Mother Teresa nods. He serves them each a humble sandwich of tuna on brown bread. Meanwhile, the sainted woman looks down to see gluttons in Hell devouring steaks, lobsters and wine.

The next day God invites her to join him for another meal. Again, it's tuna on brown bread. Again, she sees the denizens of Hell feasting.

The next day, as another can of tuna is opened, Mother Teresa meekly says, "I am grateful to be here with you as a reward for the pious life I led. But I don't get it: All we eat is tuna and bread while in the other place they eat like kings."

"Let's be honest," God says with a sigh, "for just two people, does it pay to cook?"

313

Two starving men are wandering in the desert when in the distance they see a tree, apparently covered in bacon rashers. One of the men dashes towards it, but is shot dead.

As he expires he gasps to his companion, "Don't come any closer. It's not a bacon tree. It's a ham bush."

DOREEN CONNER

Two dogs are walking down the road. One dog says to the other, "Wait here a minute. I'll be right back." He walks over to a lamp post, sniffs it for about a minute, then rejoins his friend.

"What was that all about?" the other dog asks.

"Just checking my messages."

I went on a 45-day diet. It's going great.
I've already lost 30 days.

A man goes on holiday to the Holy Land with his wife and mother-in-law. Halfway through their trip, the mother-in-law dies.

The man goes to see an undertaker, who explains that they can ship the body home, but it'll cost £5000. Or they can bury her in the Holy Land for just £150.

"We'll ship her home," says the son-in-law.

"Are you sure?" asks the undertaker. "That's an awfully big expense."

"Look," says the son-in-law, "two thousand years ago they buried a bloke here, and three days later he rose from the dead. I just can't take that chance."

JASON TUTHILL

"It's chilly in here," the wealthy customer sniffed. "Will you please turn down the air conditioning?"

"No problem, sir," said the waiter politely.

After a few minutes, the man complained again. "Now I'm too warm."

"All right," said the waiter. But soon the customer was chilly again.

Finally a patron at a nearby table whispered to the waiter, "I commend you for your patience. That guy is certainly keeping you busy."

"No, he's not," the waiter said with a shrug. "We don't even have air conditioning."

"May I try on that dress in the window?" the gorgeous young woman asks the manager of the designer boutique.

"Go ahead," the manager replies. "Maybe it'll attract some business."

HARRY BUCK

The nurse said to the doctor, "There's an invisible man in the waiting room."

The doctor replied, "Tell him I can't see him now."

PAUL REGENESS

One Sunday a minister played hooky from church so he could enjoy a round of golf, leaving his assistant to conduct the service. He drove to a faraway golf course to avoid bumping into any parishioners.

Looking down, St. Peter said to God, "You're not going to let him get away with this, are you?" The Lord shook his head.

The minister took his first shot, and scored a 420-yard hole in one. St. Peter was outraged. "I thought you were going to punish him!" he said to the Lord.

The Lord looked at St. Peter and replied, "So who's he going to tell?"

CLAIRE PARKER

The devout cowboy lost his favourite Bible while he was mending fences out on the range. Three weeks later a cow walked up to him carrying the Bible in its mouth. The cowboy couldn't believe his eyes. He took the book out of the cow's mouth, raised his eyes heavenward and exclaimed, "It's a miracle!"

"Not really," said the cow. "Your name is written inside the cover."

R. WILBERT

The patient walked into the doctor's surgery: "You've got to help me, Doc. It's my ear. There's something in there."

"Let's have a look," said the GP. "My goodness, you're right. There's money inside."

The doctor proceeded to pull out a fifty-pound note.

"I don't believe it," the practitioner exclaimed, "there's more in there."

Out came another fifty, a twenty and some tens. Finally all the notes had been removed.

The doctor counted the money: "One thousand, nine hundred and ninety pounds."

"Ah, yes, that sounds about right," nodded the patient. "I knew I wasn't feeling two grand."

A doctor answered the phone and heard the familiar voice of a colleague on the other end of the line say, "We need a fourth for poker."

"I'll be right over," the doctor answered.

As he was putting on his coat, his wife asked, "Is it serious?"

"Oh, yes," the doctor answered gravely. "In fact, there are three doctors there already."

DOROTHEA KENT

Two guys were discussing modern trends on sex and marriage. "I didn't sleep with my wife before we got married," Roy said. "Did you?"

"I'm not sure," Bobby replied. "What was her maiden name?"

JONATHAN DURIA

St Peter greets a man at the Pearly Gates. "What have you done to deserve entry into heaven?" he asks.

"Well, on a recent trip into the countryside, I came upon a gang of bikers threatening a young woman," says the man. "So I went up to the biggest, toughest biker and punched him in the nose. Then I kicked over his bike, yanked his ponytail and

"I think Mary is getting suspicious about all the long walks."

ripped out his nose ring. When I had finished with him, I turned to the rest of the gang and said, 'Leave this woman alone or you'll have to answer to me!'"

St Peter was impressed. "When did this happen?"

"Just a couple of minutes ago," said the man.

MICHAEL COFFEY

"Every time I drink a cup of coffee, doctor, I have a stabbing pain in my right eye. What should I do?"

"Take the spoon out of your cup."

STEVE JARRELL

Albert comes home, plops down in front of the TV and says to his wife, "Quick! Get me a beer before it starts." She rolls her eyes and brings him a beer.

Fifteen minutes later he says, "Get me another beer. It's going to start any minute now."

His wife is furious. "Is that all you're going to do tonight? Sit in front of that television drinking beer? You have to be the world's laziest, most–"

He interrupts her with a heavy sigh. "Well," he says. "It's started."

Two atoms are walking down the sidewalk when they accidentally bump into each other. "I'm really sorry!" the first atom exclaims.

"Are you all right?"

"Actually, no," the second atom replies. "I lost an electron."

"Oh, no! Are you sure?"

"I'm positive!"

VYAS SARWESHWAR PRASAD

Bill walked into a bar with a lump of Tarmac under his arm. "What can I do for you?" asked the bartender, looking him up and down. "A beer for me," Bill replied, "and one for the road."

NIGEL PENN

Clementine is driving home one night when her car is hit by a bad hailstorm, leaving hundreds of dents. The next day she goes to a garage for a repair estimate. The repairman winks at his workmate and tells Clementine that if she blows into the exhaust pipe really hard, the dents will just pop out.

After she arrives home, she blows with all her might into the exhaust pipe. Her housemate asks what she's doing. Clementine explains the repairman's tip. "But it doesn't work," she says, pausing to catch her breath.

"Duh!" replies her friend. "You have to roll up the windows first!"

M. VAUGHAN

The curvy redhead limped into the doctor's office complaining about a tricky knee. The doctor stooped down, peering at the knee, and asked, "Now what's a joint like you doing in a nice girl like this?"

JOHN DRATWA

Late one night the political candidate came home and gave his wife the glorious news: "Darling, I've been elected!"

"Honestly?" she replied.

"Now," the politician said, frowning, "why bring that up?"

"At this point the Western influence starts to show."

Going into a toyshop, a girl asks the price of the Barbie Teacher doll. "Ten pounds," answers the assistant kindly.

"And how much does Barbie Doctor cost?"

"Also ten pounds," says the saleswoman.

The little girl asks the prices of other versions of the same doll: it is always the same. Then her eyes fall on the doll that really attracts her attention.

"How much does Barbie Divorcée cost?" she asks.

"Fifty pounds," answers the saleswoman.

"Why is it so expensive?"

"Because Barbie Divorcée includes Ken's house, Ken's car and his computer."

KARLA MIER

Jack stumbled into the house.

"What's wrong?" asked his wife.

"I had a great idea," he gasped, smiling proudly. "I ran all the way home behind the bus and saved myself 90 pence."

His wife frowned. "That's just like you, Jack, always thinking small," she said, shaking her head. "Why didn't you run behind a taxi and save yourself ten pounds?"

JEFF SHAW

One day, the general noticed one of his soldiers behaving oddly. He would pick up every piece of paper he saw, read it, frown and say, "That's not it," and drop it.

After a month of this, the general finally arranged to have the soldier tested. The psychologist found that the soldier was deranged, and wrote out his discharge from the Army.

The soldier picked it up, smiled and said, "That's it."

Ten men and one woman are hanging on to a rope dangling down from a helicopter. The weight of 11 people is too much for the rope, so the group decides one person has to let go.

No one can decide who it should be, until finally the woman volunteers. She gives a touching speech, saying she will sacrifice her life to save the others because women are used to giving up things for their husbands and children.

When she finishes speaking all the men start clapping.

MARGARET PITMAN

Barbara couldn't understand why she was losing so badly at Trivial Pursuit. Nevertheless, she persevered, rolling the dice and landing on Science & Nature. Her question was, "If you are in a vacuum and someone calls your name, can you hear it?"

Barbara frowned, then asked, "Is it on or off?"

Bursting into a bank, the robber points a gun at the cashier and bellows, "Give me all your money or you're geography!"

"Surely you mean history?" corrects the cashier.

"Look," snarls the thug, "don't change the subject."

MIRIAM HARTILL

317

On their first date, a man asked his companion if she'd like a drink with dinner. "Oh, no, what would I tell my Sunday school class?" she said.

Later, he offered her a cigarette. "Oh, no, what would I tell my Sunday school class?" she said again.

On the drive home, he saw a hotel. Deciding that he had nothing to lose, he asked if she wanted to stop in there.

"Okay," his date replied.

"What will you tell your Sunday school class?" he asked, shocked.

"The same thing I always tell them. 'You don't have to drink or smoke to have a good time.'"

GEORGE NORDHAM

A businessman taking an efficiency seminar presented a case study on his wife's routine for cooking breakfast: "After a few days of observation, I determined what was slowing her down and suggested ways to speed up the process."

"Did it work?" the teacher asked.

"It certainly did. Instead of taking her 20 minutes to cook my breakfast, it takes me only seven."

Lou, Sam and Joe walk into a bar and each order a pint. Just as they're about to take their first sip, flies land in each of their drinks.

Lou, the most squeamish of the trio, pushes his beer away in disgust.

Sam, the thrifty one, fishes the fly out and drinks his beer.

And Joe, the lush, drags the fly out, holds it over the beer and yells, "C'mon, spit it out! Spit it out!!"

A young woman was describing her date to a friend. "After dinner," she said, "he wanted to come back to my flat, but I refused. I told him my mother would worry if I did anything like that."

"Then what happened?" asked her friend.

"He kept insisting, and I kept refusing," the young woman responded.

"He didn't weaken your resolve, did he?" the friend asked.

"Not a bit. In the end, we went back to his flat. I thought, let his mother worry."

A monk joins an austere order where the brethren are only allowed the minimum of food and clothing and may speak only two words a year. At the end of the first year the monk goes to see the abbot. "My son," says the abbot. "You have been here for a year now and are allowed two words. What will they be?"

"I'm cold," the monk replies.

Another year goes by and the monk goes to see the abbot again.

"You have been here two years now, and are allowed another two words. What will they be?"

"I'm hungry," replies the monk.

At the end of the third year, the monk goes to see the abbot again.

"You have been here three years, my son. You are allowed another two words. What will they be?

"I'm leaving," says the monk.

"Thank goodness," says the abbot. "You've done nothing but complain since you got here."

MARTIN ATKINSON

A church bulletin blunder:

"Morning sermon: Jesus Walks on Water.
Evening sermon: Searching for Jesus."

Acknowledgements

Every effort has been made to trace and contact copyright holders prior to publication. If notified the publisher undertakes to rectify any errors or omissions at the earliest opportunity.

PAGE 266-7 Thanks to Jonathan Bastable for original translation of "Malingerers" by Anton Chekhov PAGE 22-3, 282-3 Craig Brown: extracts from *This is Craig Brown* (Ebury Press, 2003), reprinted by permission of the Random House Group Ltd. PAGE 52-3 Guy Browning: extracts from *Office Politics: How it really works* (Ebury Press, 2006), reprinted by permission of the Random House Group Ltd. PAGE 208-9 Will Cuppy: "Swan-Upping, Indeed!" from *How to Attract the Wombat* (Dobson Books, 1950), illustrated by Ed Nofziger, copyright © Will Cuppy 2002, reprinted by permission of David R Godine, Publisher, Inc. PAGE 102-3 Richard Curtis & Ben Elton: extract from *Blackadder II*, copyright © Richard Curtis and Ben Elton 1985 from *Blackadder: The Whole Damn Dynasty* (Michael Joseph, 1998), collection copyright © Richard Curtis, Ben Elton, John Lloyd and Rowan Atkinson 1998, reprinted by permission of Penguin Books Ltd. PAGE 16-7, 124-5 Michele Hanson: extracts from *Living With Mother* (Guardian/Virago, 2006), copyright © Michele Hanson 2006, reprinted by permission of Guardian News and Media. PAGE 78-9, 232-3 Maureen Lipman: extracts from 'Only Kidding' in *How Was It For You?* (Robson Books, 1985), copyright © Maureen Lipman 1985, and from 'Lock, Stock and Barbecue' in *Something to Fall Back On* (Robson Books, 1987), copyright © Maureen Lipman 1985, reprinted by permission of the author and the Mulcahy & Viney Agency PAGE 38-9 David Nobbs: extract from *The Fall and Rise of Reginald Perrin* in *The Reginald Perrin Omnibus* (Arrow, 1999), reprinted by permission of the Random House Group Ltd. PAGE 90-1 John O'Farrell: extract from *Global Village Idiot* (Doubleday 2001/Black Swan 2002), reprinted by permission of the Random House Group Ltd. PAGE 162 Jimmy Perry and David Croft: extract from *Dad's Army: The Complete Scripts* edited by Richard Webber (Orion, 2003), reprinted by permission of the Orion Publishing Group. PAGE 138-140 James Thurber: extract from "The Kerb in the Sky" in *The Secret Life of Walter Mitty and Other Pieces* (Penguin , 2000) originally published as *The Thurber Carnival* (1965), text and illustrations by James Thurber, copyright © 1973 Rosemary A Thurber, reprinted by permission of the Barbara Hogenson Agency, Inc.

Art credits

AM Alberts 25, 218
Dave Allen/www.CartoonStock.com 65, 112
Charles Almon 128, 215, 281
Mark Anderson 57, 82, 150
Myke Ashley-Cooper/www.CartoonStock.com 293
Aaron Bacall 121, 175
Ian Baker 45, 83, 92, 173, 188, 245, 249, 255, 278, 300, 312
Mike Baldwin/www.CartoonStock.com 18, 20, 41, 120, 181, 241, 262, 296
Tim Bolton 84
David Brown/www.CartoonStock.com 274
Marty Bucella 246
Patrick Byrnes 10
John Caldwell 8, 32, 37, 47, 77, 98, 135, 189, 228, 240, 272, 289, 301
Scott Calvert 7, 27, 30
Canary Pete/www.CartoonStock.com 193
Dave Carpenter 87, 134, 159, 164, 195, 251, 269
Ken Catalino 40, 152, 219, 243
Gareth Cowlin/www.CartoonStock.com 235
Roy Delgado 59, 61, 62, 81, 116, 126, 154, 202, 205, 210, 216, 226, 259, 315
Ronaldo Dias/www.CartoonStock.com 238
Benita Epstein 64, 109, 117, 179, 279
Feggo 316
Noel Ford/www.CartoonStock.com 101
Randy Glasbergen 46, 146, 174, 170
Clive Goddard/www.CartoonStock.com 28
John Grimes 50, 122, 172
Ralph Hagen/www.CartoonStock.com 14, 70, 123, 153, 158, 166, 180, 192, 211, 250, 305
Jarodo/www.CartoonStock.com 165
Phil Judd/www.CartoonStock.com 186
Jerry King/www.CartoonStock.com 68
Joe Kohl 131, 147
Jeff Lok 26
Mike Lynch 14, 19, 60, 73, 86, 108, 130, 136, 200, 217, 260
Patricia Madigan 115, 167, 168
Scott Arthur Masear 56, 142, 187, 197, 204, 212, 220, 229, 234, 256, 280, 298, 317
Peter Mueller 76, 294
Mary Nadler 149, 271
Tom Plant 16-7, 52-3, 78-9, 102-3, 138-9, 162-3, 184-5, 232-3, 266-7
Dan Reynolds 13, 89, 96, 97, 106, 182, 191, 237, 253, 265, 270, 275, 284, 285, 295, 303, 304, 307, 310
Dan Reynolds/www.CartoonStock.com 107, 234, 268, 276, 291, 309
Royston Robertson 22-3, 38-9, 90-1, 118-9, 124-5, 208-9, 282-3
Royston Robertson/www.CartoonStock.com 246
Norm Rockwell 144
Harley Schwadron 42, 48, 51, 160, 170, 223, 258
Mike Shapiro 113, 311
Vahan Shirvanian 69, 94-5, 151, 207, 213, 314
Steve Smeltzer 66, 177, 297, 306
Elwood Smith cover, 1, 2, 4, 5, 15, 44, 55, 67, 75, 105, 114, 137, 152, 176, 194, 206, 225, 261, 286, 308
Mike Stokoe/www.CartoonStock.com 224
Russell Tate/iStockphoto.com 20 (frame), 70 (frame), 123 (frame), 276 (easel)
Thomas Bros. 29, 31, 34, 155, 156, 290
Carla Ventresca 24, 214
Kim Warp 11, 110, 199, 203
WestMach 287, 288

A Laugh a Minute is derived from *Laughter, The Best Medicine*, © 2006 The Reader's Digest Association, Inc.

This edition was published by
The Reader's Digest Association Limited,
11 Westferry Circus, Canary Wharf, London E14 4HE
www.readersdigest.co.uk
© 2007 Reader's Digest Association

Reprinted 2009

We are committed both to the quality of our products and
the service we provide to our customers. We value your
comments, so please do contact us on 08705 113366
or via our website at: **www.readersdigest.co.uk**
If you have any comments or suggestions about the content of
our books, email us at **gbeditorial@readersdigest.co.uk**

Concept Code: US4679/IC
Book Code: 400-347 UP0000-2
ISBN: 978 0 276 44306 0
Oracle Code: 250011346H.00.24

**Reader's Digest
General Books**

Editorial Director
Julian Browne

Art Director
Anne-Marie Bulat

Head of Book Development
Sarah Bloxham

Managing Editor
Nina Hathway

Picture Resource Manager
Sarah Stewart-Richardson

Pre-press Account Manager
Dean Russell

**Product Production
Manager**
Claudette Bramble

Production Controller
Katherine Bunn

Origination
Colour Systems Limited,
London

Printed and bound in China

**Reader's Digest
Project Team**

Editor
Rachel Weaver

Art Editor
Julie Bennett

Text rights
Connie Robertson

Proofreader
Lynne Davies